FEDERALISM AND FEDERATION
IN WESTERN EUROPE

Federalism
and
Federation
in Western Europe

Edited by
Michael Burgess

CROOM HELM
London • Sydney • Dover, New Hampshire

© 1986 Michael Burgess
Croom Helm Ltd, Provident House, Burrell Row,
Beckenham, Kent BR3 1AT
Croom Helm Australia Pty Ltd, Suite 4, 6th Floor,
64-76 Kippax Street, Surry Hills, NSW 2010, Australia

British Library Cataloguing in Publication Data

Federalism and federation in Western Europe.
    1. Federal government – Europe 2. European
    federation 3. Europe – Politics and
    government – 1945-
    I. Burgess, Michael
    321.02'094   JN15

    ISBN 0-7099-3955-8

Croom Helm, 51 Washington Street, Dover,
New Hampshire 03820, USA

Library of Congress Cataloging in Publication Data
Main entry under title:

Federalism and Federation in Western Europe.

    Includes bibliographical references and index.
    1. Federal government–Europe–congresses.
2. Federal government–Europe–case studies–congresses.
3. Europe–politics and government–congresses.
4. Constitutional history–congresses. 5. Comparative
government–congresses. I. Burgess, Michael, 1949–
JC355.F36   1985   321.02'094   85-28028
ISBN 0-7099-3955-8

Printed and bound in Great Britain by
Biddles Ltd, Guildford and King's Lynn

CONTENTS

Preface

Part One

Part Two

PREFACE

The idea for this book emerged from a workshop which I
directed at the Annual Conference of the European
Consortium for Political Research at the University of
Salzburg, Austria, in 1984. The workshop was entitled
'Comparative Federalism and Federation in Western Europe'
and I would like to thank all of the workshop
participants, some of whose contributions could not be
included in this book, for helping to stimulate and
crystallise many of the ideas and arguments which appear
in the following text.

I would also like to thank the Nuffield Foundation
for their financial assistance in the form of a research
travel grant awarded during 1980-1982. This provided the
foundation upon which I was able to develop and extend my
research into comparative federalism and federation in
Western Europe. My debt to Adrian Lee, Head of the
Department of Social and Political Studies at Plymouth
Polytechnic, must also be acknowledged. Without his
support and encouragement during recent years this
research would not have been possible.

July 1985

In memory of my father
and for Adam and his Liverpool grandmother

PART ONE

1. INTRODUCTION

Michael Burgess

Since something like half the world's population, over half of the land surface of our planet and a good many of its most powerful states in the contemporary international political system are governed by federal political systems, it has never been difficult to justify the academic study of federations. They are part of political practice and behaviour. As tangible political entities they are easily amenable to political analysis. And, indeed, the academic literature on federations throughout the world during different historical periods is both rich and abundant. It has waxed and waned according to the perceived successes and failures of federations, while approaches to the study of federation have been determined by the changes which have occurred in the discipline of political science itself. These changes have shaped and continue to mould our intellectual expectations and understanding of federal political systems in a particularly significant way: they define both the limitations and the possibilities of research endeavours.

The theme of this book may be seen as at once both modest and ambitious. It is modest to the extent that its empirical concern is Western Europe - and, indeed, not even the whole of Western Europe - and it is ambitious in the sense that it attempts firmly to establish the connecting links within this territorial arena between two distinct conceptual phenomena, namely, federalism and federation. For the purpose of clarification let us make a few further brief observations. First, the nature of our subject impels us to underline not the differentiation of the West and East European political systems, but instead the underlying unity and continuity of a particular European political tradition. European federations may display markedly different institutional and structural characteristics according either to the overtly ideological prescriptions of Western liberal democratic capitalism and Marxism-Leninism or to the military realities of the years between 1939 and 1945 and the subsequent vagaries of international power politics, but these only imperfectly obscure a fundamental continuity of European federalism. This genre of federalism is both rich and unique in its particular multidimensionality of historical, intellectual, social, economic, cultural and political strands. In a specific sense, then, the title of this book may be a misnomer. Federalism and federation do not actually recognise the military realities of Europe in 1945 as conclusively destroying and dispensing with what is a deep-rooted

European political tradition. Centuries of thought and practice cannot be obliterated almost overnight.

Our second observation is equally pertinent. Federation - the study of federal political systems - is something with which we are instantly both familiar and comfortable. Federations are, after all, tangible institutional facts. But while political scientists, and American scholars in particular, feel at home grappling with the intricacies of inter-governmental relations, centralising and decentralising trends and the currently fashionable centre-periphery relationships, there is a conceptually discrete area of political analysis which is arguably more difficult to evaluate and operationalise when we seek to pinpoint both the raison d'etre and the sustaining dynamic of federation. This area of political analysis is federalism. We shall discuss this concept in some greater depth in Chapter 2, but it is instructive at this point in our introductory discussion to remind ourselves that the particular federalism with which we are concerned in this book is European federalism. Federalism, both as a word and a concept, is not synonymous with either intergovernmental relations or decentralisation. It is conceptually discrete from such phenomena. To use the word in such a terminologically lazy and slipshod manner is to impoverish the concept and to add to the conceptual and methodological confusion characteristic of the last thirty years. In the European tradition of federalism the quality of our concepts will be filled out and developed according to the unique, albeit changing, configuration of social, economic, political and cultural forces which together constitute what it is to be 'European'. And what is 'European' is indigenous to Europe; it must be examined through European conceptual lenses.

The federal principle, then, is a spatially global notion and a universal principle in its penetrative, pervasive qualities. It has been both historically and intellectually valid since man first began to organise human relations. However, the purpose of this book is to descend from the general federal principle through the ages in different parts of the world to the particular focus of our attention, namely, eight states in Western Europe where the conjuncture of federalism and federation may be most visible and, hence, amenable to empirical investigation.

Part One concentrates upon the various manifestations of West European federalism in Belgium, Spain, France, Ireland and (historically) Great Britain. As we shall see, such federalisms exist, and have existed, as a coherent body of political ideas about the reorganisation of the state and as a political movement - expressive of these ideas - advocating federation. These chapters demonstrate that such federalisms are idiosyncratic and do not necessarily lead to federation. They may, on the contrary, fall far short of guaranteed access to the central decision-making process and constitutional entrenchment, but are they to be assessed as federal failures ? What are we to make of their endeavours in this direction ? Perhaps the needs and requirements of their particular differentiations did not stretch to federation. The various contributions to Part One call attention to this possibility and also raise a number of interesting research questions arising out of the interface between federalism and federation.

Part Two rivets our attention upon the three West European federations: Austria, Switzerland and West Germany. Each of these studies highlights the essentially symbiotic relationship between federalism and federation. Whether we spotlight the conditions for renewed territorial mobilisation in Austria, political bargaining and negotiation in Swiss constitutional reform, or institutional dysfunctionalism in West Germany, the interface between federalism and federation is manifest. Federations are not magicked into existence. West European federations were created to solve particular problems at a particular point in each State's development. What were these problems to which federation appeared as the appropriate solution ? What sort of demands were being articulated and by whom ? What, in simple terms, was the origin of intent ? The three contributions to this section of the book have, in their different ways, sought to illuminate the changing relationship between their particular federation and its sustaining federalism. Every federation, after all, must be simultaneously sustained by the twin driving-forces of differentiation (or diversity) and integration. These are opposing, but not necessarily contradictory, forces. When we consider the West European tradition of federalism and federation one question is of crucial importance: how are these particular diversities and differentiations constitutionally entrenched ? Guaranteed access to the central decision-making process can be guaranteed only via constitutional entrenchment. Otherwise the constituent units of the larger federal union would be vulnerable to the changing whims of the overarching Centre. In short, federations must have some minimal distinguishing hallmarks which serve to differentiate them from non-federal political systems.

In these few introductory pages we have already traversed a large and, some might say, infinite subject area. Debate about what are the dependent and independent variables will proceed as it always has: contentiously.

Introduction

Our chief concern is this Introduction is to sensitise the
reader to our concepts and terminology. Normative
judgements about the subject must remain normative. No
claims are made here either for the perceived moral
virtues or the putative ideological benefits of federalism
and federation. There have been numerous studies which
have done so, just as there have been many arguments
against both federalism and federation. But this book
does attempt to emphasise the importance of two
perspectives: first, that federalism is not to be
dismissed as a vague, abstract idea unrelated to practical
politics; and, secondly, that federation is an empirically
valid way of structuring multiple identities. Our subject
is grounded in political practice. Federalism is
unquestionably ideological in the sense that it is a
prescriptive guide to action. It seeks to achieve
federation. Federations constitute the institutional and
structural techniques for achieving the distinctive goals
of a variety of federalisms. They are, in this sense,
both the goal and the means of obtaining it. Let us now
turn to the initial conceptual discussion which informs
the core of the book and examine how it weaves its way
into our subject to identify and underline the distinctive
West European tradition of federalism and federation.

2. FEDERALISM AND FEDERATION IN WESTERN EUROPE

Michael Burgess

Among those eminent scholars who have contributed to the academic debate about federation since it began with K. C. Wheare's pioneering study, entitled Federal Government, in 1946, there seems to be a general agreement, laced with lament, about the absence of a genuine theory of federation.[1] During the early years of the great debate most writers used the terms 'federalism' and 'federation' as synonyms which were lazily interchangeable. Thus I. Duchacek observed in 1970 that 'there is no accepted theory of federalism'.[2] He meant 'federation', but his observation was, none the less, pertinent. Indeed, in 1977 it was endorsed by another acknowledged scholar of federation, M.J.C. Vile, who noted that:

> A theory of federalism hardly exists today .... because much of the theoretical effort of the last thirty years has been devoted to the discussion of the definition of federalism in such a way as to leave little or no basis upon which to build any sustained theoretical structure.[3]

Vile, too, meant 'federation', but his remark was equally pertinent. It was his reflection upon the succession of professional revisions of approaches to the study of federal political systems, based mainly upon shifting emphases and marginal redefinitions, which dated back at least to W. S. Livingston's provocative article, 'A Note on the Nature of Federalism', first published in 1952.[4] This game, as Vile asserted much later, is now played out. There seems little point engaging in further intellectual disputes about the nature and meaning of federation which are liable to be sterile. We shall proceed, instead, from a different conceptual angle.

Our purpose in this chapter is twofold: to examine our subject by adopting the conceptual distinction between federalism and federation; and to apply this important distinction to eight states in Western Europe. This approach is both refreshing and revealing in a number of significant ways. First, it explains much of the conceptual and methodological confusion characteristic of the last thirty years, most notably the tendency in this literature to discuss federalism when it is federation that is meant. As we shall argue in this chapter, these terms are not synonymous and should not be used interchangeably. Secondly, the conceptual distinction opens up new lines of enquiry. It is possible to investigate both young and established political systems from a fresh perspective. The absence of federation must not blind us to the presence of federalism. Thirdly, and in the specific context of this book, our approach serves to underline the existence of a distinct West European tradition of federalism and federation which is starkly different from the more familiar Anglo-American tradition.[5] Finally, and although it is beyond the aims of this book, it is an approach which more readily facilitates comparative analysis. I have written about this elsewhere, but suffice it to stress here that this distinction enables us to move nearer towards a more sophisticated conceptual framework for the comparative study of federalisms and federations.[6]

Conceptual refinement, then, opens up new and interesting empirical possibilities. Our principal concerns are thus not confined to the three established federations of Western Europe - Austria, Switzerland and West Germany. They extend to a number of other West European states - Belgium, Spain, France, Ireland and Great Britain - which are shown to have peculiar ideas and features of federalism. First, however, we must return to our initial conceptual distinction between federalism and federation.

Federalism and Federation : The Concepts Examined

The conceptual distinction between federalism and federation is not new. It has been implicit in much of the literature on the subject for many years. Indeed, Livingston implicitly acknowledged the distinction in his first published attempt in 1952 to move away from Wheare's somewhat static and legalistic interpretation of federation.[7] On the subject of regional political integration in Western Europe it has also been conspicuous in being central to the drive for a more binding political union. Federal ideas or, more specifically, the federal principle, have always been at the heart of the debate about the future of West European integration. But the importance of the distinction between federalism and federation was not fully appreciated and it was never persistently pursued.

The most recent exponent of the distinction is Preston King whose book, Federalism and Federation, published in 1982, called attention to federalism as an explicit ideological and/or philosophical position.[8] Let us look first at federation. According to King, federation is defined as 'an institutional arrangement, taking the form of a sovereign state, and distinguished from other such states solely by the fact that its central government incorporates regional units in its decision procedure on some constitutionally entrenched basis'.[9] This definition is unlikely to provoke a storm of controversy but it is worth momentarily to reflect upon a few of its implications. The federal principle is, above all, an organising principle, and it follows logically from this that federation is the organisational form which corresponds to this principle. Vile depicts it as 'a cluster of techniques .... constitutional, legal, political, administrative and financial which serve to maintain or erode the balance between mutual independence and interdependence between levels of government'.[10] Leaving aside the vexed question of equilibrium in this definition,[11] it is clear that a broad measure of agreement has emerged: federation is a specific organisational form which includes structures, institutions and techniques.

What, then, serves to distinguish federation from other forms of state? Here, again, there is widespread consensus among scholars. Vile clearly views federation as being a decentralised political system having a fully constitutional government. King, too, is unequivocal about the distinguishing hallmark of federation: it is the accommodation of the constituent units of the union in the decision-making procedure of the central government 'on some constitutionally entrenched basis'. In so far as this is achieved, the federation 'is to be viewed as non-absolutist, as constitutional, in this sense as a democracy'. It is 'a case of corporate, self-rule which is to say as some form of democratic or constitutional government'.[12] It is unclear precisely how helpful this terminological lenience can be to our present discussion. There are, after all, many forms of democratic and constitutional rule, and federation is only one of these. Before we conclude our short discourse on federation, then, let us briefly consider the question of constitutionality raised here since it seems pivotal in the task of classification.

The gist of recent scholarly analyses of
federation regarding their constitutionality is that
it is constitutional autonomy which matters rather
than the particular division of powers between
central and regional governments.[13]   A variety of
ways exist of affording special or entrenched
constitutional representation in the decision
procedure of the central government. This is clearly
evidenced by the institutional and decision-making
differences between federations as, for example,
Austria and Switzerland. But if the notion of fully
constitutional government is so crucial to the
classification of federations, how is this notion
defined? King appears noticeably reticent on this
point. He acknowledges the importance of stipulating
the nature of a federation as a particular legal or
constitutional type, but leaves us with the rather
puzzling assertion that the stipulation involved
'must be of a constitutional kind'. The only
explanation he offers is that such constitutional
stipulations necessitate 'some notion of
institutional arrangements sufficiently fixed and
stable (indeed entrenched) to require some unusual or
extraordinary procedure to overturn them,
irrespective of whether these arrangements are
written on paper or firmly imprinted on men's minds.
To go further than this King considers that some
'resuscitated concept of constitutionalism' would be
essential.[14]

Is it not possible to be more precise about this
cardinal feature of federation? Surely all that is
necessary is some modest clarification. Over twenty
years ago this subject was discussed in very clear
and simple terms by C. J. Hughes whose 'Theory of
Confederacies' has been both engulfed and
overshadowed by the accumulated weight of the
subsequent literature on federation.[15]   Hughes' view
is that federation is a classification. It is a
particular species of the genus 'fully constitutional
government' which means that it specifies certain
ways that authority (some would say power) is
distributed and exercised by government in a state.
To say that a state is 'federal' thereby implies that
it is distinguished by a particular form of
government and that this is its basic defining
characteristic. The differentia that mark off the
species 'federation' from the rest of the genus are,
for example, institutions, and a local police power
which facilitate 'the preservation of diversity of
culture, ... ways of life, of religion, social
institutions, educational policy, language and codes
of law'.[16]

The genus 'fully constitutional government' is
identified as 'the sort of government wherein law is
a sort of seamless web'; this means that 'the
government can itself be under the law, and the
sanction that prevents it acting illegally is that
there would then be a sort of breakdown of law whose
end would be difficult to foresee'.[17] It is
difficult to avoid the conclusion that the notion
'fully constitutional government' really means a form
of Western liberal democratic state; this would be
the political tradition which emphasises the law and
the constitution in the old-fashioned Dicey and Bryce
sense of the subordination of government to the law.
If we are to follow this line of reasoning we might
have to conclude either that only federations whose
constitutional type conforms to Western liberal
democratic values and stipulations may be deemed as
such or that these federations constitute a
sub-category within the overall institutional fact of
federation. This would determine, for example,
whether or not the Soviet Union is to be considered a
federation, irrespective of its own constitutional
claims. In this respect King is surely correct to
argue that this kind of issue can only be resolved -
and a firm position adopted - by entering the debate
about constitutionalism. As in King's book, it is
well beyond the purposes of this chapter to attempt
to do so.

Our discussion of federation, then, demonstrates
that - at least in Western liberal democracies -
there is a distinctive organisational form or
institutional fact which exists to accommodate the
constituent units of a union in the decision-making
procedure of the central government by means of
constitutional entrenchment. Some conceptual
problems with federation remain to be resolved but
for our general purposes it has been defined and, as
King would put it, it has been given 'some reliable
and fairly fixed sense'.[18] Let us now turn our
attention to federalism and examine its distinctive
features before moving on to look at how it manifests
itself in Western Europe.

Federalism informs federation and _vice versa_,
but it is also intricately woven into the discussion
of 'pluralism' and 'plural societies'. Without
wishing to enter this particular debate, it is, none
the less, important to emphasise the links between
these separate phenomena. The assertion that
federalism is in some sense either a form or
sub-category of pluralism is commonplace among
political scientists. King is categorical about

this: 'Pluralism reflects a much broader theoretical
concern than federalism. But federalism can still be
fitted within it'.[19] Similarly Lijphart ties
federalism to pluralism in a number of interlocked
ways. His work on segmental cleavages within
societies and on consociational democracy as both an
empirical and normative model suggests strong links
with federalism which can be analysed on
non-territorial as well as on territorial principles.
We shall return to this aspect of federalism later
when we briefly consider its tessellated European
historical and philosophical lineage.

For the moment let us focus broadly upon the
meaning of federalism shorn of its unique European
cultural and historical context. Here our discussion
is both endangered and bedevilled by other rival
perspectives. Federalism can be taken to mean
ideological position, philosophical statement and
empirical fact. Mindful of our conceptual
distinction between federalism and federation, let us
here take federalism to mean the recommendation and
(sometimes) the active promotion of support for
federation. This can take the form of an overtly
prescriptive guide to action and/or a normative
judgement upon the ideal organisation of human
relations and conduct. It can also be viewed as
empirical fact to the extent that it recognises
diversity - broadly conceived in its social, economic
and political contexts - as a living reality,
something which exists independent of ideological and
philosophical perceptions. This is what is meant
when some federalists claim that social life is by
nature federal. The way people live their lives and
organise themselves is intrinsically federal, it is a
natural social reality expressive of multiple roles,
aims and identities.

Each or all of these perspectives of federalism
are both contentious and contestable. Some
Anglo-American views may recoil from notions of
political ideology for obvious reasons, while others
may argue that social federalism underestimates the
importance of the state as a coercive unifying and
homogenising force. But our definition, it must be
remembered, was intended to be wide-ranging. Only
when we consider its application to specific cultural
and historical milieux can we begin to fill out the
concept with particular meaning. Like federation,
federalism is rooted in its context and meaning
derives from context. We must locate the concept in
its distinct setting : historical, cultural,
intellectual, philosophical, social, economic and

ideological. Here we can begin to appreciate its huge multidimensional complexities. King summarised the phenomenon succinctly and in so doing drew attention to the subtle relationship between federalism and federation when, in a provocative essay, he observed :

> Federation might best be understood in terms of the problems to which it has constituted a set of historically varying answers. If we understand the problems, the understanding of structure more clearly follows.[21]

King prompts us to direct our attentions toward the nature of problems to which federation has appeared as a solution. In doing this our discussion of federalism and federation is both deepened and extended. We are compelled to acknowledge that these concepts are part of political belief, practice and behaviour. This is patently obvious when we pose questions such as: what do the advocates of federation seek to achieve or what do these actors understand by federation ? As King astutely elaborated in his later work, 'the observer's criteria (cannot) be totally at odds with those professed by actors and proponents within federations since this would imply that federal institutions involve no element of conscious self-direction'.[22] The symbiotic nature of federalism and federation could hardly be underlined more sharply. After all, 'for all of its institutional character, a federation is still governed by purpose, and this reflects values and commitments'. Federation as either organisational form or institutional fact 'reflects commitment to entrenchment'.[23]

Our discussion so far has not fully explored the relationship between federalism and federation but it does provide us with several interesting insights into our subject and it offers potentially new avenues of enquiry. Although, as King notes, there may be federalism without federation, 'there can be no federation without some matching variety of federalism'.[24] But which forms of federalism have been, historically, successful and which are likely to be so today ? Again, federations differ significantly in structure partly, though not only, because their respective federalisms differ, but this must not ignore what Vile considers to be the most important question, namely, the problem of change and development.[25] Since King is keen to emphasise the intimate connections between institutions and

behaviour - the former being a complex of practices
which are rule governed and recommend forms of
behaviour - it is understandable why this approach
might be especially revealing in terms of change and
development. 'Federations', he argues, 'move, they
change, and this movement is equally reflected in the
views of those who operate and study them'; thus if
they 'betray some moral or normative orientation'
(sic. federalism) this will 'change over time within
each federation and will vary as between them all'.[26]

Federalism and federation are locked together in
a constantly shifting and changing matrix where
belief and practice, perception and reality,
intermingle with external stimuli to produce highly
complex and variegated forms of the federal
principle. The federal principle is itself a simple
principle but it incorporates a wealth of contextual
meaning. This kaleidoscope meaning must be examined
through conceptual lenses which are sensitised to
each distinctive setting. Since our particular focus
is federalism and federation in Western Europe, we
shall now apply this conceptual distinction to the
specific mosaic that constitutes Western Europe.
Here our twin concepts can be enriched and enlivened
as they absorb the heady mixture of the European past
and present.

The Complexity of the West European Tradition

One of the most interesting and potentially useful
applications of the conceptual distinction between
federalism and federation in Western Europe concerns
the interstate and intrastate perspective, or what
C. Pentland calls the 'international-domestic
cleavage'.[27] As a strong prescriptive or normative
orientation, federalism may be conceptually valid in
the sense that it obviates the need for a qualitative
break between an international and a domestic federal
system. Classic federalist theory, according to
Pentland, has two major components: it is a theory
of international pacification concerned mainly with
issues of peace and security; and it is a theory of
domestic political organisation.[28] But if we utilise
federalism in the way that we have discussed it above
then it is difficult to see why a qualitative break
between these two major components is necessary. If
federalism is taken to be the dynamic organisational
principle of federation - the driving force of
federal union - it is equally applicable at both
interstate and intrastate levels in Western Europe.

For our purposes in this book the interstate perspective would suggest the idea of a federal Europe. It would, more specifically, be a focus upon federal relations between states in Western Europe. Reference to federalism and federation in the context of West European political integration will be made in the concluding remarks of this chapter. It is an important dimension of our subject. But it is the intrastate perspective of federalism and federation which is more central to our concerns. Intrastate federalism in Western Europe narrows our focus to look in this book at Belgium, Spain, France, Ireland and (historically) Great Britain, and it simultaneously extends it to uncover a striking underlying continuity in the federal tradition across states in Western Europe. In Western Europe the tradition of federalism is present both within and across states, whether they have federal or non-federal political systems. Intrastate federation, on the other hand, would focus, inter alia, upon questions of centralisation and decentralisation within the federal state and in Western Europe it would perforce limit our investigation to the three acknowledged federations: Austria, Switzerland and West Germany. Intrastate federalism, then, is the key which can unlock the door to an indigenous political tradition which draws upon uniquely European modes of political thought and socio-economic organisation stretching back several centuries. It is a useful reformulation and development of our original conceptual distinction.

Since it is now time to explore and illuminate the rich diversity of federalism in the West European tradition we can conveniently return to the notion of pluralism which we introduced earlier in our discussion. Indeed, it is imperative that we do so if we are even to begin to understand and appreciate the depth of this tradition. Pentland has already identified the historical source of this tradition in admirably concise terms, believing it to be:

> quite different, tracing its origins to medieval European society and denying the federal principle its more familiar associations with the legal constitution of a territorial state. This tradition of thought .... is .... abstract and philosophical ....; its analytic bias is toward small groups and sociological variables and its prescriptive bias is towards fundamental social reorganisation both below and beyond national boundaries.[29]

Federalism here is taken to be a general principle of social organisation and finds its way quite easily into theories of pluralism. But it is important at this point to clarify the nature of the relationship between federalism and pluralism.

Is federalism one of the many varieties of pluralism or is pluralism to be regarded as an aspect of federalism ? The answer in general terms is that both interpretations may be valid. It may simply be the case that each concept requires different kinds of analysis. King's position, as we have already seen, is perfectly clear, but another recent contributor to the debate, D. Nicholls, has adopted the reverse position: 'the pluralist movement can be regarded as an aspect of federalism .... pluralist writers are the inheritors of a long tradition'.[30] Pluralism, for Nicholls, emphasises 'the social life of citizens as it manifests itself in the family, the church, the sporting or cultural group and the civic association', has the same purpose as federalism, and may even be the greatest contribution to the federal idea'.[31] Nicholls' primary aim is to investigate the work of English pluralist thinkers but his analysis may provide a clue to our query about West European federalism and pluralism.

The English tradition of pluralism, dating back to the late nineteenth and early twentieth centuries, 'when the state was becoming increasingly active and powerful',[32] offered both a critical analysis of the state and a series of proposals for its reconstruction. Political authority should be organised in a manner which accurately reflects the natural diversity of society. This social differentiation springs from freely formed bodies and associations of citizens which do not owe their existence to the state. If at this point we shift our attention to continental Europe, we can identify a similar tradition stretching back at least four centuries. Indeed, many English pluralist writers and intellectuals have drawn on this tradition.[33] It is widely acknowledged to have begun with the ideas of Althusius who first formulated the theoretical foundations of a differentiated society in the early seventeenth century. It is not our purpose to discuss these ideas in detail here, but it is useful to have some rough guidelines about his views in order to provide the contextual background to a distinctive European political tradition.

The ideas of Althusius were grounded in the medieval conception of organic structure. His was a theory of society based upon natural law whereby

individuals freely organised themselves into
associations, both religious and secular, which were
the fundamental element of the state. These
associations, or intermediate bodies, were a complex
amalgam of religious groups, guilds, communes,
corporations, leagues of towns, merchant associations
and many other organisations which antedated the
modern state and owed nothing to it for their
existence. They constituted the living practice of
society. Althusius accordingly identified the
family, the association, the commune, the province,
and the state as a kind of rising hierarchical nexus
of complex social institutions which together created
the state, were incorporated within it and
effectively intervened between it and the individual.
Small wonder, then, that Althusius has been variously
regarded as a medieval corporatist, an early
pluralist and a primitive federalist.

These ideas may have lain dormant, lost in
history, had they not been resurrected during the
late nineteenth century by the German jurist and
legal historian, Otto von Gierke, who thereby rescued
Althusius from oblivion.[34] The idea that the various
communes, guilds, corporations and other associations
were independent of the state (as were individuals)
yet of the same nature as the state was thus already
deeply rooted in the continental European tradition
of political thought by the time Gierke revived it.
As S. Ehrlich has recently emphasised in his
impressive work on pluralism, the towns and various
other associations had developed the conception of
their own distinct personality long before the modern
centralising state first emerged. Their origins and
activities did not depend on their being endowed with
the status of legal persons by the state. They were
'really existing autonomous bodies which, relative to
the state, were capable of self-government and were
self-governing in fact'. Alluding to Gierke's views,
'groups, whatever their organisation, and hence legal
persons, too, were .... real entities in which (there
existed) a sphere of freedom other than that which
can be obtained within the framework of the state'.[35]

If we take the ideas of Althusius and Gierke to
be in the intellectual mainstream of a strong
European philosophical tradition which sees groups
and associations as the basic social unit of the body
politic, we can understand why many contemporary
writers regard pluralism as historically and
philosophically more comprehensive than federalism.
After all, Althusius and Gierke did not seek to
invent a new theory of associations: they sought

instead to revive the role of free associations which
had been active before their absorption and
suffocation by the modern state. As philosophical
statement and historical fact, then, European
pluralism may perhaps be taken to have a longer
progeniture than federalism, at least in the way it
has been defined above. Federalism retains its
character as a 'normative orientation' but in
relation to pluralism it may best be
contradistinguished as an ideological position.

Whichever position we adopt concerning
federalism and pluralism in Europe, our brief
discussion of these two phenomena makes it easy to
understand why so many political scientists regard
these terms as synonymous. It is difficult to draw
firm boundaries between them. From a number of
different standpoints they may be viewed as
substitutable concepts. For our purposes, however,
this short survey is invaluable for a different
reason. It serves to highlight the rich protean
nature of the federal concept in Europe. The
indigenous European federal tradition incorporates
various elements with varying degrees of visibility
during different historical periods. Given Europe's
turbulent past during the last four centuries alone
it would be surprising if the legacies of previous
social modes of behaviour and custom, and the scars
of old religious conflicts, were not absorbed into a
European tradition which is distinct. This is why
such notions as personalism, subsidiarity,
corporatism, pluralism and solidarism are as
important in this tradition as the more familiar idea
of territoriality which has typically dominated
Anglo-American approaches to the study of federalism
and federation.[36] In the European tradition of
federalism and federation the notion of territory has
to be set alongside non-territorial,
functional-associational concepts grounded, as we
have seen, in a long historical and philosophical
lineage.

This account of European federalism is, of
course, only cursory. It merely scratches the
surface of a rich, complex and deeply rooted
tradition. However, it does suggest that King's
conceptualisation of federalism ought to be deepened,
enriched and extended. This concept in its European
setting exhibits a much more organic, societal
quality than its more instrumental, mechanistic and
liberal constitutional Anglo-American partner.
King's conceptualisation of federalism, taken
literally, would overlook the kind of European social

differentiation sketched out here. To underline the
point: federalism is the organisational principle of
federation, but in the European tradition it is also
an important principle of social organisation. This
is why elements of Catholic social theory -
personalism and subsidiarity - are still vital clues
to an understanding of this tradition with its
'bottom-up' conception of political authority and of
the state structure. Indeed, if we were to approach
European federalism from the standpoint of a
developmental analysis of religious associations we
would doubtless obtain a very interesting perspective
of the organisational capacities of Catholicism and
Calvinism to mobilise, protect, promote and insulate
their various group identities in the corporatist
mould.[37]

If we descend from the general to the
particular, as the subsequent chapters of this book
proceed, we can also see how these various elements
of the European tradition of federalism wax and wane
in their domestic state settings. The economic
decentralist nature of Proudhon's version of
federalism, for example, is no less important a
feature of this mixed tradition, particularly in
France and Spain, than the skeletal characteristics
which we have already outlined.[38] The idea of
'cultural communities', built upon the 'personality
principle', propounded by Otto Bauer and Karl Renner
as a solution to the nationalities problem in the
Austro-Hungarian Empire would also fall within this
rubric. As Lijphart has recently observed, 'Austria
is formally a federal Republic, but its system of
segmental autonomy is mainly of the non-territorial
form'.[39] So, too, with federations. They each
exhibit institutional and structural features
uniquely reflective of their own federalisms.
Switzerland, with its collegial form of government,
is an obvious example. No federation, of course, is
immune to change and each will develop new techniques
- or negotiate new political bargains - in response
to contemporary pressures whether they be general
demands for the decentralisation of decision-making,
as in Switzerland in the 1980s, or the particular
reassertion of a constituent identity as with
Vorarlberg in Austria. Before we conclude our
sketch outline of the European tradition of
federalism and federation we must not overlook the
existence of interstate federalism in connection with
regional political integration in Western Europe.
This, too, has a long progeniture and in its
contemporary West European context it adds to the

complexity of the overall European federal tradition.
As Chapter Seven demonstrates, this specific body of
federal ideas has recently experienced a notable
revival in its drive for a reconstructed European
Community centred upon the nebulous concept of
'European Union'. The years between 1972 and 1985
have been critical for the future of the European
Community; the vague European idea has been gradually
distilled into a set of practical proposals which,
while not constituting a blueprint for federation,
are none the less expressive of federal ideas.
Federalism remains doggedly resilient in this
arena.[40]

Conclusion

This chapter has examined the conceptual distinction
between federalism and federation, and indicated some
of the advantages which accrue from its consistent
application to Western Europe. It is not an
innovative distinction but, as King has astutely
observed, most writers continue to make no
distinction at all.[41] Our persistent determination
to maintain a distinction between these two concepts
doubtless raises new problems in the study of federal
theory and practice. It is not the case, for
example, that every federalism will always lead to
federation. Perhaps, as in the instances of Belgium
and Spain discussed in this book, the federal
prescription may not fully determine itself. It may
stop short of federation simply because of elite
resistance or due to its own atrophy. It may even be
bribed by concessions designed to weaken its mass
appeal. Such problems which arise as a consequence
of this conceptual distinction, however, need not
deter us from pursuing the distinction. Every
approach has its price and ours is no exception.
    One of the major advantages of using this
conceptual distinction between federalism and
federation lies in the area of comparative politics.
In the preface to his Federalism: Origin, Operation
and Significance published in 1964, William Riker
lamented about his own refusal to attempt a
comparative study of modern federal systems. The
difficulties seemed insurmountable. Riker identified
many imponderables which he felt vitiated the
exercise at its source. He reduced these
uncertainties to the need for 'more information about
history, the sensitivity to culture, and the
linguistic competence to examine all these societies'
which claimed to be federal - a task well beyond the

ability of the 'isolated scholar'.[42] Today,
twenty-one years after Riker's lament, we can perhaps
sound a note of cautious optimism about the
feasibility of this project. The conceptual
distinction employed here suggests that both
comparative federalisms and federations are now
practicable and heuristically worthwhile areas of
study. This book does not intend to offer such
comparative analyses but it does suggest that the
individual case studies which follow are amenable to
such a treatment. If it helps in the smallest way to
stimulate such studies then our modest contribution
will have been all the more worthwhile.

Federalism and Federation

Notes

1. K. C. Wheare, Federal Government, (London, OUP, 1946)

2. I. D. Duchacek, Comparative Federalism: The Territorial Dimension of Politics, (London, Holt, Rinehart and Winston, 1970), p.189.

3. M.J.C. Vile, 'Federal Theory and the 'New Federalism'', in D. Jaensch, (ed), The Politics of 'New Federalism', (Adelaide, 1977), p.1.

4. W. L. Livingston, 'A Note on the Nature of Federalism', Political Science Quarterly, Vol.67, (1952), pp.81-95.

5. For an interesting discussion of the ways in which Anglo-American concepts have failed to comprehend the European federal tradition, see K. R. Luther, 'The Inadequacies of the Anglo-American Debate for the Comparative Analysis of Federalism and Federation in Western Europe', paper given at the Annual Conference of the European Consortium for Political Research (ECPR), University of Salzburg, Austria, 1984.

6. See my paper entitled 'Comparative Federalism and Federation: Is There a Sound Basis for Comparison ?', paper given at the ECPR Annual Conference, University of Salzburg, Austria, 1984.

7. Livingston used the term 'instrumentalities' to try to break away from Wheare's rigid approach. See Livingston, 'A Note on the Nature of Federalism', pp.81-95.

8. P. King, Federalism and Federation, (London, Croom Helm, 1982).

9. Ibid, p.77.

10. M.J.C. Vile, 'Federal Theory and the 'New Federalism'', p.3.

11. This is a highly contentious issue. In an earlier essay, Preston King argued that federal supremacy did not leave much room for an effective theory of balance. See P. King, 'Against Federalism', in R. Benewick, R. N. Berki and B. Parekh, Knowledge and Belief in Politics, (London, 1973), pp.151-176. According to M. Stein, 'Federal Political Systems and Federal Societies', World Politics, Vol.20, (1968), p.727, it is R. L. Watts, New Federations: Experiments in the Commonwealth, (Oxford, 1966), who is responsible for introducing the notion of equilibrium absent from Livingston's earlier argument.

12. King, Federalism and Federation, pp.91 and 140.

13. R. Dikshit, The Political Geography of Federalism: An Inquiry into Origins and Stability, (Delhi, 1975), p.4.

14. King, Federalism and Federation, p.145.

15. C. J. Hughes, 'The Theory of Confederacies', Sixth World Congress of IPSA, Geneva, (1964), pp.1-14.

16. Ibid, p.13.

17. Ibid, p.13 and C. J. Hughes, Confederacies, (Leicester University Press, 1963), p.5.

18. King, Federalism and Federation, p.90.

19. Ibid, p.75.

20. A. Lijphart, Democracy in Plural Societies: A Comparative Exploration, (London, Yale University Press, 1977), pp.42-43.

21. P. King, 'Against Federalism', p.153.

22. King, Federalism and Federation, p.14.

23. Ibid, p.146.

24. Ibid, p.76.

25. Vile, 'Federal Theory and the 'New Federalism'', p.3.

26. King, Federalism and Federation, pp.14 and 75.

27. See C. Pentland, International Theory and European Integration, (London, Faber and Faber, 1973), p.158.

28. Ibid, p.158.

29. Ibid, pp.159-160.

30. D. Nicholls, The Pluralist State, (London, MacMillan Press, 1975), p.32.

31. Ibid, pp.10-11 and 32.

32. Ibid, p.10.

33. For an excellent analysis of the way in which continental European pluralism seeped into mainstream English intellectual thought during the early years of the twentieth century, see S. Ehrlich, Pluralism On and Off Course, (London, Pergamon Press, 1982), Ch.3.

34. Ibid, p.78. For a useful summary of Gierke's importance, see pp.69-80.

35. Ibid, pp.71-75.

36. On personalism, see F. Kinsky, 'Personalism and Federalism', Publius, Vol. 9, No.4, (1979), pp.131-156. On the links between the other elements and Catholic social theory, see A. Freemantle, (ed), The Papal Encyclicals In Their Historical Context, (New York, Mentor-Omega, 1963) and M. Fogarty, Christian Democracy in Western Europe, 1820-1953, (London, Routledge and Kegan Paul Ltd., 1957). One outstanding exception in the Anglo-American tendency to overlook key social elements in the European tradition of federalism is Daniel Elazar. Elazar's research on federalism is clearly sensitised to the European tradition outlined here. See, for example, his Federalism and Political Integration, (Israel, Turtledove, 1979).

37. This reflection was prompted by my recent acquaintance with H. Bakvis, Catholic Power in the Netherlands, (Kingston and Montreal, McGill-Queen's University Press, 1981).

38. See R. Vernon, The Principle of Federation by P. J. Proudhon, (London, University of Toronto Press, 1979).

39. Lijphart, Democracy in Plural Societies, p.43.

40. For a short summary of the influence and development of federal ideas in connection with 'European Union' in the European Community, see M. Burgess, 'Federal Ideas in the European Community: Altiero Spinelli and 'European Union', 1981-1984', Government and Opposition, Vol.19, No.3 (Summer 1984), pp.339-347. See also the author's 'Altiero Spinelli, Federalism and the EUT: On the Trail of a Long Progeniture' in J. Lodge (ed), Whither Europe ? - European Union: The European Community in Search of a Future, forthcoming (London, MacMillan Press, 1985).

41. King, Federalism and Federation, p.20.

42. W. H. Riker, Federalism: Origin, Operation, Significance, (Boston, 1964), preface, p.xii.

3. BELGIUM: A REGIONAL STATE OR A FEDERAL STATE IN THE MAKING?

Frank Delmartino

Introduction

A while ago, the French newspaper, Le Monde, consecrated an article to Belgium on the occasion of the 150th anniversary of its independence under the title: 'Belgium: 150 years of a 'provisional' nation'.[1] Indeed, when it was created, the State of Belgium could not have survived except for an international compromise between the great powers of the time and its future was far from being assured. A century and a half later, the institutional structure still seems to be provisional, but the compromise this time has to be found within the country. Our present purpose is to sketch the major lines of this search for a new equilibrium between the constitutive components : the cultural communities and the regions.

This dismembering of the unitary state could well be studied from the historical point of view by citing the deep roots of the Belgian divorce and the innumerable proposals, compromises, and failures that mark out a half-century of controversies. Others would prefer to analyse the juridical crystallisation that resulted from the political debate. The consecutive revisions of the Constitution in 1970 and 1980, and the institutional reform laws of 8 and 9 August 1980, do indeed provide revealing comment on the true scope of the reform of the State. Without rejecting these approaches, which are essential for a proper understanding of the problem, we would like to situate the process of regionalisation in the more general framework of the relations between the centre and the periphery of power.

Even though it is unique in many respects, the Belgian experience cannot be isolated from the double movement affecting the modern State. As S. Cassese (1981) has noted, there is a pendular movement between the dispersion and the concentration of power. On the one hand, there is a centrifugal movement of governmental functions upwards and downwards, notably the internationalisation and the regionalisation of many public functions. On the other hand, there is a new aggregation of powers thus dispersed in mixed administrative organs in which the different levels of power are represented. It is interesting to note that none of these re-aggregations occurs in authentically State organs.

It would be premature to conclude from this the downfall of the State. We would note, rather, that the Nation State no longer constitutes the ultimate and perfect figure of historical evolution, but is situated in a period of transition. Y. Meny (1981) expressed this succinctly when he observed that the Nation State constitutes the consolidation phase that follows the fragmentation phase and precedes that of differentiation.

This differentiation is already in motion and is characterised in Western and Southern Europe by a rather clear tendency toward dispersion of power. The reform of the State in Belgium being situated in the framework of this pendular movement, the elaboration of a quasi-federal system is of particular interest. We will limit ourselves to the essential explanatory elements and to general information concerning the ongoing reform in order to stress more the characteristics and the orientation of the process of regionalisation.

A Growing Awareness

How can one explain the apparent disaggregation of a country that is situated, paradoxically, at the point of convergence of a coalescing Europe, and of which the territory does not exceed that of the major regions of its neighbours (30.000 km, 10 million inhabitants) ? The foundation of this regionalisation movement is constituted, in our opinion, by a growing awareness of the differentiation of the country.

For more than a century since the achievement of independence in 1830, the unity of Belgium was never seriously challenged thanks to a dominant, French-speaking bourgeois class in both the North and the South of the country. The underlying heterogeneity, cultural and socio-economic, was thus concealed or at least it did not clearly manifest itself politically. The reason for this was the electoral system based on property-holding, which left the government of the country to a rather restricted elite.

The diversity, nevertheless, was obvious. In the North of the country, the vast majority of the Flemish population continued to speak its mother tongue and even formed a numerical majority within the Belgian State. However, to have access to public positions on whatever level, it was necessary to speak French. French was not only the common language for mutual comprehension, but it was in particular the cultural language, the sign of a desired or attained social level. For a considerable number of Flemish immigrants in Brussels, for example, the uprooting led to Frenchification, which furnished the capital, the origins of which were Flemish, with a French-speaking majority.

In Flanders itself, the romantic movement of the nineteenth century, like everywhere in Europe, made the people aware of their origins. But the Flemish Movement took on an exceptional scope following the First World War. A legal system, a public administration, and an educational system in French were still tolerable. But to die for a country whose leaders, and more specifically the officers, did not speak the language of the majority of its citizens, in their role as soldiers, was no longer acceptable. Thus the movement, born on the front of Flanders: Here is our blood, when will we have our right?

This right was acquired progressively. After the introduction of universal suffrage in 1919, the numerical majority thrust themselves forward. Thus, various 'linguistic' laws were passed in 1932 and 1963, tending to fix the Flemish territory, to introduce Dutch into public administration and the legal system, and particularly to establish secondary and higher education in the mother tongue. The effect of this was the creation of an elite that respected its own cultural heritage and that became progressively more involved in the public administration and political affairs of the country. The definitive breakthrough of the socio-cultural emancipation movement came in 1970, when the autonomy of the French and Dutch cultural communities was recognised in the Constitution.

Nevertheless, we must not isolate the growth of Flemish self-awareness from the socio-economic context of the period. Wallonia was already industrialised in the course of the nineteenth century and many Flemish workers settled there or commuted daily, weekly, or seasonally. Between the North and the South of the country, therefore, there was not only a cultural barrier. Just as important was the differentiation in socio-economic development. This advantage was reversed toward the middle of the present century when the industrial sectors and the infrastructure of Wallonia became more and more obsolete, while Flanders, well situated with respect to the sea and having been industrialised later, was better able to resist the beginnings of the economic crisis.

The Walloon renewal was conceived from then on less and less in the national context, 'dominated' by a Flemish majority in Parliament, even though the government remained in a constitutionally guaranteed equilibrium.[3] A large consensus was formed in the South of the country to take the economic and social future of the region in their own hands. It is thus Wallonia in particular that has demanded the regionalisation of the country in order to reshape its economy according to its own lights. Indeed, the high degree of industrialisation has favoured the dominance of Wallonian Socialist ideology and the analyses and objectives it recommends, notably as regards the active intervention of the government in the economy. Flanders, however, has always relied on the traditional currents of the free market.

This review, with few nuances because of its brevity, is intended to indicate the complexity of the explanatory factors involved in the institutional reform of the country: Flanders desiring above all to have far-reaching cultural autonomy and guarantees for the Flemish minority in Brussels; Wallonia demanding economic and social autonomy in order to confront the acute crisis from which it is suffering and for which it intends to remedy in its own way; the residents of Brussels bouncing back and forth between their national vocation as the capital and their sense of belonging, by a majority, to the French cultural community.

However, the factors that determine the difficult dialogue between the Communities within the Belgian State are not only ethnic and cultural. There are also other cleavages involved in the oppositions, frustrations, and suspicions that complicate the process of balanced nation-building. The uneven economic development and decline and the ideological-political contrasts constitute important elements of the communitarian dossier. It is precisely because of these mutually reinforcing cleavages that the creation of a broad national authority in the present crisis period is so difficult. Belgium threatens to be cast adrift institutionally and is thus searching for formulas that can reconcile unity and diversity.

A Crisis of Identity and Legitimacy

Assuming that this crisis of the state has not been caused by one single factor but by the interaction of various elements, we are attracted to the analytical schema that has been provided by the Political

Development school.   In the line of Pye (1967) and
Binder (1971), Y. Meny (1981) has successfully
clarified the modernisation crises of the European
states.   Without going into the identity, legitimacy,
participation, distribution and penetration crises
that he postulates, we think that a temporary placing
of the Belgian case in this conceptual framework is
illuminating.

Throughout the nineteenth century, a very
pronounced feeling of national identity contributed
to nation-building in Belgium.   An identity crisis
did not manifest itself until the turn of the century
when the Flemish population began to demand the
'right to be different' and thus threatened the
dominant position of the French-speaking in general
and of the Walloons in particular.   A famous
statement made in 1912 by a Walloon leader, a future
minister of state, J. Destree, may be cited in this
regard.   His 'open letter to the King' opened with:
"Sire, there are no Belgians.   There are only Flemish
and Walloons".

Examples from other countries have shown that
cultural diversity can coexist with institutional
assimilation on the condition that constitutional
guarantees are given to the parties composing the
whole.   If, however, the differentiation is not
recognised in time, a grouping, a cultural community,
a region, will refuse to identify with the values,
the culture, the language of the dominant group, thus
challenging the legitimacy of the State.   This is
what has happened, first in Flanders and then, in a
different way, in Wallonia.   In view of the
structural aspects of this socio-economic decline,
the loyalty of the Walloon population toward the
Belgian State has been sorely tested.   Although in the
past Wallonia had no problem in identifying with the
State because it participated fully in political and
economic decision-making, the situation has been
reversed for quite some time.   The State is suspected
of withholding from Wallonia political participation
as well as the financial means to which it believes
it is entitled.   Thus, in the final analysis, the
institutional crisis that is taking place in Belgium
seems to us to be caused by this double attack on the
legitimacy of the unitary State.

Twofold Cultural Autonomy, Threefold Socio-Economic
Regionalisation

Although several factors had long been pointing to
the end of the unitary State, it was not until 1970
that this reform movement broke through

institutionally. Reading the governmental
declaration before Parliament, which also had the
status of constituent assembly, the Prime Minister,
G. Eyskens, declared: "The unitary State has been
surpassed by events. The communities and the regions
must take their place in the new governmental
structures, which must be better adapted to the true
situation of the country".

The government thus proposed that the
constituent assembly modernise the State by
abandoning the unitary structure and by
constitutionally recognising the two major cultural
communities as well as the three economic regions, in
which was situated the agglomeration of Brussels.
The constitutional amendment would be limited,
however, to directive principles, which would be
later implemented by laws voted by a qualified
majority of the Parliament, that is, by a two-thirds
majority of the assembly as a whole and by a simple
majority of each linguistic group.

As regards cultural autonomy, the government
thus succeeded in having the constituent assembly
recognise the cultural communities and grant to each
an assembly composed of the members of parliament
belonging to the respective linguistic groups.[4]
Regionalisation, however, did not yet seem 'ripe
enough' to be implemented. During the 1950s and
1960s several proposals were developed by a variety
of committees. They all tended to the
decentralisation of the unitary State, but while some
envisaged a decentralisation in favour of the
provinces, others favoured the formation of regional
entities on a socio-economic basis, sometimes
crossing linguistic frontiers.

Ultimately, the linguistic cleavage prevailed,
reducing the Belgian regions to three, i.e., an
exclusively Flemish region, an exclusively
French-speaking region (Wallonia), and the Brussels
region, which is bilingual, although with a
French-speaking majority. The reform of the State in
the cultural domain and the socio-economic
regionalisation thus converged with one exception:
the capital.

Article 107 quator was written into the
Constitution: Belgium consists of three regions: the
Walloon region, the Flemish region, and the Brussels
region. The law grants the regional organs it
creates and that are composed of elected
representatives the authority to govern the matters
it determines'. For this special law, a qualified
majority was required. It was not obtained before

1980, i.e., at the time when it was decided to detach
the Brussels problem from a general agreement on
institutional reforms. The reform of August 1980
thus still did not include a solution for Brussels.
    The critical problem is not purely and simply
linguistic, even though linguistic considerations led
the Flemish to reject the administrative expansion of
the city beyond the current nineteen communes. It
must be realised that Brussels is a bilingual island
in Flemish territory, even though many
French-speakers are settled in the peripheral
communes. Some of these communes have
'administrative facilities' for the immigrants. And
there are some that demand attachment to the capital.
    The central question, however, is whether
Brussels will be accepted fully as the third region,
and on this point not only the Flemish but also many
Walloons are somewhat hesitant. As everywhere in the
world, the sympathy for the capital and its residents
is not general, but it is feared mostly that there
will be a reduction of the autonomy granted to the
major regions if this autonomy must be shared with
Brussels. The needs of the capital, but also the
resources of the Brussels agglomeration, are by
nature sharply different from those of the two other
regions. The problem is thus above all political:
should Brussels be accepted as a partner in a
regionalised state, or should the capital be
considered an agglomeration with a special status
under the authority of the central government ? The
answer is not simple, all the more so because it will
be necessary to find an equitable arrangement for the
participation of the Flemish minority in the power.

An Unbalanced Reform

Thus, the 1980 reform was only possible because of
the postponement of a solution for Brussels. The
government of M. Martens, a coalition of three
traditional parties, had a two-thirds majority in
Parliament and considered the moment opportune for a
breakthrough. Moreover, this government was formed
after a failure in the discussions between the
'traditional' parties and the so-called
'communitarian' parties, i.e., those having regional
autonomy as a central point in their political
programme. Christian-Democrats, Socialists and
Liberals were thus united, in the beginning of 1980,
in a kind of government of national unity to achieve
a reform to the extent that it was 'ripe' and to put
the problem of Brussels back into the institutional

icebox. The discontent generated by communitarian
troubles was such that this formula - disconcerting
in its simplicity - was accepted with relief in the
North and the South, except, obviously, by the party
for the defence of the French-speaking in Brussels.

Thus, in a few months, an institutional reform
was designed, a good part of it on already existing
foundations but still incomplete and provisional. We
have already mentioned the cultural autonomy.The
cultural councils, composed of members of parliament,
had been operating since 1971 but had no real power
of control over the national ministers.

An attempt to institute regional councils
provisionally in 1974 failed because these councils
were only able to issue 'advice', which satisfied
nobody. In addition, the creation within the
government of ministerial committees for
communitarian and regional affairs instituted a de
facto regionalisation. Even though not controlled by
a regional parliament before which they would be
responsible and supported only by an embryonic
regionalised administration, this intra-governmental
reform accomplished an important task. The
institutional reform of 1980 would ratify these
experiences and delimit and balance the respective
responsibilities from the democratic point of view by
establishing a parliamentary assembly for each
regional executive.

In conformity with the 'magic' formula of two
communities and three regions, it would have been
necessary to erect five parliamentary assemblies and
five executives. Brussels remained in suspense, so
there remained only two regions to be given a council
and an executive. But in Flanders it was decided to
grant communitarian and regional authority to one
single assembly and to one single executive. In
Wallonia - an agreement on this point having not been
reached but remaining possible for the future - a
Walloon regional council and executive were
established in addition to the council and executive
for the French cultural community. As the reader may
have noted, simplicity and equilibrium between the
regions are not the most striking characteristics of
this institutional construction:

Belgium: Regional or Federal State ?

National Parliament	National Government
Flemish Council	Flemish Executive
Council of the French Community	Executive of the French Community
Walloon Regional Council	Walloon Regional Executive
	The Brussels regional executive is within the national government, not having been included in the institutional reform.

And, as of 1984, to complete the process, there must be added:

Council of the German-speaking Community	Executive of the German-Speaking Community

Some Characteristics of the Reform

A detailed study of the reform of August 1980 would obviously exceed our present scope. We will thus limit ourselves to some characteristic aspects which illustrate primarily the degree of regional autonomy.
'The political regions', according to the definition of Paul Romus (1979), 'have an autonomy guaranteed by the constitution and exercise some of the prerogatives of the central government. This type of region possesses a parliament and a government competent for an entire series of matters.' The Belgian communities and regions fit these general characteristics. They have parliamentary assemblies, the councils chosen directly by the electorate and executives elected by the councils from among themselves.[5] Since the legislative elections of 1981, these executives have left the national government - except, of course, for Brussels - and the regional and central responsibilities became thenceforth incompatible.
The decreed power is exercised collectively by the council and the executive. A decree has the force of law. It can abrogate, supplement, modify, or replace the legal dispositions in force. As there is no constitutional court in Belgium, a procedure had to be devised to decide conflicts of authority. The Council of State plays an important role here, but attention is focused primarily on the Court of

Belgium: Regional or Federal State ?

Arbitration, provided for by Article 107 ter of the[6]
Constitution and operational since the end of 1984.
This court is composed both of senior politicians and
jurists. The importance of this court of arbitration
for the preservation of the unity of the state is
thus emphasised. In addition, conflicts of interest
are submitted to a joint commission composed
proportionally of representatives of the central
government and of the regional executives.

While these procedures manifest a dialogue of
equals between the centre and the periphery, the
financing of the regions reflects the dominant
position of the State. Even though the regions have,
in principle, their own taxation and rebates on taxes
and levies, the regions have been financed up to the
present by budgetary credits, hence subsidies, as
part of the State budget. Thus, the field of
regional action is strongly determined by the
financial means made available by the State.
Juridical autonomy, therefore, is counterbalanced by
financial dependence.

Finally and in particular, we must mention the
responsibilities transferred to the communities and
the regions. With regard to cultural autonomy
introduced in 1970, cultural matters have been
enlarged, and the communities have also been given
responsibility since 1980 over 'personalisable'
matters. Let us specify these two categories.

The cultural matters comprise in particular:

- radio and television broadcasting;
- the fine arts, the cultural patrimony,
  museums, and libraries;
- adult education and cultural development;
- physical education, sports, leisure, tourism;
- pre-school, extracurricular activities, and
  extramural education;
- professional reconversion and retraining.

Formal education is now 'communitarian' only in
principle, the control remaining in large part in the
hands of the national authorities because of the
delicate equilibrium between the free and the state
educational systems. Even though two ministers - one
for each linguistic regime - are responsible for it,
the maintenance on the national level of a sector
that is so important from all points of view shackles
the development of the cultural communities.

By way of compensation, the communities play a
constitutionally guaranteed role in international
cooperation. In virtue of this disposition, the

Flemish community, for example, has concluded a
treaty with the Netherlands on the unification of the
Dutch language.

The 'personalisable' matters concern the policy
of health and direct aid to people: social welfare,
family policy, policy concerning the handicapped, and
the reception and integration of immigrants.   While
cultural matters were transferred without
restriction, this is not the case for most of
'personalisable' matters, which have been much less
affected up to the present by socio-cultural
differentiation.   As a general rule, the organic
framework, and the financing of these sectors remain
national, the 'communitarisation' appearing only in
the concrete application.   Decreed and regulational
measures, obviously, can be taken in this regard so
that specifically communitarian policy can gradually
take shape.   Nevertheless, the type of transfer of
authority here differs fundamentally from what took
place in cultural matters.

The authority over 'personalisable' matters of
the two major communities also covers Brussels, and
it is here that the true significance of this
neologism appears.   Indeed, according to their
membership in one or the other of the communities,
the citizens of Brussels benefit from a specific
policy in this regard. Certain services, used by
everyone, are, nevertheless 'bi-communitarian' and
are managed by common agreement.

The regional authorities, on the contrary, are
exercised ratione loci in the interior of each of the
well-defined regions except, provisionally, in
Brussels.   Again, one may distinguish between sectors
(i.e. including all of the functions attached to
them) that have been transferred in their totality or
quasi-totality, and others that are characterised by
a transfer that is more or less partial.

Among the matters transferred integrally, one
may list city planning and regional development,
including urban renewal and the land-use policy along
with housing policy, rural renewal, and conservation
of nature.   Also transferred was administrative
supervision of the provinces and the municipalities.

As regards the other matters that have been
'regionalised', one must distinguish the aspects
transferred and those reserved by the central State.
In other words, responsibilities and functions were
cut out of several organic sectors and escaped
transference.   These 'exceptions' are so numerous and
particularly so important that they affect the
general character of the transfer operation.   To
restrict ourselves to a few typical examples:

- the protection of the environment with respect to general and sectoral legal norms remained a national matter;
- the production and the distribution of water was transferred, but not the major hydraulic works of national importance;
- the 'regional' aspects of energy, defined very restrictively, were transferred;
- the administration of employment policy was regionalised, but not the employment policy itself;
- the criterion for the distribution of the municipal fund was regionalised but not the determination of that fund itself.

The example par excellence of the complexity of the transfer of functions, nevertheless, is furnished by the economic policy. After having jettisoned the foundation of a regional policy in matters of economic planning and expansion, including public industrial initiatives, the special law of 8 August 1980 specifies restrictions and exceptions:

- any regulation regarding fiscal advantages is subject to the approval of the central authority;
- a financial guarantee by the government can only be granted by the national government;
- and the central government was ultimately concerned with sectoral economic policy with regard to five important domains: steel, coal; shipbuilding, glass and textiles.

Controversy rapidly arose regarding this last point, a controversy that is typical for the precarious equilibrium of the reform in its present version. The regions have successfully demanded greater involvement in the decision-making with regard to these key economic sectors, but they now must also contribute financially. Yet what is involved here are 'bottomless pits' that are endangering efforts in other areas. Still, this structural economic policy is seen as an essential component in the regional task profile. It illustrates very clearly that the traditional regionalism as it is manifested in several European countries has been far surpassed in Belgium.

Belgium: Regional or Federal State ?

Regionalism or Federalism ?

Thus it should be evident that it is not easy to
place the Belgian institutional formula under one of
the classic forms of the state. For convenience
sake, one sometimes speaks of a 'regional state', but
this term is far from clear, its purpose being simply
to indicate that the regionalised state must be
placed on a continuum between the unitary and the
federal state.
    One of these terms hardly needs clarification,
for the unitary state is sufficiently well-known in
the West European context. But what is the essence
of a federally structured state? Daniel Elazar cites
two elements: a defined structure and a defined
process. Regarding the structure, he states: 'If a
political system is established by compact and has at
least two 'arenas', 'planes', 'tiers' or 'levels' of
government, each endowed with independent legitimacy
and a constitutionally guaranteed place in the
overall system and possessing its own set of
institutions, and responsibilities, it is
deemed to be federal'[7]
    For this structure to be truly federal, however,
it must be oriented to the convergence of the
political forces, not to their divergence: the point
of departure is a 'sense of partnership' that is
expressed in the will to collaboration in
consultation, and this with respect for the
fundamental integrity of all the partners.
    A more juridical and institutional approach to
federalism is found in the classic <u>Traite de science
politique</u> by G. Burdeau.[8] Essential in his
definition are the principles of participation and
autonomy: participation of the component states in
the general policy of the federation and in the
development of its norms; self-government of the
component states without supervision of the central
government. Molitor adds a third element: the
resolution of conflict between the centre and the
periphery is entrusted to an independent authority.[9]
    The regional form of state is described by
Molitor in a negative manner, namely, as deviating
from the three cited federal principles.[10] First,
the regions do not participate in the national
decision-making. By law, however, certain
consultative organs can be provided between the state
and the regions. Their statute of autonomy is also
not designed with their participation; it is granted
to them. The autonomy of the regions is indeed not
absolute. What is essential for their organisational

structure is imposed and their legislative competence
is limited by central supervision or central
framework laws. And, finally, the state also has the
last word in the event of a conflict of jurisdiction.

From this point of view, of course, regionalism
does not differ essentially from the classic form of
decentralisation. For Molitor, indeed, it is 'the
extreme form of the decentralised unitary state'.[11]

The political and administrative reality,
however, cannot be forced into logical and conceptual
schemes. Although French regionalism satisfies
Molitor's definition up to a certain point, this is
much less the case for the Italian, Spanish and
particularly Belgian phenomena.

To illustrate this, we will set out the
essential elements of the Belgian state reform of
August 1980 with reference to the regional or the
federal state form:

REGIONALISM	FEDERALISM
Communities and regions not involved as fullfledged partners national politics.	The law provides an are not obligatory negotiation between the state and communities and regions regarding certain matters in which the regional authorities are involved.
Communities and regions were not able to participate in the out of the statute. The transfer of power partial with respect to the vital political and economic sectors.	Other decisions require prior agreement or agreement or concurring recommendation.[12] The transfer of power is integral with respect to a number of sectors. The The decrees have the force of law. Harmonization of policy without conflict is not foreseen.
The financial resources remain as yet largely concentrated on the national level.	The Court of Arbitration is independent of the central government. The conflicts of interest are resolved politically, by negotiation. The communities have the authority for international cooperation.

Belgium: Regional or Federal State ?

This brief survey of some of the basic traits of the Belgian state system since the 1980 reform is, of course, discouraging for those who had hoped to be able to make a definitive statement about the current position of the state. But such a characterisation raises problems not only in Belgium. The Italian constitutionalist, de Vergottini, has pointed out that the distinction between the current manifestations of federalism and regionalism in Europe are much more historical than juridical.[13]
Thus, to reduce such a complex political-administrative reality in each of the countries that are considered 'regional states' to a common denominator is scientifically questionable. It is much more important to keep in mind the alternating movements of dispersion and reaggregation of power that occur in both federal and in so-called regional systems. For the political scientist, a wide domain is open for investigation, what de Vergottini calls the 'federalismo-regionalismo'.

The dysfunctions of the present reform

In order to obtain an overview of the present state of affairs in this field of tension between the national state and the regional subsystems, one must go beyond the organic legislation of 1980. The institutional process does not stand still. Some dysfunctions of the reform have subsequently become obvious for everyone and the current political distribution of powers in the country provides for the specific fleshing out of the basic legislation. We will illustrate this by means of a few typical in this complex dossier.
Controversy soon arose about the scope of the transferred responsibilities. On the one hand, this was the inevitable consequence of the complex delineation of the tasks of the central and the regional authorities. In many cases, a wide margin was left, perhaps intentionally, for interpretation. Such a transfer of responsibility is not to be conceived as an exercise in the logic of statesmanship guided by a clear basic philosophy as one may expect in the working out of a new constitutional order. The regionalisation operation stood and stands rather in the heart of a political debate and reflects the compromise between the proponents and opponents of a certain 'devolution'. The striving for a political equilibrium here obviously does not always lead to a balanced administrative order. Inevitably, therefore, this

leads to conflicts in a context that is not particularly prone to cooperation. One tends to interpret one's own spheres of responsibility in a maximalist sense.

Central and regional authorities thus stood in opposition to each other, both armed with an equivalent legal arsenal. After all, the national law does not supersede the regional decrees, and the central government cannot annul decisions of the communitarian or regional executives. The conflicts of authority thus accumulated and formed a heavy political and psychological burden for the already very precarious communitarian relations. The Court of Arbitration only began to function at the end of 1984, so it is yet to be seen how the decisions of this highest legal college will be received politically. The conflicts of interest for their part must still be settled politically, and it is obvious that this is no sinecure in a climate of animosity and mistrust. Some of the invoked 'interests' have primarily a psychological and electoral significance, so that an equitable settlement is not _per se_ really desired by everyone.

However, the position of the national government as an equal partner with the communities and the regions is seen by many as particularly illogical and dysfunctional. In many matters, the national government is impotent and at the mercy of communitarian caprices. In addition, the communities and regions complain that the 1980 reform was not implemented according to its spirit by the central government and that it is very reluctant when it comes to transferring personnel and financial resources.

This lack of clarity in the institutional relations is aggravated by the current party system. There are no national political parties at present which stand up for the interests of the country as a whole. This endangers, of course, the political legitimation of the national policy. Each politician, including the prime minister, is dependent on an electoral base that is situated in only one part of the country. In debates that concern community matters, therefore, the ministers of the central government are caught between their national mandate and the desires of their voters. It speaks for the statemanship of many of them that this situation has not yet made the country ungovernable. Nevertheless, it is an untenable position.

National solidarity, the essential connective tissue for every state, is being sorely tried. In

sectors that are particularly sensitive to the
economic crisis, it has even been lost to a certain
degree.   Every region is trying to pull the blanket
of governmental investment to itself and casts a
jaundiced eye on any possible favouring of the
'rival'.   Compensations of all kinds are thus
demanded and granted to the point of absurdity.
Obviously, this competitiveness does not promote the
most rational policymaking, so that considerable
malaise reigns over the inadequate forms of political
organisation.   It must be pointed out, however, that
the extremely difficult circumstances of the
socio-economic crisis-specifically as regards
economic development and employment-cast the
inefficient task delineation of the various
governmental organs in sharp relief.

Toward a federal state ?

Ever more voices are being raised in support of a new
form of the state, and virtually nobody still
believes that the 1980 reform was either definitive
or final.   On the contrary, a thorough revision is
again needed.   In the light of the above, it is
obvious that not only politicians but also leaders
from the socio-economic circles, i.e., from industry,
are demanding more clarity and action.
        From the many recent studies, colloquia, and
individual statements, we have selected, by way of
illustration, an authoritative statement by the
former chief of cabinet of the prime minister, who
was himself involved for years in institutional
reforms.   During a scientific congress sponsored by
the Flemish Institute for Political Science devoted
to the 1980 and (1990) reform of the state, O. Coenen
asked whether we could really wait until 1990 with 'a
federal state without federal authority'.   The
communities and regions have been organised in the
meantime, however inadequately, but the state has
been institutionally and politically dismantled.
Reference was made in particular to the lack of any
hierarchy between laws and decrees as well as to the
lack of national political parties.   'The achievement
of the 'federal' model of 1980', Coenen stated, 'can
only be realised if the national legislature and
government are actually formed on a national
basis'.[14]   Consideration was given to the reassembly
of the party families across the linguistic border in
order to provide a truly national substratum for
national institutions.

Apart from the chances of realisation of this proposal, about which there are divergent opinions, it is interesting for our argument to note that the attention is no longer only focused on the question of what responsibilities can be transferred to the communities and regions but also what the future institutional position of the state must be. The term 'federalism' (or 'con-federalism') is being heard ever more often, but it is used with divergent meanings.

Traditionally, the concept of 'federalism' in Belgium was used by political groups who demanded a form of political autonomy for their region. Both Flemish and Walloon autonomists proclaimed it already before the Second World War with a clear view to dismantling the Belgian State.[15] Support for federation was thus much more a political slogan than a consistently thought through principle of state structure.

Since the 1960s thought about the desirable structure of the state has entered the spotlight of political attention, and several formulas have been debated: 'federalism with two' (Flanders and Wallonia), 'with three' (the same plus Brussels), 'provincial federalism' (on the basis of the nine provinces), and so on. Federation then, stands for a form of the state in which far-reaching autonomy would be granted to the component parts. The stress here is still on the centrifugal forces. And also in governmental circles, one generally speaks of 'federalisation' when one means the distribution of powers to communities and regions.

Up to now, such use of the term 'federalism' in Belgium is directly contrary to what is understood by it outside.[16] Now that the autonomy of the component regions has largely been obtained, more thought is being given to the reconstruction of the authorities that have to bind the whole together. Thus, 'federalism' is gradually emerging in its classical meaning. It is still unclear how close the collaboration between the component parts must be. Therefore, some would opt for the term 'confederation', because they would stress the international legal personality of the sub-states.[17] However that may be, the trend is unmistakably in the direction of the preservation of the state. Radical separatism does not seem to be an alternative any longer. In the pendular movement that Cassese describes, Belgium has probably gone past the extreme point of dispersion of power.

Nevertheless, the institutional problem is by far still unresolved by this change of course in governmental conceptions. The institutions, as they emerged from the 1980 reform, are tuned neither to the regional nor to a truly federal model of state organisation. As shown above, characteristics can be cited that have every appearance of administrative decentralisation, while other responsibilities go further than those of many sub-states in federal systems. Belgium, therefore, urgently requires a decision: it must work out its own kind of "equiordinazione", as de Vergottini calls it, a balanced organisation of power between the global political-administrative system and its component parts.

It is obviously not the role of political science to recommend options regarding desirable state forms, but a scientific contribution could, with foreign experiences taken into account, consist of pointing out a few essential conditions for a regionalised or federalised state to function adequately. One of these conditions is solidarity between the parts of the country, for which the centre must play a coordinating role. In Spain, for example, the unequal distribution of prosperity is considered a political challenge for the entire country. The affirmation of the right to regional autonomy is therefore asserted in the same breath with the duty of solidarity. A 'fund for inter-territorial compensation' has to prevent the more prosperous regions from fencing off their wealth. But between the regions themselves, cooperative agreements can be concluded, with the approval of the central authority. The Spanish constitution of 1978 tried in this way to give form to the fundamental principle of unity-in-diversity.

Another condition is consensus between the most important political forces of the country as regards the future development of the regional autonomy. For one of the causes of the unclear delimitation of responsibilities and resources between centre and periphery is the lack of a balanced vision of long-term development. In political circles, one is already very satisfied when a majority is found in parliament to enact a constitutional amendment or to approve an organic law. In order to obtain this majority, it is not unusual that compromises are necessary that endanger the coherence of the entire concept. A clear majority for a decentralisation movement, as is the case now in France, is rather rare. But also between the majority and the opposition fundamental agreements can be reached about the long-term development. In the middle of 1981, the centre-right majority and the social democratic opposition in Spain reached such an agreement. This is the so-called LOAPA agreement, which has since been elevated to law, whereby it was decided to divide all of Spain into regions and also to harmonise the regional policy. Consequently, the further operationalisation of the regional institutions has encountered no significant problems on the occasion of the change of government.

Another condition for a good "equiordinazione" is related to the organisation of the division of responsibilities, and this as regards both legislative and executive powers. The transposition of a still unresolved struggle between the centre and the periphery for influence and power into a juridical and administrative state structure can only institutionalise the confusion and simultaneously undermine the entire system. The problem is not solved by requesting a Solomon-like judgement from an external authority concerning conflicts of jurisdiction. Possibly still more important for the stability and the equilibrium of a state structure is a division of responsibilities that rests on a consistent policy philosophy and applies administrative effectiveness criteria. A flexible constitutional framework, such as that in Spain, whereby the division of tasks is not determined 'ne varietur' but can be adapted to the capacity of the individual regions and to the developments in the centre-periphery play of forces, naturally promotes a balanced settlement. But it is still essential that the actors be prepared to engage in constructive dialogue in such a way that the state framework and the fundamental harmonisation mission of the centre is not questioned. Otherwise the regionalist-federalist flag can no longer be flown, and one is confronted with a state-dissolving dispersion of power.

Conclusion

What form of state organisation will ultimately emerge as the 'Pact of the Belgians' is as yet unclear. Nor can it be predicated how this construction will be able to be classified. In any case, the problem continues to be studied, even officially, as is indicated by the establishment of a 'Study Centre for the Reform of the State'.[18]

Belgium: Regional or Federal State ?

The objective of this Centre is 'to make
evaluations and proposals in view of the possible
continuation, adaptation, improvement, and/or
revision of the State Reform'.

In general, it is expected that the first result
will be a more consistent delimitation of the
regional responsibilities. Paradoxically, in a
sense, this is perhaps the best contribution that can
be made to the achievement of a balanced state
structure in which it is not skirmishes on the front
line of responsibilities that dominate but rather the
attainment of the objectives that are common to the
entire political-administrative system. An
institutional formula that would thus relate the
component parts of the country to each other and
rally the forces would, in our opinion, certainly
rely on the tradition of 'federalism', even if not
all the elements of a 'federation' are present.

Notes

1. *Le Monde*, 21 September 1980.

2. The German-language minority in Belgium (65,000 people) now also fullfledged cultural autonomy, so that finally three communities were formed, each with a deliberative organ and an executive.

3. Art. 86 bis of the Constitution.

4. Art. 3 bis, 3 ter, and 59 bis of the Constitution.

5. In anticipation of the constitutional amendment regarding the present Senate (i.e., the First Chamber in a bi-cameral system), the Councils of the Communities and Regions are composed of directly elected members of the national parliament in the respective areas.

6. The Law of 28 June 1983 concerning the organisation, the jurisdiction, and the operation of the Court of Arbitration.

7. D.J. Elazar, The Ends of Federalism: Notes towards a Theory of Federal Political Arrangements. In: M. Frenkel (ed), *Partnership in Federalism,* (Bern, 1977), pp.25-26.

8. G. Burdeau, *Taite de science politique,* (paris, 1980), Vol.II, Part III, Chap. II.

9. A. Molitor, 'La regionalisation dans les Etats de l'Europe Occidentale', *Administration Publique*, (1981) no. 4, p.211.

10. Ibid., p.212.

11. Ibid., p.213.

12. Cf. Art. 6, 4 and 5, and Art. 80 of the Special Law of 8 August 1980 for Institutional Reform.

13. G. de Vergottini, 'Modelli comparati di autonomie locali',*Organizzazione e diritto delle regioni*, (Rome, 1982), p.76.

Belgium: Regional or Federal State ?

14.   O. Coenen, 'De besluitsvormingsmecanismen op
national en gewestelijk vlak. Een federale staat
zonder federaal gezag,' Res Publica, (1984)
no. 3, pp. 333-348.

15.   Cf. Jan Van Rompaey, 'Essai de synthese de
l'evolution de la reforme de l'etat en Belgique
de 1961 a 1979,'Federalism: History and Current
Significance of a Form of Government, (The
Hague, Martinus Nijhoff, 1980), pp.97-123.

16.   Cf. above, the definition of D.J. Elazar.

17.   Thus M.Quevit, 'Une confederation belge:
Solution institutionnelle equitable pour la
Flandre, la Wallonie et Bruxelles',
Res Publica, (1984), no.3,pp.351-362.

18.   Royal Decree of 14 March 1983.

REFERENCES

L. BINDER (ed.)(1971),

Crises and Sequences in
Political Development.
Princeton University
Press.

G. BURDEAU (1980),

Traite de science
politique.
Tome II: L Etat.
Paris, L.G.D.J.

S. CASSESE (1981,

Etats, regions, Europe.
In: Pouvoirs, Revue
francaise d'etudes
constitutionnelles et
politiques. No. 19,
pp.19-26.

O. COENEN (1984),

De besluitvormings-
mecanismen op national
en gewestelijk vlak.
Een federale staat
zonder federaal gezag?
In: Res Publica,
1984, no.3, pp.333-348.

G. DE VERGOTTINI (1982),

Modelli comparati di
autonomie locali.
In: Organizzazione e
diritto delle regioni.

D.J. ELAZAR (1977),

The Ends of Federalism:
Notes towards a Theory
of Federal Political
Arrangements.
In: Max Frenkel (ed.),
Partnership in
Federalism. Bern, Peter
Lang, pp. 25-56.

Y. MENY (1981),

Crises, regions et
modernisation de
l'Etat. In: Pouvoirs,
Revue francaise
d'etudes
constitutionnelles et
politiques. No 19,
pp.5-18.

Belgium: Regional or Federal State ?

A. MOLITOR (1981),   La regionalisation dans
                                les Etats d'Europe
                                occidentale.
                                In: Administration
                                Publique, 1981, no.4,
                                pp.205-227.

L.W. PYE (1967),   Aspects of Political
                                Development.
                                Boston, Little Brown.

M.QUEVIT (1984),   Une confederation belge
                                Solution equitable pour
                                la Flandre, la Wallonie
                                et Bruxelles.
                                In: Res Publica, 1984,
                                no.3, pp.351-362.

P. ROMUS (1979),   L'Europe et les regions
                                Bruxelles, Editions
                                Labor.

J. VAN ROMPAEY (1980),   Essai de synthese de
                                l'evolution de la
                                reforme de L'Etat en
                                Belgique de 1961 a
                                1979. In: Federalism:
                                History and Current
                                Significance of a Form
                                of Government. The
                                Hauge, Martinus Nijhoff
                                pp.97-123.

4. THE NEW SPANISH STATE STRUCTURE

Antoni Monreal

Introduction

During the nineteenth and twentieth centuries, state
and nation building in Spain were dominated by
unitary-centralist ideas. With some outstanding
exceptions this was also true of Spanish liberalism.
Both the moderate and the progressive elements within
Spanish liberalism adopted a centralist model of the
developing state structure, albeit for different
reasons. In general, the centralist orientation
derived from the belief that territorial powers
differentiated from the powers of the central state
would have constituted a serious obstacle to the
reforms which Spanish liberalism sought to implement.
Thus, throughout the nineteenth century, liberalism
and centralism were allies in the fight against the
Ancien Regime interest which protected the old local
rights and privileges.
     The outstanding exceptions to this general trend
of liberal thinking were, however, significant in a
particular sense. The more radical wing of the
liberal movement was republican and nineteenth
century Spanish republicanism was federalist. The
First Republic was proclaimed in 1873 as a distinctly
Federal Republic and the constitutional structure
designated the state to be Federal. The main
federalist influences upon republicanism were
American and French. The new constitutional project
was presented to the legislature with an explicit
reference to 'the great founders of the Federation in
the modern world' and republican propaganda abounded
with literature which popularised the federal
structure of the United States. Proudhon epitomised
the French influence upon Spanish federalism in the
nineteenth century. His political philosophy was
translated into Spanish by Pi y Margall, one of the
Republic's Presidents, who was philosophically
anarchist but politically reformist. He understood
the federal state to be an organisation which would
guarantee individual liberty and promote far-reaching
social change. The republican movement in general
was federalist because it saw in the Federal State a
means by which the creation of several new
territorial centres of power would fragment and
weaken the central state power. In this way the
notion that 'decentralisation is liberty and through
liberty we are men' was put into practice.

Proudhon's views about political power and the state were thus an important element incorporated into Spanish federalism.[1]

The federalists were clearly in the majority in the Republican party but they remained a minority voice in Spain. When the First Republic collapsed in 1874 amidst public disorder and social crisis, republicanism was widely discredited and, along with it, federalism. With the disappearance of republican federalism all of the non-centralised plans for the state structure that had been supported by national political parties disappeared. Thereafter political decentralisation was promoted from the geographical and political periphery of the Spanish state. In particular, the peripheral nationalist movements in Euzkadi, Catalonia and Galicia pursued this goal at the end of the nineteenth, and at the beginning of the twentieth, century.

In 1914 administrative decentralisation represented another experiment with the state structure, but it was restricted to Catalonia as a centralist response to the autonomous claims of the Catalan nationalist movement. It created management services in the specific areas of education, communications and culture, and was deemed successful from the standpoint of economic and administrative efficiency. The Catalans accepted these gains but were undeterred in their overall quest for political autonomy. When the Second Republic was proclaimed in 1931 as the 'Integral' state, which conceded political autonomy to those regions which desired it (without resorting to federal status), an effective compromise seemed to have been reached between the rival competing perspectives. Under the impact of Austrian and German influences the 'Integral' state permitted regional political decision making which ended centralism without introducing federation.[2] It resulted primarily from an agreement made between the peripheral nationalist movements which favoured a federal system and the centralist political forces which sought unification. The peripheral nationalist movements had crystallised as the driving force behind widespread support for a politically decentralised state structure. Catalonia in 1932 and Euzkadi in 1936 reorganised themselves as autonomous regions, while Galicia's similar efforts were thwarted by the civil war.

Both the First and the Second Spanish Republics attempted to establish non-centralist models of the state structure, and military intervention effectively terminated these experiments. However,

these attempts, together with the creation of the new
Autonomous State since 1978, demonstrate that the
dominant centralist tradition was able neither to
produce uniformity nor express diversity: it did not
succeed in abolishing a cultural and social diversity
rooted in history and tradition, and it failed even
to contain it peacefully within the state. Indeed,
during the latter years of the Franco dictatorship,
centralism displayed itself as a powerful stimulant
for the most radical and violent peripheral
nationalist forces. After 1978 the Spanish political
system experienced profound change which has reshaped
the type, form and structure of the state. The
purpose of this chapter is to examine the main
changes which have resulted in a new Spanish state
structure set against this historical introduction
and to comment upon the nature of the new state.

The Imperative of Political Decentralisation

The new Spanish Constitution defines the state as
'social and democratic in terms of rights' and its
form as a 'parliamentary monarchy'. Its structure is
founded upon the recognition that within the
framework of unity in the Spanish nation the
Constitution guarantees 'the right of autonomy to the
nationalities and regions' of which the Spanish
nation is composed. Not only has there been a sharp
break with the centralist unitarism characteristic of
the Franco regime but there has also been a
distinctive departure from the centralist tradition
inherent in the Spanish state - a long-standing
tradition only briefly interrupted by the First
Republic (1873-74) and by the Second Republie
(1931-1939).
    The formation of the non-centralist state
structure after 1978 is due, first, to the existence
of three powerful sub-state nationalist movements in
Catalonia, Euzkadi and Galicia. These were the three
'historic' nationalities which composed the different
political parties and groups most vociferous in
opposition to the Franco regime. In fact the
binomial democracy-autonomy movement was in such
conflict with the binomial dictatorship-centralism
forces that the negotiated reform process, which in
1976-1977 brought Spain from dictatorship to
democracy, was conducted in a manner designed to
secure a state structure acceptable both for the
historic nationalities and for the variety of other
political elements involved in the complex work of
transition. The result was a state structure based

upon the principles of unity and autonomy. This
model structure certainly contained features typical
of other states, such as Italy, but it none the less
retained its own unique characteristics in an overall
sense.[3]

The pressure from sub-state nationalist
movements, however, was not the only explanation for
the creation of a politically decentralised state
structure: there was also widespread elite support
for a penetrating reform of the Spanish
administration. In this sense the principle of
decentralisation seemed the most appropriate to
modernise an administration remarkably inefficient
and discredited by public opinion. Finally, we must
recognise that the decision to reorganise the whole
of Spain into Autonomous Communities[4] was taken, on
the one hand, due to a desire to avoid future tension
between geographical areas and, on the other hand,
because this approach would make their recognition
more general, thus softening the resistance that
might be generated by giving autonomy to the historic
nationalities.

In reality the Autonomous Communities exhibit a
wide variety of social, economic and cultural
differences. From a narrow socio-economic
perspective there are some glaring disparities. For
example, Madrid's Autonomous Community occupies 1.59%
of Spanish territory and has 12.44% of the total
population, but only 1.47% of its labour force works
in agriculture whereas Extremadura takes up 8.25% of
Spanish territory, has 2.23% of the total population,
but employs 38.02% of its labour force in
agriculture. These disparities become clearer still
if we consider the contributions which the various
Autonomous Communities make to the Gross National
Product. Catalonia, for example, has a figure of
19.93% and Madrid one of 16.49% while Cantabria and
Navarra fluctuate between 1.35 and 1.45% and Rioja
contributes 0.37%. Furthermore the world recession
has had an unequal impact upon these areas. In
Andalucia 29.62% of the labour force is unemployed
while in Catalonia it is 21.55% and in Euzkadi it is
22.27%. Since the Spanish national average
unemployment figure is 20%, it is clear that areas
like Galicia, with 11.25% unemployed, are much less
economically depressed than most other Autonomous
Communities.

Even among the four Autonomous Communities
created by a different system from the rest and
having more independent decision-making powers, the
economic indicators do not display homogeneity. The

percentages of the labour force working in industry
in these areas show wide divergences: in Euzkadi
40.09, in Catalonia 37.66, in Galicia 16.34 and
Andalucia 16.13. Similarly the percentage figures
for those working in agriculture are : Euzkadi 6.60%,
Catalonia 6.62%, Andalucia 20.40 and Galicia 45.98.
·Together these four Autonomous Communities have
36.04% of Spain's total population and contribute
44.77% of its GNP. Small wonder, then, that some
regions of Spain viewed political decentralisation as
a means to achieve increased economic development.[5]

Of the seventeen Autonomous Communities created
in 1978 only a handful have an inherent history and
tradition, and hence a differentiated culture and
language which form the basis of a conscious national
identity. In these areas there are clear
manifestations of a determination to preserve and
promote their own unique identities. Significantly
only two of these Autonomous Communities - Euzkadi
and Catalonia - have political party systems which
are radically different from the national
configuration. Indeed, the close relationship
between the national and the regional party systems,
out of which the new state structure grew and which
it is intended to reinforce, may be partly why
neither of the two main Spanish political parties -
the Socialists and Conservatives - is the majority
party in Euzkadi and Catalonia. At present twelve
Autonomous Communities are governed by the
socialists, three by the conservatives and two by
nationalist parties.[6]

In practice the process of change from a
centralist state structure to one based upon
political decentralisation has been implemented at a
relatively rapid pace when compared with, for
example, the Italian case. In a remarkably short
period of time, from 1978 to 1983, seventeen
Autonomous Communities were established and regional
elections held in each of them. Moreover, the
necessary commissions required to establish the
respective jurisdictions and competences of the State
and the Autonomous Communities and to make an
economic evaluation of them were quickly in
operation. We must now turn to examine the new
Spanish state structure.

The New State Structure

Although the 1978 Spanish Constitution makes the
existence of a politically decentralised state
structure possible, it neither defines this structure

as regional or federal nor does it in any way allow for the expression of divergent opinions.[7] From the perspective of a formal analysis, it seems evident that some elements which generally appear in a Federal state are absent in the Spanish model. The Autonomous Communities cannot intervene in an eventual reform of the constitution; the remaining powers are allocated by the Constitution to the State and not to the Autonomous Communities, the senate is a house of territorial representation having less power than the Congress in matters dealing with legislation and control of the Government; and in the approval of the Autonomous Statute (which designates the Autonomous Community) the State legislature (Cortes) directly intervenes.

However, these arguments can be counterbalanced by others equally significant. It the Autonomous Communities cannot intervene in the constitutional reform process, they do have a legislative initiative; if the residual power is attributed to the State and not the Autonomous Community, it should be remembered that either through the system of implicit powers or through the constitutional reform process it is not unusual to hand over the residuary power to the member state; while it is true that the Senate has less power than the Congress, this does not mean that it does not have important functions; and if the State legislature (Cortes) intervenes in the approval of the Statutes of Autonomy, it is also true that those Autonomous Communities which have been approved by Article 151 of the Constitution have characteristics similar to those which we would expect to find with conventional legislative pacts.

If we go beyond a formal comparative analysis of the new Spanish state structure with both Federal and Regional states, there are some features which are common to each of them. First, given the nature of the previous political regime, only a non-centralist state structure could make the State power legitimate. In other words, the new state structure had formally to recognise the diverse identities of well-defined territorial units which could effectively dispose of the political decision-making power. If we consider both Federal and Regional states in this respect it is clear that their legitimacy is founded upon the same basis: they are considered legitimate precisely because they are Federal or Regional. Thus the Federal state, the Regional state and the Autonomous state each has the common task of making the state power legitimate by creating various territorial centres of power.

Secondly, not only do the Federal, Regional and
Autonomous states confirm legitimacy by their
fragmentation of power and its dispersal to various
political centres, but they also make political
decisions for the different territorial units of
which they are composed by the same means (at the
highest level of approving acts) and by the same
organisation - essentially via their own legislative
and executive branches. In short, the very nature of
their political autonomy is the capacity to make
political decisions. This was a point present in the
Italian model and the Spanish acknowledged it by
making a careful distinction between administrative
decentralisation and political autonomy. The latter
is distinguished in terms of its very nature: the
capacity to choose between a number of possible aims.
The law is the jurdical instrument by which the
choice comes into existence and the achievement of
the interest of every territorial unit is the aim of
the political autonomy. The Constitutional Court
recognises the political autonomy of nationalities
and regions, and distinguishes it from the
administrative autonomy of local councils.

A politically decentralised state must have the
capacity to make political decisions. In Spain this
capacity is maintained, on the one hand, by the
political institutions which enable the Autonomous
Communities to govern themselves (essentially a
legislative house, an administration and a president)
and, on the other hand, by the totality of the
competences (powers and functions) which the
Autonomous Community is given. Both the political
institutions and the competences are established in
the Autonomous Statute which in turn indicates that
without the approval of the Autonomous Community -
either by its legislature or by the legislature and
its electorate via referendum - the Statute cannot be
modified. Only a constitutional reform would cause
the constitutional and statutory guarantee of the
Autonomous Community to disappear from an organic and
a functional standpoint.

However, even if the political institutions of
the Autonomous Community remain constant, the
competences are variable. Here we are not referring
to the fact that the competences of different
Autonomous Communities can be different because the
Constitution and the Autonomous Statutes determine
them; rather we are emphasising the fact that the
area in which the established competences are to be
exercised in an Autonomous Statute will be greater or
lesser according to three principal factors: the

political attitude of the State; the political
attitude of the Autonomous Community; and the
attitude of the Constitutional Court. In short, the
area of competences will be determined by a
combination of elements of a political and a
juridical nature. Thus it can be affirmed, first,
that the political decision-making capacity of the
Autonomous Community is variable to a great extent
because the competences assumed by the Statute can be
exercised in a number of shifting dimensions, and,
secondly, because (from the standpoint of
constitutional and statutory confirmation) there is
no reason to think that the capacity to make
political decisions necessarily has to be either
inferior to or less than that which is enjoyed by the
member state of a conventional Federation.

But if the variability of the Autonomous
Community's decision-making capacity is based upon
the way that competences are distributed between the
State and the Autonomous Community by the
Constitution, how is this achieved ? Certain
intricate provisions incorporated in the Constitution
provide the answer. They can be briefly summarised:

a)   Article 148 establishes a list of matters
     over which the Autonomous Communities may
     assume control.

b)   Article 149 establishes a list of matters
     over which the State has exclusive control.

c)   Article 149.3 establishes that the
     Autonomous Communities can take charge of
     matters (via their respective Statutes) not
     expressly given to the State by the
     Constitution.

d)   Article 149.3 gives the remaining power
     (not assumed by the Statutes) to the State.

e)   Articles 150.1 and 150.2 facilitate the
     delegation of powers by various means from
     the State to the Autonomous Communities.

These constitutional provisions require
elucidation if we are fully to understand their
implications for the new state structure and we shall
now turn to examine and clarify them.

Our first observation concerns the question of
competences. The limit of competences of the
Autonomous Communities varies according to the way in

which they became autonomous; in other words, the way in which the Autonomous Statute was approved. For example, four Autonomous Communities (Euzkadi, Galicia, Catalonia and Andalucia) have been formed along the lines of Article 151 of the Constitution and can assume competences up to the limit established in Article 149. The rest have had to limit themselves to the terms of Article 148 at least during their first five years of existence. Secondly, although the competences assumed by the Autonomous Communities can vary considerably, in practice they are very similar. In the case of the four Autonomous Communities mentioned above their similarity of competences derives from their Statutes which were designed to gain the maximum power possible. And the same relative homogeneity, albeit at a different level, can be found in the powers obtained by the remaining thirteen Autonomous Communities created under Article 143. Thirdly, besides being the constitutive norm of an Autonomous Community, the Statute of Autonomy is where the competences are established: competences which can be exclusive, shared or concurrent, and be either legislative or executive.[8] However, in practice it remains ambiguous whether or not the competence is exclusive, what the scope of the shared and concurrent functions is, and how far the decision-making power of the Autonomous Community can oscillate. Indeed, the decision-making power can fluctuate precisely because the level of the competences is subject to a high degree of indeterminacy. But it is here that the role of the Constitutional Court is pivotal. The Court has the authority to judge the constitutionality of the laws and to resolve conflicts between State and Autonomous Community competences. When it asserts the right to interpret the Constitution it does so by determining the 'quantum' of decision-making power to be allocated to the Autonomous Communities and thus it contributes decisively towards the shape of the state structure which may develop either towards or away from the Federal model. When conferring competences either to the state or to the Autonomous Communities its decisions are both binding and final.

Because of the Court's strategic position its decisions regarding the distribution of competences, particularly those deemed 'exclusive', 'shared' or 'concurrent', are especially significant. When it confers an exclusive competence upon an Autonomous Community the Court does not base its judgement upon the fact that this competence has already been defined in the Statute of the Autonomous Community; rather it defines the character of the competence in each case by an assessment of whether or not the interest is that of the Autonomous Community or of the State.[9] The Court has already emphasised the ambiguous sense in which the exclusive competence idea is used both in the Constitution and in the Autonomous Statutes,[10], and it has stressed that 'even the exclusive Autonomous competences should be set within a constitutional framework'.[11] In short, this means that in cases of conflict the Court can decide whether or not a competence is exclusive without necessarily referring to the text of the Autonomous Statute. This serves at best to create considerable indeterminacy in constitutional matters and to underline the crucial role which the Constitutional Court can play in Spain.

The shared or concurrent competences can be dealt with in the following manner: when, in Article 149.1, the Constitution gives exclusive competences to the State, in some clauses it does so in order that the State might dictate 'the bases' or 'basic legislation' or the 'basic norms', but leaving matters which do not correspond to these three categories as part of the functions of the Autonomous Communities - as long as these functions are also indicated in the Statute of the Community in question (as has been the case for the four Autonomous Communities formed under Article 151 of the Constitution). The importance of this aspect of constitutional arrangements can be fully appreciated when we note, on the one hand, that the extent of the Autonomous Communities' jurisdiction is in practice delimited by that which is 'basic' and, on the other hand, when we group the fundamental nature of the functions in question: the bases and coordination of the general planning of economic activity; the bases and general co-ordination of health matters; the bases of the legal system of Public Administration; the basic legislation concerning environmental protection; the basis of the mining and energy sectors; and the basic norms dealing with the structure of the press, radio and television (Article 149.1, sub-sections 13, 16, 17, 18, 22, 25 and 37). To summarise, this indicates that the outstanding importance of the functions outlined above and the open-ended nature of the 'basic norms' criterion will have a direct bearing on the way in which 'bases' is interpreted, and this in turn will widen or narrow the political decision-making power of the Autonomous Communities.

How, then, has the Constitutional Court interpreted this question of shared or concurrent competences? The explanation lies in three separate approaches. First, although the Court acknowledges that it is impossible to give 'a precise and an a priori definition of the concept of basic conditions or bases',[12] it comes very close to achieving this when it states that bases:

> should be understood according to the general criteria which regulate a legally defined sector or which deal with juridical matters common to all of the State. This can be interpreted both positively and negatively: the positive aspect is that aims, goals and the general orientation for all the State are manifested and characterised by the unity of the State and the equality among its members; the negative aspect, for the same reasons, defines the limits within which the competences of the Autonomous Community's political organs can move, and which even when they are defined as exclusive, the Constitution and the Statute leave thus limited.[13]

On the other hand, the Court states that the reason why the State has exclusive power over the bases:

> is because such bases should give a normative and uniform regulation, the same for all of the Nation which assures that, in matters of general interest superior to those of each Autonomous Community, there be a common normative denominator .... from which each Autonomous Community can develop its own competences.[14]

The Court has also affirmed that beyond a formal criterion:

> the notion of bases or basic norms should be extended as a material notion, and consequently, these basic criteria or principles, whether or not they are formulated as such, are those which can be reasonably deduced from the standing legislation.[15]

The function of the approval of the bases is defined as 'a general determination of the minimal technical requirements and minimal conditions in order to establish common characteristics'.[16] Clearly, the

Court considers that basic legislation conferred
exclusively to the State is an instrument which, due
to State integrity and equality among citizens,
establishes a normative regulation which is common to
a particular matter. This must be applied within
certain minimum terms and it seems clear that the
bases 'can be deduced from the standing legislation'.
However, it is equally clear that such legislation
does not precisely define what should be understood
as 'basic'. If we glance at any of the functions
outlined above the Spanish legislature has not
approved a definitive law about the 'bases' since the
Constitution came into effect in 1978.

The Court's second approach to shared or
concurrent competences is much more precise. It has
established that even though the Constitution
recognises the approval of basic legislation only by
an Act, this does not ignore the relevance of
by-laws. The Court has stated its position thus

> Given the fundamental and general character of
> the basic norms, they can only be established
> posterior to the Constitution by act;
> nevertheless there can be some matters in which
> the Government can use it power to make by-laws
> to regulate by Royal Decree in a complementary
> way, some basic aspects of a certain matter.[17]

The way in which the by-law is used is unclear: its
complementary nature in relation to an Act is
repeatedly emphasised so that it may be used only
'when indispensable'.[18] Nevertheless, what the
Government cannot do is 'to define in general terms
and by Royal Decree that which is basic'.[19] Thus it
seems that both acts and by-laws are methods to
define what is 'basic' in such a way that not only
the legislature but also the Government can exercise
an important influence. Both are able, within
certain limits, to determine that which is 'basic' as
well as what scope it may have.

Thirdly, a limit is clearly indicated on basic
legislation: 'it is necessary to keep in mind that
the establishment by the State of the bases ....
cannot develop to such a degree that it leaves the
content of the correlative competences of the
Community vacant'.[20] In other words, 'never should
the determination of the bases nor the general
co-ordination develop to such an extent as to leave
the corresponding competences of the Communities
vacant'.[21] These two statements unequivocally affirm
that the basic legislation should leave enough room

for the legislative and executive competences of the
Autonomous Communities to develop as long as they
form part of the Statute of Autonomy. However, as
regards the chronological relationship between the
basic legislation by the State and the development of
competences by the Autonomous Communities, it is
important to note that the Autonomous Community 'is
not obliged to wait for basic post-constitutional
legislation'[22] and that 'the non-existence of State
norms cannot be understood as an implicit prohibition
for the Autonomous Communities to try to regulate a
matter which has not been the object of State
regulation'.[23] In this sense the Autonomous
Communities can indirectly mark out the scope of that
which is 'basic', but it is the State norms which
will ultimately prevail.

In summary, the Constitutional Court plays a
fundamental role in the development of the new state
structure in Spain.[24] It is able to do this by
having the last word on the distribution of
competences between the State and the Autonomous
Communities. This allows it to enlarge or restrict
the decision-making capacity both of the State and of
each Autonomous Community, and hence enables it
actually to establish both the major and the minor
decision-making capacities of each power centre. In
some ways a judicial decision is used to solve what
is a political conflict.

Conclusion

The Constitutional Court's present orientation is
indicated by two significant achievements. First, it
has preserved the state structure despite many
attempts by the political parties to modify it.[25]
Secondly, in all that concerns the delicate task of
distributing competences, it has protected and
maintained the capacity of the Autonomous Communities
to make political decisions. However, it is still
too soon to make an accurate overall prediction about
the future of this decision-making capacity because
both restrictive and expansive tendencies co-exist
within the state structure. The prospects for the
Autonomous Communities are, in this respect, simply
unknown. Indeed, the Spanish state structure is open
to many different developments. The Autonomous
Communities, or at least some of them, may obtain a
degree of political decision-making similar to some
member states of a Federation or they might move
closer to the Italian model with their
decision-making capacity much reduced. The Spanish

constitutional design permits both developments. For
the moment the orientation of the Constitutional
Court's jurisprudence is to look for a balance
between both of these alternatives.

Notes

1. For detailed information about Spanish
    federalism and the political ideas of Pi y
    Margall, see G. Trujillo, Introduccion al
    Federalismo Espanol: Ideologia y formas
    constitucionales, (Madrid 1967); I. Molas,
    Ideario de Pi y Margall (Madrid 1966); and
    C.A.M. Hannesy, The Federal Republic in Spain:
    Pi y Margall and the Federal Republic Movement,
    1868-1874, (London 1962).

2. See 'Discurso del presidente de la comision
    redactora' in R. Sainz de Varanda,
    Coleccion de Leyes Fundament ales, (Zaragoza
    1967).

3. On the Italian state model, see L. Paladin,
    Diritto Regionale, (Padova 1979); C. Lavagna,
    Diritto Publico, (Torino 1983); and
    M. S. Giannini Las Regiones en Italia, (Madrid
    1984).

4. There are seventeen Autonomous Communities in
    total. Four of them - Euzkadi, Catalonia,
    Galicia and Andalucia - were created by a
    different system from the other thirteen and
    this is why they have more competences than
    them. The remaining thirteen are: Aragon,
    Asturias, Baleares, Canarias, Cantabria,
    Castilla-La-Mancha, Castilla-Leon, Comunidad
    Valenciana, Extremadura, Madrid, Murcia,
    Navarra and Rioja.

5. Except for the percentage of unemployment, which
    corresponds to the second quarter of 1984, all
    the statistics date from 1983. See
    Anuario Estadistico de Espana, Instituto
    Nacional Estadistica, (Madrid 1983) and
    Anuario El Pais, (Madrid 1984).

6. For the electoral statistics of the Communities,
    see Anuario Estadistico de Espana, Instituto
    Nacional de Estadistica, (Madrid 1983), Anuario
    El Pais, (Madrid 1984), and Cuadernos de la
    Vanguardia, Equipo de Sociologia Electoral,
    Universidad Autonoma de Barcelona, (Barcelona
    1982).

7. In general it is referred to as a State of
    Autonomous Communities, but this has not
    prevented many writers and commentators
    describing it as Federal. For example,
    Gumersindo Trujillo has called it a 'federal-
    regional' structure in his 'Federalismo y
    regionalismo en al Constitucion Espanola de
    1978: el Estado federo-regional' in
    Federalismo y Regionalismo, (Madrid 1979) and
    the same definition was used later in his LOAPA
    y Constitucion: El projecto de LOAPA desde la
    perspectiva de su constitucionalidad, (Vitoria
    1982). A. Rubiales has described the state
    structure after 1978 as 'federalizable' in 'Las
    Comunidades Autonomas: Tipologia y mapa
    territorial' in Documentacion Administrativa,
    182, (1979). For a comparative viewpoint, see
    J. Ferrando Badia, El Estado unitario, el
    Federal y el estado regional, (Madrid 1978).

8. Concerning the distribution of powers and
    functions, see S. Munoz Machado, Derecho Publico
    de las Comunidades Autonomas, (Madrid 1982);
    J. Salas, 'Els poders normatius de la
    Generalitat' in Taula deCanvi, extra 2,
    (Barcelona 1980); L. Vandelli, El ordenamiento
    espanol de las Comunidades Autonomas, (Madrid
    1982); and E. Garcia de Enterria et al,
    La distribucion de las competencias economicas
    entre el poder central y las autonomias
    territoriales en el Derecho Comparado y en la
    Constitucion espanola, (Madrid 1980).

9. Seutencia del Tribunal Constitucional (STC),
    2 Feb. 1981, p.3.

10. STC, 16 Nov. 1981, p.1.

11. STC, 23 Nov. 1982, p.1.

12. STC, 28 Julio 1981, p.5.

13. STC, T Abril 1983, p.4.

14. STC, 28 Enero 1982 p.1 and 28 Abril. 1983, p.2.

15. STC, 28 Julio 1981, p.5.

16. STC, 20 Mayo 1983, p.5 and 20 Julio 1984.

17. STC, 28 Enero 1982, p.1 and 9 Marzo 1984.

18. STC, 20 Mayo 1983, p.3, 25 Octubre 1983 and
    28 Junio 1983.

19. STC, 28 Abril 1983, p.2.

20. STC, 28 Enero 1982, p.1.

21. STC, 28 Abril 1983, p.2.

22. STC, 28 Enero 1982, p.1.

23. STC, 8 Feb. 1982, p.2.

24. For more information, see J. Sole, 'La
    Jurisprudencia del T.C. y el Estando de las
    Autonomias' en Catedra de Derecho Politico,
    Anuario de Derecho Politico (Barcelona 1983).

25. STC, 5 Agosto 1983, esp. p.4. a, b and c.

5. FEDERALIST AND REGIONALIST MOVEMENTS IN FRANCE

John Loughlin

Introduction

Any comparative study of federalism and federation demands that the systems being analysed are sufficiently similar to some and different from others for us to be able to make any comparison at all. A federal state has usually been contrasted with a unitary state and France has long been regarded as the classic example of the latter. It would seem, therefore, that France would be an excellent model against which to test the alternative model of the federal state. In other words, if we can lay bare a set of criteria, such as the degree of centralisation of the state, which define the unitary nature of France as such, then, in a negative way, we can be on the path to understanding a non-unitary state.

The enterprise, however, is not as easy as this, since centralisation and decentralisation, may have many different meanings. There may be a high degree of political centralisation with a correspondingly high degree of industrial and administrative decentralisation and deconcentration. What is more interesting, perhaps, than drawing up a list of abstract criteria by which we may define a unitary state, is to examine those social movements within the state which have adopted an ideology of federalism and which seek to install federal institutions. By looking at the origins of such movements, their success or failure in achieving their aims, and their relationship to other political forces, we may come away with a clearer idea of the nature of the society from which they emerge and the state which they seek to modify.

This is the main purpose of this chapter. It does so by examining French federalist movements in the period following the Second World War.[1] However, it does so by relating them to another set of social movements which emerged at about the same time and whose aims to some extent overlap with those of the federalists.[2] The very possibility that such movements may influence the behaviour of more powerful social actors such as Government Ministers and Civil Servants should lead us to modify our understanding of the 'unitariness' of the French state. This may thus provide at least some of the empirical elements necessary for the elaboration of a set of concepts necessary for any venture of comparison.

The Myth of Jacobinism

Before dealing with the contemporary period, however, it would be useful to look a little more closely at the myth of Jacobin France evoked above. It is true that France has had a highly centralised administration - the prefectoral system - since the time of Napoleon. On the other hand, throughout much of the nineteenth century and, indeed, well into the twentieth, the central government has been much more tolerant of the local society (the 'periphery' or 'region') than the myth would have us believe.[3] There often existed a de jure centralism and a de facto toleration of local cultures.

One possible explanation for this is the predominantly rural character of French society, a character which it retained until the contemporary period. The majority of French people were peasants, often living in semi-autarchic local societies. These peasants related to the state via the mediation of local elites - notables or Catholic clergy[4] - who 'represented' them in the sphere of politics. Some of these local societies, such as Brittany, the French Basque Country and Corsica, also possessed distinct cultural traditions, that is they differed 'ethnically' from their French compatriots of other linguistic groups and from the predominant French culture as defined by Paris. But rather than trying to crush these ethnic minorities by making them conform to an a priori model of 'Frenchness' as the myth would have, the governments in Paris, for most of the modern period since the French Revolution, saw them as bulwarks of social conservatism[5] and for that reason tolerated them. Such a conservative stratum of society was important in a country marked by frequent revolutions and changes of regime. It was sufficient that the mediating elites imbibed the dominant French culture while at the same time maintaining contact with the local culture.

For most of the time, almost everyone seemed to accept this situation since there were few revolts against the central power since the Revolution.[6] Revolts occurred when the government threatened the prerogatives of the notables or clergy. Then the latter would wave the regionalist banner and stir up unrest among their clienteles. An example of this was the anti-clerical campaign in the early years of the Third Republic which sparked off regionalist movements in places such as Brittany and French Flanders. Regionalists, however, were usually small numbers of literary or intellectual elites such as

the romantic literary movements, the Felibrige,
founded by the Provencal poet, Mistral. More radical
autonomist and nationalist movements appeared,
especially in the inter-war period.[7] But these, too,
represented a minority of the ethnic populations.
Some of their members eventually collaborated with
the decentralisation programme of the Vichy regime,
and others with the Nazi and (in Corsica) Fascist
Occupants of France.

Federalism was also the ideology of an
intellectual elite, although it could be argued that
the Proudhonian tradition (well represented within
the Paris Commune) and the anarcho-syndicalist
traditions of the French labour movement represent
forms of federalism with a popular base.
Contemporary French federalists find their
ideological inspiration in the writings of
Montesquieu, and especially in De Tocqueville,
Proudhon and Sorel.[8] It is this specifically French
form of federalism which distinguishes them from
their American, German or Italian counterparts.

From this brief historical summary of the
antecedents of contemporary federalism and
regionalism two points stand out: first, federalist
and regionalist traditions do exist in France;
secondly, these traditions tend to be elitist since
the masses of French people and the Parisian
governments co-existed peacefully. It is only in the
period following the Second World War that these two
ideologies would attract a wider audience, although
this support has always remained a minority of the
French people. This is true even in those regions
marked by a high degree of ethnicity, that is,
possessing a distinct language and folklore. In
order to understand the nature of these movements,
the links between them, and their place in the
political life of contemporary France, it is
necessary to examine whether there exists a set of
conditions common to the growth of both of them in
the post-War period. The Discrediting of the
Nation-State

During the Occupation some federalists compromised
with the Vichy regime which had its own programme of
decentralisation akin to the conservative
provincialism of the nineteenth century. Others,
however, participated in the Resistance against the
Occupant. It was in these Resistance circles that
there occurred a widespread rejection of traditional
nationalism and of those elites who had been
associated with it. The destruction caused during

the War was seen to be a consequence of this
nationalism and there was a widespread desire to
rebuild a new society on different, more humanistic
and universalist, principles. It was then but one
step from rejecting traditional nationalism to
rejecting the nation-state itself since many felt it
was the worship of the nation-state which had led to
the slaughter of two World Wars and the crimes of
Nazism. This questioning of the nation-state after
the Second World War was one of the primary impulses
of the European movement and was an important factor
in ensuring the initial successes of European
integration. To this distrust of the nation-state
must also be added the fear of communism which
reached the height of its influence in France in the
late 1940s. Most federalists, like their
non-federalist friends in the European movement, saw
the construction of Europe as also being a bulwark
against the Soviet Union.

It was in this context, then, that the early
federalist movements flourished. It has been
estimated that in 1948 there were seventeen
federalist groups in France each with between 50 and
4000 members.[9] All these groups adhered to a
coordinating body called the Union francaise des
federalistes (UFF). Alain Greilsammer has
distinguished three tendencies:

   a)   a socialist tendency, grouped around the
        review La Republique moderne, called the
        Cercles socialistes et federalistes pour les
        Etats Unis d'Europe;
   b)   a liberal tendency whose most important
        group was the Comite d'action economique et
        douaniere; and finally
   c)   a Right-wing tendency the most important
        group being La Federation-Mouvement
        federaliste francais.

In fact, it would seem to be the Right-wing tendency
which was the most important numerically and
Greilsammer describes its principal concerns as
being: 'regionalisme, revalorisation des
municipalites, retour a un certain corporatisme
economique, lutte contre le communisme, combat pour
le renouveau spirituel de la France, etc.'[10]
What united all these groups in their early
years was their commitment to building a new Europe
and a new France. Within the European movement they
represented a particular tendency. Their aim was a
federal Europe and this opposed them to the unionists

(who sought the creation of a unitary European state)
and the functionalists (such as E. Haas) who thought
that economic factors should predominate over
political ones and that integration would come about
as the inevitable consequence of a so-called
'spill-over' effect.[11] Most federalists wanted some
kind of federation of 'regions', that is, of units
smaller than the present nation-state and, hence,
were opposed to the creation of a giant European
state. To achieve this they wished to place
political factors before economic ones, that is,
create institutions first. For the same reason,
their desire to create a federation of something
other than the existing nation-states, they opposed
the idea of a Confederation of the existing European
states. Once again their reasoning was based on the
idea that the old European nation-state was
discredited.

The French federalists were agreed, then, on the
necessity of building a new Europe, in which the old
nation-states would be superseded. They divided on
the question of strategy. The more moderate,
socially conservative tendency, the Federation
Mouvement federaliste francais, saw the most
effective form of action as being that of lobbying
politicians in parliament. They were not very
concerned with mobilising masses of people. In other
words, the MFF continued the elitist tradition of the
earlier federalists. Moreover, the MFF tended to
accept the steps already taken towards European
integration, such as the setting up of the European
Coal and Steel Community, even if these were not in
accord with strict federalist principles (since they
involved the governments of existing nation-states).
In other words they were pragmatists and became known
as possibilists.

It was the subsequent failure to carry forward
the process of integration in Europe and especially
the failure of the Europe Defence Community that led
to a decline in the federalist movements. With the
decline there was a series of violent polemics
between the different tendencies and eventually a
split. The MFF had already left the UFF in 1953 and
in 1955 there was a split at the international level
in the Union europeenne des federalistes when the
possibilists decided to found the Action europeenne
federaliste (AEF). In 1959, the UEF became the
Mouvement federaliste europeen (MFE). The MFE,
although divided within itself on questions of
doctrine and tactics, came to represent what was
known as maximalisme. The French section led by

Alexandre Marc adopted a more revolutionary position
with regard to society than did the MFF. Another
important difference with the MFF was on the question
of tactics. Whereas the latter, as we have seen,
remained elitist the MFE wished to mobilise the
'masses' and promoted the idea of a European
Constituent Assembly. Nevertheless , despite these
differences of doctrine and tactics,both tendencies
came together on occasion to conduct joint
campaigns,especially in defence of European
institutions against Gaullism.

Federalism, Regionalism and Ethnic Minorities

Both possibilists and maximalists agreed that the way
forward to building Europe was, paradoxically, to
'return to the sources' of society, that is, to those
forms of society in which man could find his full
developemnt - the family, the commune, the region and
the association. This was in opposition to the
'proletarianisation and 'atomisation' of man
experienced in great metropolitan centres such as
Paris. The federalists called this movement back to
the sources the 'dialectic', which was not to be
confused with the Marxist dialectic of the class
struggle which they categorically rejected. On the
contrary, the dialectical movement of the federalists
was more akin to corporatism although they rarely
called it this. In any case, this was the
philosophical and strategic background to the
federalist interest in regionalism. When
J. F. Gravier, a geographer, published his famous
work Paris et le desert francais in 1947, this made a
strong impact on the federalists. In it he
forcefully expounds the theme of the 'gigantism' of
Paris which came about to the detriment of the
provinces. Gravier then proposed a programme of
decentralisation to remedy the problem.
        Gravier's work also caught the attention of
another group in French society: those who espoused
the political philosophy of regionalism and who
actually lived in the 'regions', such as, Bretons,
Basques and Corsicans. Regionalism, in fact, had
become a discredited philosophy immediately following
the War because some local autonomists and
nationalists, like some federalists, had collaborated
with the Occupant. This collaboration had occurred
because of the autonomists' hatred of the French
state and the espousal of Fascist ideology by some of
them. Autonomists had been active in assisting the
Occupant track down, torture and murder Resistance

men and women.[12] Because of this activity, all those
who had been associated with regionalism or
autonomism were under suspicion, even those who had
remained loyal to France. When words such as
Gravier's were listened to attentively by the
moderate centre-left who eventually took control of
the Fourth Republic, this gave the regionalists a way
back into the mainstream of public life.
Furthermore, the theme of 'European unity', regarded
as progressive and forward-looking, could become a
suitable mask for individuals and groups which had
been more characterised, at their best, by passeisme
and provincial folklorisme and, at their worst, by
collaboration with Nazi and Fascist Occupants.

The Socio Economic Transformation of French Society

The themes of regionalisation and decentralisation
were sympathetically considered by those in
government circles. In fact, in the late 1940s and
early 1950s, when the centre-left had successfully
excluded both Communists and Gaullists from political
power, a programme of industrial decentralisation was
adopted and applied to French society. This was, in
fact, a consequence of the application of the
Marshall Plan and represented an attempt to use the
spatial or geographical resources of France in a more
efficient manner. Prior to this the structures of
the French economy had barely changed since the
beginning of the century. The primary sector
(agriculture and forests) was still very large
compared with other European states, such as Great
Britain and Germany. Industrialists were
conservative and the entrepreneurial spirit was
lacking. The great achievement of the Fourth
Republic, despite its governmental instability, was
to effect an important transformation of these
socio-economic structures and lay the basis for the
economic expansion of the Fifth Republic. The credit
for this goes to politicians such as Robert Schuman
and technocrats such as Jean Monnet whose brainchild
was a series of economic plans. It was in this
context of economic transformation and expansion,
tied to the programme of European reconstruction,
that the Fourth Republic's decentralisation programme
must be situated. In other words, the governments'
primary concern was not the 'region' and its
problems, but rather the French state as a whole and
its place within Europe. Nevertheless, it could be
argued that the very fact of adopting a programme of
decentralisation represented a kind of victory for at

least some of the federalists, in particular those of
the moderate MFF - (La Federation).

It was these three factors - the discrediting of
the nation-state, the regionalist theses of the
federalists (Gravier), and the transformation of the
socio-economic structures of French society through a
programme of decentralisation - which may be seen as
the immediate causes of the return of regionalism to
French political life. But who were the
regionalists? To answer this question, it is
necessary to look briefly at the nature of these
local societies.

Prior to the economic transformations of the
Fourth Republic, there existed in France two distinct
kinds of society, each marked by a different mode of
production.[13] On the one hand, there was an
urbanised industrial capitalist society (Paris, the
East and North East, Lyon). On the other hand there
were rural societies marked by the preponderance of
the small peasant holding in which the economic unit
was the extended family. In some of these rural
societies there was also a differentiation because of
'ethnic' factors such as a distinct language, history
and folkloric customs. Examples of such societies
are Brittany, the French Basque Country and Corsica.
It is in these three regions that the regionalist
movements have been strongest since the Second World
War and where they have embraced the entire range of
possibilities of regionalist ideology from moderate
regionalism to violent separatism. However, milder
regionalist movements, mainly concerned with
preservation of the local language, have sprung up in
Alsace, French Flanders, French Catalonia and
'Occitania'.[14] These 'ethnic' societies, mainly on
the periphery of the Hexagon, were marked
traditionally by conservatism and were held together
by a form of corporatist ideology - Catholicism in
Brittany and the Basque Country, a 'clan' system in
Corsica. It was this corporatism which ensured the
survival of these societies as cohesive units into
the twentieth century. The local society related to
the nation-state via the system of mediating elites
of which we have already spoken.

In the period following the Second World War,
these societies were threatened with a rapid break-up
as the economic transformation began to take effect.
This threat came from the rural exodus, penetration
by new industries, the advent of mass tourism and the
shaking up of the traditional morality with the
onslaught of the modern mass media.[15] Regionalism was
mainly the political response of those notables who

had been the mediating elites between their local
societies and the state. They were concerned to
protect their own interests in their societies and
attempted either to halt the process of change, as
their forebears had tried, or to minimise its effects
on their societal positions. Their strategy was
two-fold: to mobilise the local population and by
doing so to put pressure on the central government.
Examples of such movements were the C.E.L.I.B.
(Comite d'etudes et de liaison des interets bretons)
in Brittany, important since it provided a kind of
model for other regions, Enbata in the French Basque
Country, and the Mouvement du 29 Novembre in
Corsica.[16] Of all these groups, the CELIB was most
successful. It was their activities that were partly
responsible for the adoption by the Guy Mollet
government in the early years of the Fourth Republic
of a series of Plans d'Action Regionale (PAR) which
were intended to promote the economic and social
development of the regions in the context of European
integration. Gravier himself was directly involved
in the drawing up of these Plans.

It is out of place here to discuss fully the
significance and consequence of this programme of
industrial decentralisation. What is of interest to
us in this chapter is that, as has been noted, the
federalists also saw the necessity of a form of
regionalism and decentralisation. But in their
attitude to the regions and the problem of
regionalism they were divided. The kind of
regionalism favoured by the CELIB, that is, an
accommodation with the central power in an attempt to
wring concessions from them was also favoured by the
moderate MFF (La Federation). In fact, according to
Greilsammer, the MFF regarded the problem or
regionalism as being more important then the problem
of Europe. Furthermore, he states that 'La
Federation est restee liee au C.E.L.I.B. de Joseph
Martray, qui effectue frequemment en Bretagne des
campagnes similares aux sienne'.[17] The MFF set up
its own organisation to promote its regional
policies, the Mouvement national pour la
decentralisation et la reform regionale (M.N.D.R.).
This correspondance between the MFF and moderate
regionalist groups such as the CELIB is not
surprising given the conservative character of both
groups. Both had their origins in Catholic social
philosophy, which was, in fact, a form of
corporatism. Both had a similar strategy, at least
on one level - the attempt to influence politicians
and civil servants at the level of the central power

- although the CELIB differed in so far as it
attempted to mobilise the local population, or at
least, its professional and cultural associations.
Furthermore, both groups seemed to be happy to accept
the regionalisation programmes of the Fourth Republic
and, in fact, were partly responsible for them.

It may be tentatively concluded, therefore, that
there was a meeting of minds and a pooling of tactics
by regionalists and federalists during the early
1950s in response to the socio-economic
transformations taking place in France at both the
national and local levels. The two movements,
however, should not be completely identified. The
regionalists, such as the CELIB, Enbata or the
Mouvement du 29 Novembre, were more concerned with
their own regions than with the problem of European
integration, and this may have been espoused by some
of them for purposes of camouflage. Moreover, the
federalists saw regionalism not as an end in itself
but as a step in a wider transformation of society -
the creation of a federal Europe. The federal
movements were also in decline when movements such as
the CELIB and Enbata were in the ascendant. Finally,
both the federalists and regionalists contained
different tendencies which may be described as
moderate and radical rather than Right-wing and
Left-wing, since both moderate and radical tendencies
had Right and Left wings. Rather the division was
between those who were content with the reform
measures of the government and the first steps
towards European integration, and those who rejected
compromise and sought the revolutionary overthrow of
the nation-state. The latter sought the setting up
of a federal Europe des regions or Europe des
ethnies, or quite simply wished to 'liberate' their
'nation' from the 'colonialism' of Parisian
'imperialism'.

The Decline of Moderate Regionalism and the Rise
of Ethnic Nationalism

We have described regionalism as the political
response of local elites faced with the breakup of
their traditional societies under the impact of
modern capitalism with its programme of industrial
decentralisation. This response coincided with the
regionalist theses of the federalist movement and, as
we have seen, there was a certain amount of
intermingling of the two movements with regard to
personnel and tactics. When De Gaulle came to power
and set up the Fifth Republic, both moderate

regionalism and federalism declined because their
main tactical weapon - influence on the parliamentary
deputies and on the government - was removed from
them. One of the principal aims of De Gaulle was to
reduce the power of Parliament and by doing so to
neutralise the local notables whose political power,
expressed in the 'regime des partis' or the 'regime
d'Assemblee', he regarded as being one of the
obstacles to realising the 'grandeur' of France.
Furthermore, in the early years of the Fifth Republic
De Gaulle showed little interest in problems of
regionalism, a lack of interest shared by his Prime
Minister, Michel Debre. The latter went as far as to
say that 'L'amenagement du territoire a pour premier
objectif de maintenir et de developper la prosperite
des regions florissantes. La seconde ligne d'action
capitale ...[18] c'est l'amenagement de la region
parisienne.' It may seem paradoxical, then, that
many regionalists and federalists became
unconditional Gaullists (termed the 'trahison des
notables' by the more radical regionalists). In
fact, this switch to Gaullism could be seen as a
Bonapartist response on the part of the notables[19],
while those federalists who became Gaullist were
happy that the General should weaken the powers of
Parliament and the system of partis which they also
despised. In any case, as a result of De Gaulle's
accession to power, both moderate regionalism and
moderate federalism declined.

There then occurred a process of radicalisation.
The older, more conservative notable element in the
regionalist movements more or less came to terms both
with the regional programmes of the Fourth Republic
and the arrival to power of the Gaullist Fifth
Republic. But there existed within all the
regionalist movements a younger, more radical
element, who were already adopting a more critical
attitude towards Paris and its regional programmes.
This younger element was mainly a student
intelligentsia attending universities such as Rennes,
Bordeaux, Marseille and, of course, Paris. Uprooted
from their traditional societies, the conservative,
rural societies of Brittany, Corsica and the French
Basque Country, they became alienated from the
increasingly atomised society they found around them.
This feeling of deracinement and alienation was
intensified with the arrival of the authoritarian
Fifth Republic of De Gaulle. At the same time, the
young intellectuals were being submitted to political
and philosophical influences which their elders had
not known. The process of decolonisation (the

dismantling of the French Empire), and especially the
successful struggle for independence in Algeria,
convinced them that the description of France as the
'one and indivisible Republic' need not be taken too
seriously. One of the reasons for refusing
independence to Algeria had been that it, too, shared
in this unity and indivisibility but then, under De
Gaulle, it was finally granted. It was but one step
to the conclusion that if this were true for Algeria,
it may also be true for Brittany, Corsica or the
Basque Country as well as for the other oppressed
'nations' of France such as Occitania, Alsace, French
Flanders and French Catalonia. Furthermore, the
political ideology of Marxism exercised a widespread
hold on French intellectuals at this time. Marxism
allowed the radical regionalists to interpret the
relation between their societies and the French state
(or 'Paris') in a radically new way, that is
according to the theories of uneven development and
unequal exchange.

All these influences - the phenomenon of
deracinement, the process of decolonisation, and the
intellectual tool of Marxism - were directly
reponsible for the formulation of the theory of
'internal colonialism', whose principal ideologue was
the Occitanian activist and university professor,
Robert Lafont.[20] Internal colonialism saw the ethnic
regions as 'nations' which were colonised and
oppressed by an imperialist power - the French state.
Furthermore, the 'internal colonialism' thesis also
provided the young radicals with a strategy that
differed from that of the moderate regionalists.
Whereas the latter had not put into question the
adhesion of their region to the French Republic, the
former began to elaborate a critique that did just
this. However, only a minority finally adopted a
stance that sought complete 'national liberation',
and only a minority of these wished to do so by
violent means. The majority of this radical tendency
were more concerned with obtaining statutes of
autonomy within the French Republic. Such groups
were the MOB (Mouvement pour l'organisation de la
Bretagne), which split when its Left-wing members set
up the UDB (Union democratique bretonne) and the
Right-wing remainder became Strollard ar Vro. In
Corsica, the autonomists also split into Right and
Left factions: the Left-wing FRC (Front regionaliste
corse) founded by Charles Santoni and the ARC (Action
regionaliste corse - later Action pour la renaissance
de la Corse) of Max and Edmond Simeoni which was
later banned and changed its name to the UPC (Unione

di u Populu Corsu).[21] The Basque Enbata retained the
same name and organisation but it was controlled at
first by the moderates, then at a later date by the
radicals and nationalists. Finally, in all these
areas a violent separatist tendency appeared: the
FLB-ARB (Front de Liberation de la Bretagne-Armee
Republicaine Bretonne) in Brittany, the FLNC (Front
de Liberation nationale de la Corse) in Corsica, and
Iparretarak in the French Basque Country.

It is out of place here to submit these
movements and their ideologies, in particular the
ideology of 'internal colonialism', to a searching
critique.[22] What is of interest to us in this
chapter is the link, if any, between this phenomenon
of radicalisation and the federalist movements. We
have already pointed out the correspondence between
the moderate federalism of the MFF tendency and the
moderate regionalism of groups such as the CELIB and
the early Enbata. The French section of the MFE, led
by Alexandre Marc, Denis de Rougemont and an
ideologue on the question of ethnic minorities, Guy
Heraud, adopted a more revolutionary stance with
regard to both Europe and national minorities. The
MFE was more concerned with the integration of Europe
than was the MFF, which eventually used its resources
to promote the regional question. Nevertheless, the
MFE developed its own distinctive approach to the
regions and the problem of national minorities. In
contrast to both the moderate regionalists and
federalists, the MFE carried further the critique of
the French nation-state which it saw as imprisoning
the several 'nations' or 'ethnies' to be found within
their borders. The basic French units of the Europe
some of the maximalists wished to construct were the
'natural' ethnic communities distinguished by their
own language, culture and history from the 'French'
nation (or 'Francie', as Robert Lafont termed it).
It is obvious that such a political ideology would be
of great interest to the emerging radical autonomists
and ethnic nationalists and, conversely, the radical
federalists would be interested in the emerging
movement of ethnic nationalism.

It would seem to be the case that there was a
correspondence between the radical federalists and
the ethnic nationalists similar to that which existed
between the MFF and the moderate regionalists.
First, there was an intermingling of personnel. This
was made easier by the fact that some of the leading
radical federalists originated from within the ethnic
minorities. Guy Heraud was an Alsatian, Robert
Lafont, an Occitanian militant, and Morvan-Lebesque,

a Breton, were among the founders of the Comite de
liaison pour une action federaliste (CLAF).
Secondly, there was a cross-fertilisation on the
level of ideas. The 'internal colonialism' thesis
was the brain-child of Lafont and was accepted with
little criticism by the radical federalists. It
forms the underlying assumption of the work
Pour une France Federale by the radical federalist
Pierre Fougeyrollas.[23] For the latter, Europe can be
constructed only with the liberation of these
minorities from French 'imperialism' and, conversely,
the minorities can be liberated only within the
context of a new Europe. Heraud had produced his own
theory of 'ethnicity'[24] but accepted Lafont's thesis
only with some reservation.[25] It could be argued
that the radical federalists provided the radical
regionalists (autonomists and ethnic nationalists)
with a theory which could then serve as a mobilising
myth. Lafont applied the theory to Occitania,[26] the
UDB to Brittany in their booklet Bretagne = Colonie[27]
while in Corsica the FRC reproduced the thesis in
Main basse sur un ile.[28] On the other hand, the
emerging ethnic nationalism gave the federalists a
stick with which to beat the French nation-state, a
beating which was greatly appreciated by the radical
regionalists many of whom now wished to overthrow the
nation-state and denied its legitimacy.

It is important, nevertheless, not to completely
identify the two movements, as was the case with
their moderate counterparts. While the radical
federalists placed the problem of ethnic minorities
within a European context, the radical regionalists
tended to see no further than the bounds of their own
region and its relation to 'Paris'. In other words,
one of the characteristics of ethnic nationalism and
autonomism is not to look over one's hedge even at
other 'nations' 'oppressed' within the Hexagon. In
any case, if the radical regionalists were
federalists, it tended to be within a French and not
European context. Autonomists, for example, sought a
statute of autonomy within the French Republic (the
UDB and UPC). The nationalists, on the other hand,
sought some form of independence but did not give
much thought to relations of the post-independent
state to other states. Another important difference
is that some sections of the radical regionalists
such as the UDB, the FRC and the later Enbata,
adopted, implicitly or explicitly, a form of Marxism.
This was particularly the case after the events of
May 1968. The radical federalists also swung to the
Left, but kept their distance from Marxism and

remained anti-Communist. Their inspiration was
rather Proudhon and the radical Catholicism of Peguy
and Mounier. The philosophy of even the radical
federalists remained tinged with corporatism and
their theory of 'ethnicity' was not exempt from a
certain racism.[29] Finally, the appreciation of
Europe by radical federalists and radical
regionalists differed considerably. For the former,
as we have seen, European integration of a federal
kind was at the heart of their political philosophy.
The latter tended to reject the process of European
integration which they saw as the facilitation of the
entry of multi-national corporations into Europe.
Basque and Occitanians saw their regions marked out
for tourist development by the 'marchands de soleil',
the purveyors of 'tout-tourisme', that is, groups
such as ITT and Sofitel. Bretons criticised the kind
of industrial growth that had taken place in Brittany
and pointed to its precarious nature. The programme
of industrial investment which had taken place since
the 1950s was described as the parachuting into the
region of 'pirate companies' attracted by the offer
of low wages and a work-force recently torn from the
land and therefore with little tradition of
industrial organisation and trade-union militancy.
However, it remains true that not all of the radical
regionalists adopted this Marxist critique of Europe,
although they did criticise the PAR's of the 1950s.
It is also true that the radical federalists
criticised the 'functionalist' and
'neo-functionalist' approaches to European
integration. Nevertheless, there was a basic
ambivalence on their part with regard to the
integration that had already taken place.

The Success or Failure of Federalism and Regionalism

It now remains to be seen whether these movements
were successful or not in achieving their aims. Both
the moderate regionalists and moderate federalists
were successful in so far as they did persuade the
central government to adopt a programme of
regionalisation which at least took into account the
fact that there was a regional problem. The MFF was
only partially successful in its aim of achieving a
federal Europe since it was the neo-functionalists
who eventually had their way. Nevertheless, the
moderate federalists, being possibilistes, quickly
came to terms with this situation and turned their
attention to the regional problem. On the level of
mobilisation, the moderate regionalists did have a

certain amount of success in rousing the local populations to support their demands. The moderate federalists did not even try to mobilise the population since their strategy remained that of elitist lobbying. However, this strategy must be considered to have been a failure after the arrival of De Gaulle to power which hastened the decline which had already begun with the failure of the EDC. Furthermore, the hostility of De Gaulle to any form of European integration not based on the primacy of the existing nation-states, and especially on the primacy of France, was a blow to those for whom the nation-states should be superseded. The unity of the moderate regionalists was also shattered by the arrival of De Gaulle to power and the consequence was the fragmentation and radicalisation we have already described. It may be concluded, therefore, that the moderate federalists and regionalists were partially successful in realising their aims and that, being pragmatists, they easily came to terms with the partial failure.

The radical regionalists and federalists have not fared much better. The majority of the local ethnic populations have on the whole refused to respond to the mobilising myth of the Corsican, Breton or Basque 'nations'.[30] This is even more the case in Flanders, Alsace, 'Occitania' and Catalonia. In all cases, ethnic activism has been confined to small fractions of the population such as the uprooted intellectuals who have been its ideologues and chief activists. The majority have continued to accept their 'French' identity and to support Christian Democrat or Gaullist politicians (although the Socialists did make a breakthrough in Brittany in the 1981 General Elections). Although separatist violence continues - in Corsica at a high level, increasingly in the French Basque Country, and resurgently in Brittany - the violent separatists are becoming increasingly marginal even from separatists who are non-violent and from Left-wing parties and trade-unions which had hitherto given them some support, for example, to their political prisoners.

The MFE, in contrast to the MFF, adopted a strategy of mobilising the 'masses' of Europe around the theme of European integration. This obviously included the inhabitants of the 'ethnies opprimees', whom they wished to federate into a 'Europe des ethnies'. In fact, most of their support came from urban areas outside what were considered to be the ethnic regions, although they did have some support in Alsace.[31] Therefore, the radical federalists must

be considered to have failed on several levels. Not
only did their concept of European integration lose
out to the neo-functionalist model, but the 'ethnies'
themselves did not respond to the project for the
creation of a federal France and Europe.
Furthermore, many of the radical regionalists seemed
reluctant to adopt the ideology of European
federalism. Exceptions were the MOB which became the
Strollard Ar Vo and which had an explicitly
federalist ideology. However, it is the Left-wing
UDB which has captured most of the radical
regionalist support in Brittany. In general, then,
both federalism and regionalism, especially in their
radical versions, have been singularly unsuccessful
in mobilising the ethnic populations around their
political projects.

This failure is probably a consequence of the
nature of the movements themselves and of their
interpretation of the reality of French politics and
history. The radical regionalists and federalists
presented an analysis of the French nation-state
which was based more on a new mythology than on
reality. They correctly drew attention to the fact
that France was composed of several linguistic groups
and traditional societies which had more or less
survived into the modern period. In other words,
they successfully debunked the Jacobin myth of the
'one and indivisible Republic' which was conceived in
official history as an 'eternal' reality. What they
seriously underestimated was the extent to which the
linguistic minorities identified with this ideology.
In other words, the latter had a double identity:
French as well as Breton, Corsican and Basque. Hence
the notion that they were distinct 'peoples' or
'nations' crushed by an imperialist Jacobin power
based in Paris, was, in fact, a new mythology to
replace the old, this time given intellectual
respectability in the ideology of internal
colonialism. Undoubtedly, the regions suffered grave
problems such as the rural exodus, rapid
industrialisation, and the advent of mass tourism.
The populations concerned, however, did not see the
solution to these problems in some form of 'national
liberation' or in the creation of a 'Europe des
ethnies'. On the contrary, they wished for more aid
from the state and therefore saw their resolution in
a closer connection between the local society and the
state rather than the opposite. A common theme in
regions such as Corsica is that the state has
abandoned them. Finally, it is probable that the
utopian nature of the radical federalists' schemes

was a hindrance to their acceptance by large numbers of people, especially peasants not given to romantic and literary fantasising. One example of such fantasising is the federal France of Pierre Fougeyrollas which would include regions such as Occitanie orientale and Francie septentrionale. The administrative centre would no longer be the monster city Paris but a new capital called Franceville, situated somewhere near the present Clermont-Ferrand.[32] Just as the radical regionalists underestimated the attachments of their 'peuples' to the 'one and indivisible Republic', so, too, the federalists seriously overestimated the possibility of the traditional nation-state withering away.

While the regionalists and federalists may not have been completely successful on the level of achieving their political aims, they have nevertheless played an important ideological role in modern France. It is they who drew attention to the regional problem and to the imbalance that existed between Paris and the provinces. Thanks to them, we are more aware of the existence of linguistic minorities and the possibility of the disappearance of precious cultural heritages, which until then had been despised as mere 'patois' and 'folkloric' customs. There is today a new respect for these groups and a greater willingness to preserve their distinct identities. The Right-wing governments of the Fifth Republic were less willing to do so than are their successors in the Socialist-Communist government which took office in June 1981. In fact, one of the basic planks of the Left-wing government's policies is a programme of decentralisation and respect for national minorities which they claim is more radical than anything seen in France since the setting up of the prefectoral system by Napoleon I.

Socialist decentralisation[33]

One author has defined a federal state as one which has a high degree of decentralisation.[34] If this definition is accepted, then France, under the Socialists of Francois Mitterrand, is moving toward some kind of internal federalism. This definition, however, has been rejected by Preston King on the grounds that there are many different kinds of decentralisation and that even states traditionally classified as non-federal are marked by some of these kinds of decentralisation.[35] Nevertheless, it could still be argued that the socialist reforms are leading to some form of federal system according to

King's own definition of the term which has already[36] been discussed by Michael Burgess in Chapter Two. The new reforms do in fact allow an 'entrenched representation' but what is important is what kind. So far the reforms have been applied most fully in Corsica and it is to this region that we must look in order to discern the nature and extent of this 'entrenched representation'.

In effect, the Regional Assembly for Corsica, the new body set up by the decentralisation reforms, may on its own initiative or on that of the Prime Minister, suggest modifications or adaptation on actual or pending legislation concerning the powers, the organisation or the functioning of the Region of Corsica or of any proposals concerning the economic, social or cultural development of the island.[37] The government, however, is not obliged to accept these recommendations. In other words, while the Assembly has a right to be consulted, it cannot pass any legislation of its own which would be binding in any way on the central government. This means that the principle of sovereignty, remaining entirely at the level of the central organs of power, is maintained. This position has been reaffirmed by Gaston Defferre, the former Minister of the Interior and of Decentralisation, who was responsible for the reforms.

This helps us to assess the federal status of the reforms. It would seem that many of the themes of federalism as put forward by French federalists since the Second World War are contained in the socialist programme of decentralistion: the valorisation of the 'region', the respect for linguistic and cultural minorities, the democratisation of local government institutions and a wide deconcentration of administrative powers by the abolition of the perfectoral system. This application of federalist themes has not, however, led to the creation of a federation. This is because the kind of 'entrenched representation' is such that sovereignty remains, juridically and de facto, the preserve of the central government. It would seem, then, that a further criterion among those that define a federation would be that sovereignty is d ivided both juridically and de facto, between the central and the regional levels of institutions. So far, in France, this is not the case.

Notes

1. On federalist movements see Alain Greilsammer, Les Movements Federalistes en France de 1945 a 1974, Ed. (Presses d'Europe, 1975); on regionalism and ethnic nationalism see John Loughlin, 'Regionalism and ethnic nationalism in France', in Y. Meny and V. Wright (eds), Centre-Periphery Relations in Western Europe, (Allen & Unwin, 1984).

2. Language is usually taken as the starting point for the definition of an ethnic minority. It has been estimated that seven distinct languages are spoken within France: four Romance - French, Occitanian, Catalonian and Corsican, two Germanic - Flemish and Alsatian: one Celtic - Breton: and Basque which is sui generis. Brittany and 'Occitania' (most of France south of the Loire) are geographically situated entirely within France south of the Hexagon. Flanders, the French Basque Country and French Catalonia are the minority parts of larger linguistic groups which straddle its borders. Alsace and Corsica possess distinct dialects which are linguistically close to German and Italian respectively.

3. For an example of such toleration in Brittany, see. S. Berger, Peasants Against Politics: Rural Organisation in Brittany 1911-1967, (Cambridge (Mass), 1972).

4. This is the basis of Bonapartism as analysed by Marx in the 18th Brumaire of Louis Bonaparte. Marx, however, does not seem to have taken into account the existence of such local societies and sees the peasants of all France as being a mass - like a 'sack of potatoes'.

5. Berger, Peasants Against Politics points out that this was the case even during the Front Populaire period when the Left-wing government cooperated easily with the Right-wing group the Office de Landernau in Brittany.

6. During the revolution of 1789-99 these occurred mainly in the West, e.g. the chouan revolt.

7. Studies of these movements may be found in
    C. Gras et G. Livet (eds), Regions et
    regionalisme en France (du XVIIIe siecle a nos
    jours), (PUF, 1977).

8. See Greilsammer, pp.188-196.

9. Ibid., p.40.

10. Ibid., p.41.

11. See Ernst HAAS, The Uniting of Europe,
    Political, Economic and Socal Forces 1950-57,
    (London, 1958).

12. For two conflicting accounts of this period in
    Brittany, see Y. Fouere 'Le regionalisme breton
    sous le governement de Vichy et le Comite
    consultatif de Bretagne' and M. Denis,
    'Mouvement breton et fascisme. Signification de
    l'echec du second emsav', both in Gras and
    Livet, (eds), Regions et regionalisme en France,
    pp.481-506. Fouere, a federalist, minimises the
    degree of collaboration, while Denis
    emphasises it.

13. See R. Dulong, Les regions, l'Etate et la
    Societe locale, (PUF, 1978).

14. See Loughlin, 'Regionalism and Ethnic
    Nationalism in France'.

15. In Corsica, for example, there was no local
    daily for the whole island until Nice-Matinand
    Le Provencal(Marseille) produced Corsican
    editions in the late 1950s. Interestingly, it
    is 1959 that the first Corsican regionalist
    movement, the Mouvement du 29 Novembre, founded
    by Corsican journalists appears. See
    P. Silvani, Le Corse des annees ardentes,
    (Albatross, 1976).

16. So-called because Corsica was declared to be
    fully integrated into the French nation by the
    National Assembly in 30 November 1789. The
    Mouvement contended that, in reality, the island
    was still only on the eve of integration.

17. Greilsammer, Les Mouvements federalistes, p.119.

18. Le Monde, 7 March 1961.

19. The conservative regionalists saw in De Gaulle a 'representative' of their interests before the state and the forces of industrial capitalism.

20. See, for example, R. Lafont La Revolution regonaliste, (Gallimard, Paris, 1967) and Decoloniser en France, (Gallimard, Paris, 1971).

21. On the Corsican problem see P. Hainsworth and J. Loughlin "Le probleme corse", Contemporary French Civilization, (London, 1984).

22. I have attempted to do this in 'Regionalism and ethnic nationalism in France', in Meny and Wright (eds), Centre-Periphery Relations.

23. P. Fourgeyrollas, (Ed), (Denoel, Paris 1968).

24. Notably in L'Europe des ethnies, (Presses d'Europe, Paris, 1963).

25. See 'Observations critiques sur la notion de colonialisme interieur',Europe en formation, n.193, (Avril 1976) pp.16-20.

26. See La Revendication occitane, (Flammarion, 1974).

27. Publ. (de l'UDB, 1974) (2eme ed).

28. Edit (Martineau, 1971).

29. For example, Jacques Bargiarelli, a Corsican federalist, could write that '.... de trop nombreux metissages, consequence inevitable des migrations, risquent de mettre en peril la personnalite de notre peuple' in 'De la region course a la federation europeenne', Europe en formation, n.195, (Juin 1976). This review is the principal voice of the radical federalists.

30. See Loughlin, 'Regionalism', in Meny amd Wright, Centre-Periphery Relations.

31. See Greilsammer, Les Mouvements Federalistes, p.125.

32. Fougeyrollas, Pour une France Federale.

33. See Y. Meny, "Decentralisation in Socialist France", in West European Politics, vol.7, n.1, (Jan. 1984) pp.65-79.

34. H. Kelsen, General Theory of Law and the State, (2nd ed.), (New York 1961) (trans. A. Wedberg). Quoted in Preston King, Federalism and Federation, (Croom Helm, London & Canberra, 1982) p.122.

35. Ibid., pp.122-129.

36. See below pp.14-26.

37. Loi n.82-213 du 2 mars 1982 (J.O. 3 mars 1982) et loi n.82-214 du 2 mars 1982 portant statut particulier de la Region Corse (J.O. du 3 mars 1982) and loi n.82-659 (organisation administrative) and loi n.82-659 du 30 juillet 1982 portant statut particulier de la Region Corse (competences). J.O. du 31 julliet 1982.

6.   FEDERAL IDEAS IN CONTEMPORARY IRELAND

     Neil Collins

Introduction

Ireland is not a sovereign state in that there are
two separate jurisdictions on the island. It is
difficult, therefore, to apply the major approaches
to federation which political scientists have used in
the United States, the United Kingdom, West Germany,
Austria and other countries. The question of
federation in Ireland has, however, received a
substantial fillip with the publication of the report
of the New Ireland Forum. The Forum was set up by
the Government of the Republic of Ireland to prepare
a blue-print for Irish unity. This chapter rehearses
the background to the Forum, the idea of federalism
in Ireland, particularly as presented to the Forum,
and the Report's treatment of the specifically
federal option. As the Report stated:

     The New Ireland Forum was established for
     consultations on the manner in which lasting
     peace and stability could be achieved in a new
     Ireland through the democratic process and to
     report on possible new structures and processes
     through which this objective might be achieved.[1]

     The first meeting of the New Ireland Forum took
place in Dublin Castle on 30 May, 1983, under the
chairmanship of Dr. Colm O h Eocha, President of
University College, Galway. The Forum's membership
is drawn from the four nationalist parties on the
island: Fine Gael and Labour (the present coalition
partners), Fianna Fail (the major opposition party)
and the Social Democratic and Labour Party (from
Northern Ireland). The party leaders set themselves
an open agenda, but by early 1984 their three major
options were clear. Invitations to join the Forum
were sent to the Official Unionist, Democratic
Unionist and Alliance Parties, but none of these
Northern Ireland parties accepted.
     All the various suggestions put before the Forum
(called "federal solutions" by their authors)
fulfilled the assumptions of federation outlined in
Chapter Two by Michael Burgess: the focus upon fully
constitutional government and the notion of
guaranteed access to the decision-making centre. The
idea of a contractual agreement or political bargain
was also evident. Each suggestion and the Report's

own federal option is examined below. The particular
academic interest in the current debate in Ireland
may be that it represents an attempt to forge a
particular kind of political/legal/constitutional
arrangement which may be 'federal' in nature if not
name. Indeed this chapter attempts to show that the
current legal separation between the two parts of
Ireland hides a more complex and integrated social
reality.

The Forum Report was published on 2 May, 1984.
As had been forecast it contained three options: a
unitary state, a federal/confederal state, and joint
authority. Soon after publication a disagreement
broke out between Fianna Fail and the other parties
about the status of the three options. It is clear
that a unitary state is the preferred outcome for
nationalists but Fianna Fail's leader, Charles
Haughey, has represented it as the only agreed
option. Even within his party, however, there is
significant dissent on Mr. Haughey's
interpretation. Outside Ireland the Forum Report was
greeted with intense interest by the media,
particularly in Britain and the United States. The
Department of Foreign Affairs organised an intense
diplomatic and public relations hype.

The Report's so-called federal/confederal
option is based on the existing two states. The
federal possibility is distinguished by the relative
power of the central government and a more elaborate
central parliamentary institution than that of a
confederal arrangement. The Chapter entitled
"Federal/Confederal State" is brief and mostly links
the two possible arrangements together. It is
largely concerned with constitutional form and broad
declarations of intent.

Social and Informal Organisational Structures

While legal features may be given prominence by the
Forum Report, the study of federalism draws attention
to the importance of social and informal
organisational structures. To understand the
relevance of federalism for Ireland, it is necessary
to understand the nature of these structures.

In international law, the archipelago which lies
off the north-west coast of Europe is divided
between two separate sovereign states:
the United Kingdom of Great Britain and Northern
Ireland, and the Republic of Ireland. But at
the level of private organisations, the
situation is much more untidy. Whilst most

organisations observe the frontier, and confine
their activities to one side or other of it,
many operate on either an all-Ireland or an
all-archipelago basis .... There are many other
fields where Britain and Ireland, Northern
Ireland and the Republic, are inextricably
intertwined: business, banking, the media, the
arts, many aspects of public administration
.... Anglo-Irish relations are more complex
than the more strident simplifiers on either
side are aware. Unionists are not irrevocably
opposed to any kind of all-Ireland framework:
in some fields they adopt it already.
Nationalists do not inevitably perceive an all-
archipelago framework as a throwback to tyranny:
they accept it for some purposes already. Thus
the Anglo-Irish process, which both sovereign
governments see as in their interests, is
underpinned by an already existing reality.[2]

Professor Whyte's study was initially presented
to a European academic conference and none of the
participants could think of any parallel. Even in
the Nordic Union, where cooperation is stronger than
in most parts of Europe, it is unusual for
organisations to recruit in more than one country'.[3]
Only in North America is there anything approaching
the level of cross-border linkage. This social and
organisational overlapping may have no direct
political significance in relation to a federal
solution but it does suggest some firm ground on
which politicians with such an eventual aim could
build. Let us now focus our attention upon four
related dimensions to these organisational
structures.

Economic

As Whyte suggests, there are extensive economic links
between the two parts of Ireland. Many businesses
are administered on an all-Ireland basis,
particularly in the fields of banking, retailing and
construction. Similarly, the larger trade unions
have members on both sides of the border. Although
the majority of unions operate in one jurisdiction
only, the Irish Congress of Trade Unions is an all
island body. The Forum Report noted that:

> The structure of the two economies are more
> similar today than they were 20 years ago.
> Agriculture's share of GDP has declined in both
> areas although agriculture contributes
> relatively more to the South's GDP than it does
> to that of the North.
>
> Industry's share of GDP has continued to grow in
> the South while it has declined in the North so
> that the relative size of the industrial
> sector is now roughly similar .... Structures
> of the agricultural and industrial sectors
> differed greatly, North and South. Since the
> 1960s and especially since EEC membership, these
> differences have given way to greater
> similarities in these two sectors. The service
> sector has grown considerably in both areas and
> contributes relatively more to the North's GDP
> than it does to that of the South. These
> developments are mirrored in the overall
> structure of employment.[4]

The economies of the two units are heavily
interdependent in that trade between them is very
important. Nevertheless, the external trade of both
economies with Britain greatly exceeds intra-Irish
trade. While the Forum Report itself placed little
emphasis on the social interaction, it was clearly
aware of the opportunity costs of partition:

> Development agencies in both areas accept that
> they face the major challenge of expanding and
> diversifying the economic base in industry
> and services. They aim in particular to develop
> advanced technology applications with a high
> value added content in order to meet the
> pressing demand for new employment in
> traditional industries.[5]

A central factor in the inability of the North
to match the economic growth of the South has been
the violent political struggle there. Despite this,
however, GDP per head is roughly the same in both
areas, reflecting a 'catching-up' on the part of the
South. The historical lead of Northern Ireland in
terms of personal income was often advanced as an
argument against any change in links with the UK.
Increasingly, however, the economy of the North has
become more dependent on public expenditure, or
transfer payments, from the rest of the UK. In 1982
the annual grant from Britain to Northern Ireland was

IR pounds 964 per head. This financial dependence on Britain was an important element in the Forum's discussions because it is generally recognised that the Republic could not meet the bill were Britain to withdraw its subvention for any reason. The Forum's economic consultants assumed that 'Britain would honour existing liabilities to individuals on its exchequer'. They said of a two-state federal solution that, if no external aid was available and the British subvention ceased, 'the financial imbalances .... would be so severe that the adjustment in living standards and in employment would be unconscionable'.[6] Referring to the hoped for 'reconciliation between the two major traditions in Ireland', the Forum Report asserts that 'the British government have a duty .... to make the required investment of political will and resources'.[7] The present and future economic health of Ireland as a whole is clearly strongly dependent on Britain in terms of trade and direct financial support. The Forum Report was quite categorical about this point:

> While a settlement of the conflict entailing an end to violence and the dynamic effects of all-Ireland economic integration would bring considerable economic benefits, reconstruction of the Northern Ireland economy and the maintenance of living standards in the meantime would require the continued availability of substantial transfers from outside over a period of years.[8]

Legal

Among the institutional similarities between the Republic and Northern Ireland are the law and legal institutions. The Forum Report was particularly interesting in this regard:

> A great deal of pre-1922 law remains common to both jurisdictions .... Since independence the vast bulk of legislation enacted in the South is unique to the South in response to its own needs and policies. Nevertheless, within that body of statute law down the years, there was a distinct tendency to adapt where appropriate British precedents in legislation. This has been particularly true of the commercial and tax areas for reasons that flow obviously from the very many commercial links

between Britain and Ireland. In addition, there was a tendency over the years in both jurisdictions, to cite and rely on the decisions of the English courts. When these factors are taken into account it is possible to justify the general conclusion that the law of both jurisdictions had by 1972 diverged to a quite limited extent from the common base which existed prior to 1922. However, since the introduction of Direct Rule in Northern Ireland in 1972 the process of legal integration with Great Britain has accelerated. In consequence, the tendency over the last decade for greater differentiation between North and South in the legal field is more pronounced particularly in the area of legislation.

Nevertheless, the authors concluded optimistically that:

The law and legal institutions, particularly the courts have demonstrated over the last sixty years a capacity to adapt to change, somewhat cautiously perhaps and with a tendency to emphasise continuity with the past. But in the light of their history, there can be every confidence that whatever political structures are proposed for the future, the courts and the legal system can adapt to and work within them.[10]

Another common social phenomenon between north and south has been the impact of terrorism on family, social and economic life. The Forum summarised it thus:

The violence in the North has created staggering costs in human and economic terms since 1969. Nearly every family in the North has been touched either by personal grief or injury. There are many thousands who have lost spouses, parents, children. Amongst the 24,000 injured are many thousands who continue to suffer pain and disadvantage from severed limbs or permanent disability. Thousands more have to endure psychological stress and damage because of the fear and tension created by murder, bombing and intimidation. The lives of tens of thousands have been blighted. While the South and Britain have not suffered in any comparable way they have been affected by the spill-over of violence, especially in terms of extra security and judicial measures.[11]

The violence of para-military groups has been 'organised' on an all-Ireland basis as has the corresponding response to it. The cost to the UK and Ireland, in 1982 terms, of violence in extra security, compensation and damage to tourism, between 1969 and 1982 is estimated as IR 11,840m (stg pounds 11,062m.) The implications of this financial burden and the organisation of measures to reduce it have been an important common focus for policy-makers North and South.

Political

> The situation is daily growing more dangerous.
> Constitutional politics are on trial and unless
> there is action soon to create a framework in
> which constitutional politics can work, the
> drift into more extensive civil conflict is in
> danger of becoming irreversible, with further
> loss of life and increasing human suffering.
> The consequences for the people in Northern
> Ireland would be horrific and it is
> inconceivable that the South and Britain could
> escape the serious threats to stability that
> would arise.[12]

Political institutions linking the two parts of Ireland are conspicuously few. The Council of Ireland, established by act of the Westminster Parliament in 1920 to deal with non-contentious matters of policy concerning the whole island, was dissolved in 1926, never having functioned. An attempt to reinstate the Council failed along with the Northern Ireland power-sharing executive in 1974. The island as a whole votes together in only one election, that to the European Parliament, but STV-PR is common to all Irish elections. Of the political parties represented at the New Ireland Forum, none contest elections on both sides of the border. The same is true, obviously, of all the unionist groupings. Only the minor left wing and republican parties are fully organised on an all-Ireland basis. Sinn Fein, in particular, put up candidates in both jurisdictions for the 1984 European Elections and claimed 8% of the all-Ireland vote on that basis.[13]

Ecclesiastical

Whyte's study showed that the majority of churches are structured on an all-Ireland basis. This is true of the main Protestant churches as well

as the majority denomination on the island, the
Catholics. Such organisational unity has not always
been reflected in the approaches of the churches to
political questions. Some commentators have been
particularly critical:

> The role of the churches in Ireland over the
> years has been unhelpful at best, given the high
> degree of religiosity in the country and
> hence the scope for widespread beneficial
> influence. Certainly, the platitudes have
> wafted forth with monotonous regularity, but the
> prospect of any change within the churches' own
> attitudes and practices, which could begin the
> gradual process of reducing suspicion and
> tension between the two religious communities
> has been conspicuous by its absence. Sectional
> interest and dogmatic rivalry remain the
> cornerstones of religious authority in Ireland,
> North and South.[14]

In this context the submissions to the Forum of
the various churches, but particularly the Catholic
Church, were very closely examined. For the most
part they did not contain detailed institutional
suggestions. The churches have, however, been
conciliatory in their emphasis on a common desire for
some peaceful solution. The Church of Ireland, which
is in the mainstream of the Anglican tradition, has
the majority of its members in the North and its
submission reflected their concern about the Forum's
deliberations:

> The plain fact is that partnership in Northern
> Ireland is being seriously impeded by the
> absence of a positive, realistic and honest
> approach by the Republic to the issue of Irish
> unity. And this is a situation in which the
> great majority of citizens in Northern Ireland
> are quite determined not to be absorbed into the
> Irish Republic as it at present exists. This is
> a stark fact of life.[15]

The Church of Ireland's position as an
all-Ireland body with a strong unionist tradition is
reflected in an address by Dean Griffin of St.
Patrick's Cathedral Dublin:

> Britain can never be as foreign to us as say,
> France or Germany, and neither can the Republic
> be regarded as a foreign country when seen from

Northern Ireland. Is so many ways for richer or
for poorer these two are bound together and our
supreme aim under God must be to bring together
what is valuable in both our traditions into a
creative synthesis which will enrich the lives
and endeavours of all the people in this island
thereby enabling us to play a more effective
role and to show a more effective Christian
witness in the community of nations.

The Dean said that any sincere effort to promote
reconciliation in the North has to give due
recognition to both British and Irish dimensions. He
went on:

The logical corollary to this is that any
administration or Government in Northern
Ireland, if it is to command the consensus of
all the people must include the two traditions
and must have close links with both London and
Dublin with both Britain and the Republic, for
there can be no reconciliation without mutual
respect and recognition.[16]

Although the Catholic Church is the majority
church on an all-Ireland basis, for many Protestants
it represents the majority reason for the border. As
the Forum Report notes:

There is a widespread perception among unionists
that the Roman Catholic Church exerts or seeks
to exert undue influence in regard to aspects of
the civil and legal organisation of society
which Protestants consider to be a matter of
private conscience. Despite the implicit
separation of Church and State in the 1937
Constitution, many unionists hold the view that
the Catholic ethos has unduly influenced
administration in the South and that the latter,
in its laws, attitudes and values has not
reflected a regard for the ethos of Protestants
there.[17]

The Catholic bishops made a written submission to
the Forum which received widespread criticism for its
seeming intransigence on issues affecting church-
state and inter-church relations. The written
submission, which seems to have sadly misinterpreted
the public mood, was followed by an oral submission
which was very different in tone. 'There is no way'
argued Dr. Cahal Daly, the most senior bishop in the

Catholic panel which addressed the Forum, that 'the
constitution we now have could be imposed on the
Northern Ireland Unionists'. As Chapter Two shows,
there is a strong element of federalist thought in
much of Catholic social theory and the bishops' views
were clearly compatible with the traditional emphasis
on subsidiarity and natural rights. Dr. Daly's
opinions mirrored those of Pope John XXIII writing in
general terms of natural rights:

> One of the fundamental duties of civil
> authorities .... is to coordinate social
> relations in such fashion that the exercise of
> one man's right does not threaten others in the
> exercise of their own rights nor hinder them in
> the fulfilment of their duties.[18]

Similarly the Irish Church views on the social order
are influenced by Pius XI's declaration that it is a
disturbance of proper order to turn over to a greater
society of higher rank, functions and services which
can be performed by smaller communities on a lower
panel.[19]

As one of the more conservative bishops wrote in a
polemical monograph:

> I am well aware that, in the context of a united
> Ireland, whether federal or otherwise, there
> will have to be modification in our laws ....
> to satisfy the legitimate human and political
> aspirations of all.[20]

Or, more specifically:

> Nor are we unaware, in the context of the North,
> of the possibility of a federal solution, in
> which matters like divorce, as the lesser of two
> evils, might have to be allowed.[21]

Most churchmen, who presented evidence to the
Forum, ignored specific political solutions such as
federation, but only one clerical submission rejected
a federal solution out of hand. Dr. George Dallas, a
Northern Presbyterian, argued that true
Protestantism, since it represented Christian
morality, could act as a bastion against continental
European anti-church factions. 'The best solution
.... is a unitary state .... there is no
place or need for a federal solution'.[22]

Dr. Dallas's views proved to be in the minority, within the Presbyterian Church. The General Assembly, which met shortly after the Forum Report's publication, recorded its deep disappointment at the emphasis on a unitary state as a framework for a political settlement. The Presbyterian Church with over 350,000 members in 566 congregations or parishes, is divided into twenty-two district 'presbyteries'. Three of these, with over 12,000 members, are located wholly in the Republic. The Presbyterians, like the Methodists and Baptists, represent a long Irish tradition of Dissent. Dr. William McDowell, a Dublin based cleric, told the Assembly whatever resolution to our problems, a unitary state, at this time, is not one that we can see as bringing peace and stability to our island.[23]

Dr. McDowell reminded the Assembly that, in addition to the unitary state as the preferred option of nationalists, the Forum has also examined the alternative of a federal Ireland and of a joint administration of the North by the British and Irish Governments. He had underlined the cross-border involvement of the Presbyterian Church in his own submission to the Forum, which is examined below.

Submissions to the Forum

The most vehemently anti-federalist elements in Ireland are the most irredentist nationalists and unionists. These elements are also united in their suspicion of the EC. The Irish Sovereignty Movement, for example, submitted the following view to the Forum:

> It would be totally impermissible for the parties of the Forum to give countenance to any idea that this State would be willing to abandon .... its legal and political sovereignty as part of the price of territorial reunification.
>
> No Irish party or parties have the right to make such promises explicit or implicit. Hence, we are strongly of the view that there should be no consideration of hypothetical future constitutional arrangements incorporating Anglo-Irish executive or legislative institutions or any hint that confederal constitutional arrangements might be appropriate.[24]

Apart from the nationalist extremists, the unitary state idea received most support among Fianna Fail members of the Forum. As a spokesman for Mr. Haughey explained even before the Forum was muted:

> there is no official party policy tying us to any particular form of a united Ireland. But preference has grown again for a unitary state with some legal administrative autonomy for Northern Ireland.[25]

Joint sovereignty, an idea widely canvassed in the press, was put to the Forum by Bernard Cullen and Richard Kearney, two academic philosophers:

> The Unionists demand British sovereignty over Northern Ireland. The nationalists demand Irish sovereignty over Northern Ireland. It is in the light of the foregoing arguments that we are proposing joint British and Irish sovereignty over Northern Ireland.

> Northern Ireland administered under joint sovereignty would have a bi-national cultural identity. It would be equally legitimate to hold a British or an Irish passport. There would be two national anthems and two national flags, each set of national symbols having equal prominence in all official circumstances.[26]

However, it received little support from politicians north or south. Reaching the point of harmony which would allow joint sovereignty to be accepted without coercion remains the difficulty with this, as with most other proposed solutions. The level of agreement necessary for federalist solutions is unlikely to be greater than for joint sovereignty. Federalism has, however, been a recurrent theme in the search for a way around the apparent impasse caused by conflicting nationalist and unionist aspirations.

The issue of federalism has received renewed attention in Ireland as a result of the debate surrounding the New Ireland Forum. It is, however, far from a new idea as a solution to the division of Ireland from which so much political instability arises. As early as 1921, Eamon De Valera proposed a federal solution to the problem of partition. J. Bowman[27] shows that federalism was the basis of De Valera's policy on Northern Ireland. Until 1982 the federal option was Sinn Fein's preferred solution and

it still finds favour with many republicans. For the
Unionists of Northern Ireland, however, they were
already in a satisfactory 'federation' until the
establishment of direct rule:

> The 1920 Act gave the Northern Ireland
> parliament and government a very wide range of
> powers which could be used to pursue policies
> separate and different from the rest of the
> United Kingdom. Since 1921 a process of
> preservation and growth of the powers of the
> regional legislature was made possible through
> lack of interference from Westminster ....

> The 1920 Act also gave Northern Ireland a large
> measure of financial freedom, comparable to that
> which might be enjoyed by a province in a
> federal system ....

> While remaining firmly within the United
> Kingdom, Northern Ireland thus developed with
> many of the characteristics of an independent
> state .... it is arguable that in practice the
> status of the Stormont government was closer to
> the federal model than the devolution model -
> that is, that the two governments were almost
> coordinate in powers with each other, each with
> its own sphere of influence. (The usual
> relationship in a devolved system is that the
> regional government is subordinate to the
> central government.)[28]

Indeed, a UK federation was one of the compromises
canvassed during the discussions on the Home Rule
Bill in the Autumn of 1913.[29] In most recent
discussions of federalism in relation to Ireland the
number of units has been two - either both Irish
jurisdictions, or Northern Ireland and Britain or
even Ireland and Britain. The purpose of this
chapter, however, is to examine the relevance of a
federal solution in Ireland alone, but including
suggestions for a complete reappraisal of the nature
of government on the island involving the federal
principle. Thus the federal ideas in contemporary
Ireland referred to here include those for the
breaking-up of the present units - the Republic and
Northern Ireland - and the establishment of a federal
state for the whole island involving two or more
units. A simple unitary state for Ireland or
independence for Northern Ireland are possibilities
neglected here.

It should be noted before going on to the Forum debate that a previous book examined federal solutions in Ireland.[30]   In his contribution to that volume Maurice Vile dismisses the two unit federal idea as flying 'in the face of all the experience of systems, successful and unsuccessful'. He claims that:

> Two units, each dominated by a different communal majority, would seem almost inevitably to come into head-on conflict sooner or later, with none of the mechanisms available to mediate such conflict in federations with a larger and more varied collection of units. The problem of creating a federal government which would not be either totally dominated by one unit or totally deadlocked by the other seems to be insuperable. The Catholic population in the North would gain a great deal of confidence because of the association with the South, but the Protestant majority of the North would have no allies to turn to in the game of coalition-building and would therefore tend to maintain its present attitude of a total unwillingness to compromise.[31]

His somewhat pessimistic conclusion is 'that federalism does not offer a short-term solution to the Irish problem, and indeed there are almost certainly no short-term solutions'.[32] We shall now look at the variety of submissions in order more fully to appreciate the scope and diversity of informed opinion.

Swiss Canton System

In October 1983 Mr. Sean MacBride put his proposal to the New Ireland Forum for a federal Ireland based upon the Swiss model. He pointed out that such a plan was among those canvassed in the period between the 1918 General Election and Independence in 1922:

> Now, 60 years later, I would respectfully urge the Forum to look at the Swiss system of Government as future model for a New Ireland.
>
> Our existing system of Government is top-heavy, bureaucratic, inefficient and Dublin-orientated. Why not decentralise ? Why not limit the functions of the central government to Foreign Affairs, Central Finances, Security and Health ?[33]

MacBride's status within Ireland as a radical thinker and campaigner ensured that his ideas received wide publicity. Unfortunately, MacBride's fate was not unlike O'Rahilly's; his ideas about Switzerland did not engender much further debate on federalism.

Four Provinces

In January 1984 the Forum heard a submission by Mr. Michael O'Flanagan, a former public relations officer for Sinn Fein, who left that party after a federal policy - envisaging four provincial parliaments - was dropped from its constitution. O'Flanagan's proposal would involve a return to a nine-county Ulster. Ulster is the name of the pre-modern province which covers territory now in the Republic but mostly consists of the present 6-county Northern Ireland. A nine-county unit would substantially reduce the Protestant's majority position. Ireland would, under O'Flanagan's plan, become a 4-unit federal state with a weak central government. The Forum members showed some detailed interest in these ideas. Mr. O'Flanagan himself suggested that his idea was not dissimilar to the next one highlighted here.

Regional Government

The notion of a re-division of Ireland into regions, which would find their justification in economic planning rather than history, was aired in the European Parliament during the final months of the Forum. The idea that European integration would facilitate an end to Irish divisions was often used to justify Ireland's entry to the EC. For some advocates of entry the erosion of the significance of national boundaries would facilitate unification while others hoped that making the border less important would take the steam out of the desire for re-unification. The regional plan is an extension of such ideas. Northern Ireland would be retained as a regional unit with new relations with a weak Irish central government, while the rest of Ireland would be divided into regions on the basis of economic planning needs. Each unit's relationship with Britain and the EC could vary.

A long time proponent of the regional idea, the journalist Desmond Fennell, restated the case:

> I am not saying a regional planning authority,
> or industrial development authority, or some
> gimmick like the once mooted Western Development
> Board. I am saying a regional government such
> as, in various forms, there are 20 of in Italy,
> 11 in West Germany, 26 in Switzerland and a
> number which I cannot give exactly in Spain. I
> mean, in other words, an institution with much
> the same powers as the Northern Ireland regional
> parliament and government which existed until
> 1972 ....

> This is not, let me point out once again, merely
> a matter of giving the regions, including
> Dublin, a sound self-controlled basis for
> improving their economies and their quality of
> life. It is also about introducing a
> significant degree of real democracy. Very
> decisively, it is about showing the Ulster
> British that we have some serious intention of
> accommodating them in Ireland - something which
> is not made either obvious or credible by our
> paralysed state. We are no petty people, but we
> have petty leaders, centrally and regionally,
> standing in our way.[34]

In his submission to the Forum, Desmond Fennell
seemed to acknowledge Vile's warning but still opted
for federation:

> Since it is generally accepted that the proper
> and generous way to treat ethnic minorities is
> to give them a degree of self-government, the
> united-Ireland scheme proposed must include a
> degree of self-government for those parts of
> Ireland where the Ulster British form a majority
> or a substantial part of the population. In
> theory, the two available ways of doing this are
> through devolution with a unitary state or
> through the creation of a federal state ....
> Two-unit federations have seldom been attempted
> and have never succeeded .... Political science
> and common experience teach that a federation,
> to be successful, must be composed of at least
> four or five and preferably more units.
> However, the Forum might well decide for reasons
> of tactics and simplicity - in order to show its
> openness to the federal solution - to propose a
> two-unit federation and to leave further
> examination of the federal structure until
> later.[35]

Presbyterian Options

Dr. William T. McDowell, Clerk of the Dublin Synod of
the Presbyterian Church in Ireland, presented the
Synod's views to the Forum which, unlike most
clerical submissions, paid some attention to
institutions including the possibility in the long
term of an Irish federation:

> We believe, that the following points reflect
> the feelings of most Northern Protestants: they
> recognise that a United Ireland is a legitimate
> aspiration but they would like the Nationalist
> group to recognise that Northern Ireland, as
> part of the United Kingdom, is equally
> legitimate. They react badly to the ambivalence
> of the phrase 'unity by consent' for example:
> this is said while at the same time a demand is
> made for the removal of the UK guarantee. They
> react to this suggestion in the same way as
> citizens of the Republic would if the United
> Kingdom were to pass an Act of Parliament aimed
> at uniting the Republic with it 'by consent'.
> They cannot conceive of a united Ireland as 'the
> only long term solution' as it is often called,
> for they know that many thousands in Ireland
> actively oppose this. They will only begin to
> trust the people of the South when they believe
> they do not want to take them over. The Synod
> suggested that if the Forum sincerely wished to
> help the situation in Ireland it would promote
> better understanding by working out its
> blue-print with the following in mind: (1) that
> no progress could be made until all Irishmen
> genuinely accepted each other's aspiration as
> legitimate, (2) that the Republic cease to claim
> jurisdiction over Northern Ireland and that it
> recommend that the Constitution be changed
> accordingly, (3) that the immediate task was to
> promote in every possible way and at every level
> closer cooperation between the two parts of the
> country and to encourage the formulation of
> schemes for an acceptable partnership or
> federation for a future date when the political
> climate made this possible.

A former Moderator of the Presbyterian Church
spelt out in more detail his personal proposals for
an essentially federal solution:

There should be one Ireland with two states:
Northern Ireland and Southern Ireland,
interdependent and interrelated.

The whole of Ireland would elect deputies to the
Dail/House of Deputies by the same method as at
present obtains in the Republic to meet as at
present in Dublin. This would mean
approximately 72 new deputies from the North.
Of these, approximately 45-50 would be
Unionists.

In the Government there would be power sharing
- i.e. one-fifth to one-quarter of the ministers
would be chosen from the elected Unionists,
based on approximately the proportion of
Protestants to the population of the whole of
Ireland.

A new House of Representatives (replacing the
Senate) would be set up, to which Northern
Ireland and Southern Ireland would each elect
the same number of representatives, say 30 or 40
each.

All bills would have to pass through both the
Dail/House of Deputies and the House of
Representatives, and no bill concerned with
human rights could become law unless passed by
the majority of two-thirds/three-quarters in the
House of Representatives.

Both Southern Ireland and Northern Ireland would
elect an official Head. In the South he would
be called An Uachtaran, in the North, the
Governor. Between them they would exercise
jointly the office of President for the whole
country. No bill could become law until signed
by both An Uachtaran and the Governor and either
could refer a bill to the judiciary for
guidance.

'Unionist' Community Workers

A group of unionist community workers was represented
at the Forum by Mr. Anthony Orr. He called for slow
progress to 'some form of federalism whereby the
people of the north-eastern corner of Ireland would
have some say and some part to play which would allow
a wide scope of movement between the two parts of
Ireland'.[36] As a group the community workers warned

against trying to view the situation in Northern
Ireland in logical terms. This warning presumably
applies with equal force to this chapter.

New Ireland Group

Senator John Robb is a non-elected member of Seanad
Eirann and chairman of the New Ireland Group. He
presented the Group's proposals. Forum members
referred to these as if they were federal proposals,
although it is unclear that that is what they are.
The New Ireland Group's submission urged the Forum to
support joint action by the two sovereign governments
for the setting-up of a Northern constitutional
convention charged with finding consensus during the
specified period of the convention. Their position,
however vague, can be briefly summarised:

> We should draw the Forum's attention to what we
> believe are the minimum terms of the
> establishment of New Ireland on a sound basis -
> an indefinite transition period, the right to
> dual citizenship, explicit separation of church
> and state, a Bill of Rights, an appropriate
> degree of autonomy for the people of Northern
> Ireland, the promotion of a Convention of Wales,
> Ireland, Scotland and England (WISE) to be held
> every decade, the promotion of ecumenical
> initiatives, guaranteed economic underpinning
> for the transition period, an all-Ireland
> convention constituted in such a way that
> representatives from North and South would meet
> on the basis of equality to work out a
> constitutional settlement of the island.[37]

The Report's Federal Option

Most of the federal solution put before the Forum and
outlined above laid great stress on institutional
formulae rather than on social processes. They share
a concern for declarations of intent and statements
of rights. The inquisitorial nature of the Forum's
proceedings may account for this emphasis, or in the
terms which Burgess suggests in Chapter Two, the
limitations of the concepts federalism and federation
in the Anglo/American tradition may be the inhibiting
factor. The Forum members worked diligently in the
style of a committee of enquiry taking evidence,
receiving submissions and commissioning advice. They
moved towards proposals on which an acceptable
bargain might be struck between an Irish government

Federal Ideas in Contemporary Ireland

and some authoritative Northern Ireland body at some
time in the future. A federal state was one of the
options spelt out as a way of accommodating
differences within Ireland. Federation in Ireland is
not viewed as an organic product and preserver of
differences in society, but rather as a
centrally-derived, legal bargain under which
currently insurmountable political divisions may be
by-passed. Each community's aspirations are
'legitimate' and need to be 'recognised' in the new
formula. Given this approach, it is important that
any bargain can be steadfastly entered into, rather
like a treaty; both sides must be able to fulfill the
agreed conditions. Thus, there was a great deal of
notice paid to the reactions of the British
Government to the Forum's Report. In their
deliberation very little attention seems to have been
given to developments in Irish society as a whole.

The _Irish Times_ warned in the early stages
against this danger, and argued the need for
imaginative submissions; it referred particularly to
the value of MacBride's federal paper in stimulating
fresh thought:

> Nothing can help the process better than the
> submission of good and original ideas - unless
> it be their reception by those to whom they
> are addressed with objectivity and imagination.
> The country will not readily forgive any
> politicians who approach these proceedings
> with less than open minds.[38]

No attempt has to be made in this discussion to
assess the weight or merit of the various federalist
suggestions that have been put to the Forum. Clearly
some submissions were received politely but ignored
while others forced themselves to the attention of
the Forum members by reason either of their
insightfulness or the stature of their authors. It is
useful for this discussion, however, to show the
range of proposed federal solutions. Since their
appearance before the Forum, some individuals and
groups cited above appear to have moved their
positions. Most notably Senator Robb subsequently
spoke in favour of Swiss-canton model. The Catholic
bishops may also have signalled their preference for
a federal solution rather more directly in response
to journalists' questions about their oral
submission. Nevertheless, the broad outlines of the
federalists ideas remain essentially unchanged.
Since the publication of the Report, there has been

very little discussion of the merit of federalist
ideas because attention has been focused on the
reaction of the British Government to the document as
a whole. Further, debate has been dampened by the
narrow interpretation of the Report's proposals by
the current leadership of Fianna Fail. In
particular, discussion of the federal option has been
muted by the assertion of Mr. Haughey that the
unitary state idea is the only one which his party
would accept. The federalist ideas of
De Valera have proved something of an embarrassment
to the party leadership as has the call from within
the party for a more open debate on the non-unitary
proposals. The current leadership of Fianna Fail
'wants to create a situation of dependence and a set
of economic and political structures that would make
(unionist) consent irrelevant in the face of an
inevitable outcome'.[39] They know what their
preferred outcome is and see no value in putting
forward sub-optimal solutions. The SDLP, in
particular, and the other parties to an extent, are
committed to bargaining. The unionists, they feel,
could be presented with circumstances in which
current intransigence was likely to be
counter-productive and a federal solution may well be
accepted as the best long term solution.

Events in Ireland often overtake ideas and
experiments but on this occasion, despite the
attempts to restrict debate to one option, the ideas
which the Forum advances are liable to shape the
future of Irish politics for some considerable time.
It is important, therefore, to outline in detail the
Forum Report's own federalist option:

> A two state federal .... Ireland based on the
> existing identities North and South would
> reflect the political and administrative
> realities of the past 60 years and would
> entrench a measure of autonomy for both parts of
> Ireland within an all-Ireland framework .... A
> federal .... constitution would be
> non-denominational and capable of alteration
> only by special procedures. There would be
> safeguards within each state and in the country
> as a whole for the protection of individual and
> minority rights. There would be a Federal ....
> Supreme Court .... a special Bill of Rights
> or, alternatively, all the rights already
> defined and accepted in international convention
> to which Ireland and the UK are signatories ....
> (would be) incorporated in the new federal ....

constitution. This constitution could only be
formulated at an all-round constitutional
conference convened by the British and Irish
governments. Residual power would rest with the
central government. Certain powers would be
vested in the two individual states. Each state
would have its own parliament and executive.
Authority for security would be vested in the
federal .... government in order to gain
widespread acceptability and to ensure that the
law and order functions were administered in the
most effective and impartial manner .... the
federal parliament could have one or two
chambers, a House of Representatives and/or a
Senate. Laws relating to previously agreed
fundamental issues could be passed only if they
received the support of a weighted majority of
the Senate in a two chamber system or of the
House of Representatives in a one chamber
system. The federal government would be
approved by and be responsible to the federal
parliament. The powers held at the federal
level would be a matter for negotiation but in
an Irish context matters such as agriculture,
industry, energy, transport, industrial
promotion and marketing might be more
efficiently administered on an island basis at
federal level, while other services such as
education, health, housing and social welfare
might best be administered by the individual
state. The functions of Head of State could be
carried out by a President the office
alternating between persons representative of
the Northern and Southern states. The Northern
parliament would have powers which could not be
removed by an Act of another parliament.
Existing civil and religious rights in the North
would be unaffected .... unionists would have
parallel British citizenship and could maintain
special links with Britain. Mechanisms for
ensuring full Northern participation in the ....
civil service would have to be devised.
Provision would be made for the full recognition
and symbolic expression of both traditions.[40]

Conclusion: Federalism - The Future

Fianna Fail may be manouevred into easing its
insistence on the unitary state. As Martin Mansergh
admitted in the interview quoted above:

We have a good conception, or at least a very clear conception, of what a united Ireland should be, although obviously its something that has to be negotiated so it's not something that's going to depend solely on us. Back in the mid-seventies, in Jack Lynch's day, there was perhaps a strong preference for a federal solution - give Unionists Stormont back but under an all-Ireland umbrella. The Fine Gael policy of a confederal Ireland isn't so different from that except that the all-Ireland element is more attenuated than it would be in the federal system.[41]

One party which is less likely to moderate its opposition to federalism, however, is Sinn Fein. O'Flanagan's submission to the Forum outlining a federal formula based on four historic provinces is very much a product of the eclipsed leadership of the early seventies. The repudiation of federalism was supported by a two-thirds majority at the party's 1982 Ard Fheis (party conference). The proposed nine-county Ulster federal unit would in Sinn Fein's view be dominated by the same power block which has traditionally held the nationalist community in subjection. They are quite categorical:

> Federalist policies were a sop to Loyalism. The Loyalists should be told: 'We're out to break the link with Britain. This country is one country.' The Loyalists are just a major idiosyncrasy. They should be told the truth: 'You're entitled to no more than anyone else in the country.' It's a message they have been resisting and will continue to resist, but at the end of the day it's the only just solution .... The idea of a federal Ireland and a federal Ulster sounds grand and fair, but you will have as much trouble getting Loyalists to accept a nine-county parliament as you will in getting them to accept a united Ireland, so why stop short ?[42]

Sinn Fein are to an extent insulated from movements in public opinion by their commitment to their own ideology. Their political strategy uses the ballot box but their major strength is not drawn from it. Changes in public opinion are more important to the various constitutional parties. It is interesting, therefore, to note the support for the federal option reflected in opinion polls taken

after the publication of the Forum Report. The
federation/confederation option was generally
favoured by 55% and opposed by 32% of respondents in
the Republic to a survey of 1,000 electors published
in the _Irish Times_ and conducted by the Market
Research Bureau of Ireland. The 1,000 quota
controlled sample of electors in Northern Ireland
found 29% in favour and 56% opposed. Federation or
confederation was slightly less objectionable to
unionists than the other Forum options, and supported
by more Northern Catholics and SDLP supporters than
the unitary state option.[43]

The least welcoming to all the proposals of the
Forum, including federation, are supporters of the
Democratic Unionists Party. The DUP leader, Dr.
Paisley, made a dramatic protest in Dublin on the day
the Report was published and summarised his reaction
to it at ceremonies commemorating the 294th
anniversary of the Battle of the Boyne:

> Our safety and welfare cannot be guaranteed
> under a Roman Catholic Government in Dublin ....
> Therefore we will resist to the death any
> attempt to put us into a united Ireland or on
> the road to a united Ireland. I come to join
> with you today in burying the proposals of the
> so-called New Ireland Forum .... (Northern
> Ireland) is now the last bastion of
> Protestantism in Europe and stands between the
> Vatican and her goal of a united Roman Catholic
> State of Europe.[44]

Dr. Paisley, the most popular political leader
in Northern Ireland, may eventually decide that the
last bastion of Protestantism has little enough in
common with secular Britain. Many observers have
seen an independent Northern state as attractive to
Paisley. Such a new state, it is argued by the SDLP,
would be untenable unless it negotiated with the two
existing sovereign governments for help with its
inherent political, economic and security problems.
Out of such negotiation may then emerge a federal
Ireland. Dublin would exercise reserved powers not
dissimilar to those which Westminster once had in
relation to the Stormont Parliament. The DUP leader
himself denies he wants an independent Northern
Ireland so the road to federal bargain seems blocked.
On the other hand, Dr. Paisley could not admit that
he favoured independence even if he did because it
would undermine his insistence on the insolubility of
the United Kingdom. If, however, a declaration of

independence were made necessary by a British
betrayal of Protestantism, some new political
accommodation would have to be established involving
all parts of the archipelago.

Notes

1. New Ireland Forum, Report, Dublin: Stationery
    Office, 1984, para.1.1. References to the Report
    are given to paragraphs not pages because it is
    available in several different forms in various
    Irish government publications and the paragraph
    numbers are common to all.

2. J. Whyte, "The Permeability of the United
    Kingdom - Irish Border: A Preliminary
    Reconnaissance", Administration, Vol.31 (1983),
    no.3, p.300-314.

3. Whyte, Administration, p.313.

4. New Ireland Forum, A Comparative Description of
    the Economic Structureand Situation, North and
    South - Summary Commentary, Dublin: Stationery
    Office, 1983, p.2-3.

5. New Ireland Forum, Economic Structure, p.3.

6. Davy Kelleher McCarthy Ltd., The Macroeconomic
    Consequences of Integrated Economic Policy,
    Planning and Coordination in Ireland,
    Dublin: Stationery Office, (1984), pxxx.

7. Forum Report, para. 5,3.

8. Forum Report, para 4,9.3.

9. New Ireland Forum, "The Legal Systems of
    Republic of Ireland and of Northern Ireland -
    Summary, Dublin: Stationery Office, 1983, p.3,
    based on a report commissioned as a background
    paper for the Forum and drawn up by C. K. Boyle
    and D. S. Greer.

10. Ibid, p.3.

11. Vid. New Ireland Forum The Costs of Violence
    Arising from the Northern Ireland Situation
    since 1969, (Dublin: Stationery Office, 1983).

12. Forum Report, para. 4.12.

13. Irish Times, 28 June, 1984.

14. K. Heskin, Northern Ireland: A Psychological
    Analysis, (Dublin: Gill and Macmillan, 1980),
    p.154.

15. *Irish Times*, 9 December, 1983.

16. *Irish Times*, 12 April, 1984.

17. *Forum Report*, para 4,9.2.

18. Pope John XXIII, *Pacem in Terris*, 1963.

19. Pope Pius XI, *Quadragesimo Anno*, 1931.

20. Jeremiah Newman, *Ireland Must Choose*, (Dublin: Four Courts Press, 1983), p.57.

21. Ibid, *Ireland Must Choose*, p.68.

22. *Bulletin of the Department of Foreign Affairs*, (Dublin: Stationery Office, January 1984), p.4.

23. *Irish Times*, 7 June, 1984.

24. *Bulletin of the Department of Foreign Affairs*, (Dublin: Stationery Office, January 1984).

25. Martin Mansergh in an interview reported in P. O'Malley *The Uncivil Wars*, (Belfast: Blackstaff Press, 1983), p.47.

26. *Irish Times*, 9 December, 1983.

27. J. Bowman, *De Valera and the Ulster Question*, (London: Oxford University Press, 1983).

28. D. Birrell and A. Murie, *Policy and Government in Northern Ireland: Lessons of Devolution*, (Dublin: Gill and Macmillan, 1980), pp.28-9.

29. P. Buckland, *A History of Northern Ireland*, (Dublin: Gill and Macmillan, 1982), p.13.

30. D. Rea (ed), *Political Cooperation in Divided Societies*, (Dublin: Gill and Macmillan, 1982).

31. Maurice Vile, "Federation and Confederation: The Experience of the United States and the British Commonwealth" in D. Rea *Divided Societies*, p.225.

32. *Divided Societies*, p.226.

33. *Irish Times*, 5 October, 1983.

34. Sunday Press, 29 January, 1984.

35. Bulletin of the Department of Foreign Affairs, (Dublin: Stationery Office, December 1983).

36. For a summary of these arguments, see Bulletin of the Department of Foreign Affairs, (Dublin: Stationery Office, March 1984).

37. Bulletin of the Department of Foreign Affairs, (Dublin: Stationery Office, November 1983).

38. Irish Times, (editorial), 6 October 1983.

39. O'Malley, Uncivil Wars, p.55.

40. Forum Report, para. 7.1 to 7.7.

41. O'Malley, Uncivil Wars, p.47.

42. Danny Morrison, Sinn Fein, interview reported in O'Malley, Uncivil Wars, p.282.

43. Irish Times, 22 May 1984.

44. Irish Times, 13 July 1984.

7.   EMPIRE, IRELAND AND EUROPE: A CENTURY OF
     BRITISH FEDERAL IDEAS

     Michael Burgess

Introduction: British Federal Ideas - A Double
Paradox

Federalism does not occupy a very prominent place in
the pantheon of British political ideas during the
last century. Yet a well-known paradox suggests that
it should. The British - traditionally hostile to
the application of federal ideas at home - have been
the greatest drafters and prescribers of federal
systems for others. Variations of the federal policy
have survived inter alia in Canada, Australia and
India, while relatively short-lived federations were
established in Malaysia, the West Indies, Nigeria and
the Central African Federation. As exporters of
federal ideas the British have an impressive pedigree
which is second to none.
     This irony, however, obscures another paradox
which has gone largely unrecognised. The second
paradox takes the form of a political riddle which
has spanned the last century and provides the
connecting link between British interests in the
Empire, Ireland and Europe. The riddle can be simply
stated: beneath the veneer of British hostility
towards federalism at home there lurks a continuous
tradition of federal ideas related directly to the
reorganisation of the British state. Empire, Ireland
and Europe have, at different times, prompted a
succession of British statesmen, politicians and
prominent public figures to promote the federal
cause. British federal ideas have been present in
varying forms and with varying degrees of influence
and support throughout the last century. They have
not been for export only. It is the purpose of this
chapter to call attention to a neglected tradition of
British federal ideas concerning the British state
and to assess their contemporary political
significance.

Empire

Federal ideas first became closely intertwined with
British imperial affairs just over a century ago.
They acquired an increasing relevance to Britain's
changing relationship with the white self-governing
colonies in that they furnished the prospect of an
imperial consolidation. The federal solution -
commonly referred to by the nebulous phrase 'imperial

federation' - offered the Victorians a dazzling
alternative to colonial independence and the gradual
disintegration of the self-governing empire.
'Federation or disintegration ?' were the stark
alternatives presented by the imperial federationists
of the late-Victorian era. Grossly over-simplified
though it was, this dramatic appeal continued to
arouse sporadic public interest well into the
twentieth century.

The political movement which had its origins in
the so-called 'empire scare' of 1869-1871[1] gained
formal institutional expression as the Imperial
Federation League in 1884. Founded on 29 July, 1884,
at the Westminster Palace Hotel, London, the new
political organisation was committed to 'secure by
Federation the permanent unity of the Empire'.[2] From
the outset the League was a house divided against
itself. It contained public men who could agree
about the urgent need to strengthen the bonds of
empire, but about little else. They disagreed about
both strategies and tactics. But between 1884 and
1893, when the League was formally dissolved, the
organisation represented the most important public
expression of the idea of closer imperial union
during the late-Victorian years. Over 31 local
branches were formed throughout England and Scotland
during this period and membership hovered at around
the figure of 2,000.

It is important to note that the genuine
federalists were only a tiny minority within the
League. Most imperial federationists sought an
undefined closer union either by adjustments in
Britain's traditional trade practices or by changes
in imperial defence, especially naval defence, which
would leave free trade intact. But there were
several leading politicians and influential public
figures within the movement who were quite prepared
to experiment with the federal principle in order to
consolidate British power overseas. Federal ideas
were expressed in a variety of ways. Broadly
speaking, however, they can be conveniently divided
into two categories: those ideas which constituted a
federal element or instalment, such as the Council of
Advice and the admission of colonial representatives
sitting in the British Parliament; and those
suggestions which amounted to a fully-fledged federal
union replete with a common, over-arching executive
and parliament, subordinate state parliaments and a
uniform electoral system.

Many federationists liked the idea of some form
of colonial representation in the British Parliament.

Lord Rosebery, for example, supported the admission
of colonial delegates to the House of Lords in 1884
and, again, in 1886.[3] This was not a novel
suggestion. It had been advocated by Joseph Hume as
far back as 1831 during discussions about the First
Reform Bill. Similarly the idea of a Council of
Advice of colonial agents-general, as a kind of
consultative body on imperial defence and foreign
policy questions, had been promoted by the third Earl
Grey in 1879. W. E. Forster, the first Chairman of
the Imperial Federation League, favoured this
constitutional reform in 1885 as a useful
stepping-stone in the direction of the 'ultimate form
of federation' which would give the 'imperial
federation' the same institutions as the United
States of America.[4] Some federationists believed
that important piecemeal progress towards a federal
union could be made by creating an Imperial
Zollverein - a customs union for the empire. Indeed,
this idea found favour among many leading figures
within the Conservative party who had participated in
the foundation of the National Fair Trade League in
May 1881. Others preferred to opt for a Kriegsverein
- a defence union - which would avoid controversial
tariff and trade adjustments and offer, instead, a
sound basis for a coordinated imperial defence
policy.

Overall federal union within the empire was
generally viewed as something for the remote future.
Many regarded it as desirable but too visionary
during the late nineteenth century. Only the threat
of war could translate the vision rapidly into
reality. But federalist ideas and influences were,
none the less, commonplace. British and colonial
politicians were neither as hostile nor as immune to
them as conventional wisdom would have us believe.
Comprehensive federal schemes proliferated; there
were as many schemes as there were individuals to
propound them. Throughout the years between 1870 and
1914 federal proposals littered the mainstream
periodical literature and the proceedings of the
Royal Colonial Institute (RCI) attracted many
carefully prepared federal proposals which responded
to Britain's changing international position.[5]

When the Imperial Federation League collapsed
abruptly in December 1883, federal ideas for the
empire did not disappear with it. On the contrary,
their resilience was manifested in the variety of
small pressure groups which sprouted in Britain
during the 1890s.[6] Apart from the RCI, which had
nurtured such ideas for a generation, the Imperial

Federation (Defence) Committee emerged in 1894 as evidence that the cause of imperial unity had been reorganised along more specific lines.[7] Federal ideas about empire soon resurfaced in more robust shape during the first decade of the twentieth century when the Round Table movement was formed in 1909-1910. Destined to dominate British intellectual thinking about empire- commonwealth relations until the early 1920s, the movement served as a crucial repository of imperial federationist ideas which represented a basic continuity of thought and action between the late nineteenth and the early twentieth centuries in terms of the reorganisation of the British state.[8]

Imperial federation, then, was the link which ran beneath the surface of the activities of public men like Lionel Curtis and Philip Kerr, later Lord Lothian, who were among the founders of the new political movement in Edwardian Britain. This connection was expressed by the nebulous phrase 'organic union' but it is clear the 'the discovery of some form of federation which shall be at once effective and acceptable' was the main focus for their energies.[9] Agreement upon the definition of purpose, however, did not automatically stretch to unanimity about the ultimate form of union to be pursued. Curtis's mystical faith in the Empire and his almost doctrinaire commitment to the cause of imperial federation was not shared by Kerr. The latter believed fervently in empire but he was less than sanguine about attempts to 'fit the Empire into the constitutional ideas which have suited the United Kingdom and the self-governing colonies in the past'. This, in his view, was to court destruction.[10] The empire would be lost forever.

Kerr, however, did share Curtis's interest in a reorganisation of the imperial structure and he concurred about the need to work for a common policy in defence and foreign affairs. Aware of the strength of colonial nationalism, he was not prepared to state what exact form the new political system should take; he merely acknowledged the desire for a closer, more binding, imperial union. With the exception of Curtis, the Round Table movement decided not to try to force the pace unnecessarily. Under Kerr's influence as editor of the journal, Round Table, the movement preferred to educate British and colonial public opinion in the need for constitutional reform. As always, Kerr felt more comfortable when specific schemes and blue-prints were eschewed. They were premature and unhelpful.

Only when international circumstances changed and after a long period of discussion between the British and colonial governments were concrete initiatives liable to be well received. Meanwhile federal ideas would continue to circulate and form part of that crucial preliminary intellectual spadework necessary to alter official attitudes and perceptions regarding constitutional change.

As with the imperial federationists of the late Victorian years, many Round Table enthusiasts favoured the idea of colonial representatives sitting in the British parliament while others sought to devise new executive machinery to facilitate more effective cooperation and consultation in defence and foreign policy. In this matter the Round Table was unanimous: if the dominions were to have an effective voice in imperial policy, the quadrennial colonial/conferences were palpably inadequate. Lionel Curtis was unequivocal about this. Dubbed 'The Prophet' by his contemporaries, Curtis launched himself with single-minded determination on the path towards a federal reconstruction of empire. His famous Green Memorandum, published and widely circulated in 1910, outlined the movement's aims and assumptions, and sketched out a detailed plan of imperial federation which acknowledged the separation of domestic and imperial affairs. The new institutional framework would include an Imperial Parliament, distinct from Westminster, with a directly-elected lower house and an upper house of states based upon equal representation together with an impartial tribunal to decide disputes over legislative jurisdiction between the federal authority and the colonial governments. These reforms entailed the creation of domestic government for the United Kingdom (since the new federal government would deal only with imperial matters and not with British internal affairs) and the adjustment of British status, as regards internal affairs, to that of Canada, Australia, New Zealand and South Africa. Various concessions to national sovereignty were incorporated in Curtis's scheme. He was scrupulously careful to leave the regulation of tariffs alone and he devised an ingenious method for the raising and collecting of revenues for imperial purposes. Curtis's plan, in short, contained virtually all of the institutional checks and balances which were conventionally associated with a modern federation.

A strong sense of mission propelled Curtis into the dominions during 1910 to disseminate the movement's ideas, establish Round Table groups among the elite and professional classes, and to maximise the impact of his own memorandum. He met with varied success. His influence appears to have been greatest in New Zealand and Australia, while Canadians were more reserved in their encounter with his passionate idealism. None the less, his energy and his ability to portray the movement's goals as synonymous with the vital interest of the empire as a whole elicited more than a passive response. The 'imperial problem', it must be remembered, was identified as 'the empire in danger'. The German menace and the sense of relative isolation combined to heighten dominion awareness of their vulnerability to European and Asiatic predators; it also served to focus dominion attentions upon their relationship with Britain as regards defence and foreign policy. In the event of war they would still be dependent upon Britain. Curtis's proposals and the force of his argument thus struck a responsive chord in informed colonial circles. The timing seemed opportune.

The translation of federal ideas into concrete proposals, however, carried with it obvious pitfalls. Political movements which espouse such radical objectives must tread carefully in their efforts to influence official thinking. The obstacles confronting the Round Table were large and ultimately insurmountable. Federal ideas were certainly consonant with an age which witnessed the empire at another crossroads in its political development. But they required long and careful dissemination if they were not to appear premature, ill-conceived and utopian.

This conundrum remained a weakness in the movement's armoury throughout its heyday. Federal ideas were its stock-in-trade but they were also unquestionably at the centre of its major internal disputes. They were not, however, solely responsible for the movement's failure to achieve its goal. As John Kendle has observed, 'the movement, particularly the London group, did have some influence in governmental circles in Great Britain and the dominions', not least because its members came from 'the affluent, the well-placed, the intellectual, and generally the most acceptable members of society'. Other factors helped to determine its decline: dominion nationalism, its ambitious commitment to organic union; its insular perception of empire; its archaic attitudes; and its conspiratorial image.

One unwise initiative, then, could vitiate
federal ideas at their source. Kerr was insistent
about this. His warning to Curtis was prophetic:

> if we wanted to get something done, it would be
> another matter. We don't; we want to make
> people familiar with the idea of Federation so
> that they will be all the more ready to swallow
> our gospel when it is published.[11]

The case for 'organic union' had first to be
thoroughly analysed and prepared before it could be
effectively canvassed at governmental and conference
levels. The die, however, had already been cast.
Imperial federation received a convincing and
humiliating rejection at the 1911 Imperial Conference
when the New Zealand premier, Sir Joseph Ward,
bungled his attempt to float federationist ideas for
an imperial parliament to control imperial defence
and foreign policy.
    This brief sketch of the imperial unity movement
from the 1880s to the early 1920s emphasises both the
continuity and the resilience of federal ideas in
Britain. Their influence is often difficult to
pinpoint but they have never been completely absent
from discussions about empire. It is when we turn to
the Irish question, however, that their ubiquity in
the fabric of British political ideas can be more
fully appreciated.

Ireland

During the last century the Irish question has been a
regular focus for the germination of federal ideas in
Britain. Federalism was advocated in the 1870s by
Isaac Butt and his Home Rule party but it was during
the 1880s that federal ideas began to circulate
widely among those politicians and statesmen who
sought a solution to the Irish problem. The
relationship between federalism and Ireland, however,
was never a simple one. It was subjected to numerous
other cross-currents of opinion. Two examples of the
complexity of this relationship are important in this
discussion. First, there was the link with the
integrity of the British Empire: by reorganising
Anglo-Irish constitutional relations, federalism
would guarantee the unity of the empire. In this way
an Irish separation - tantamount to imperial
dismemberment - could be avoided. Set in its
imperial context, of course, many advocates of a
reconstructed federal relationship between Britain

and Ireland viewed this as the necessary pre-requisite for a wider scheme of imperial federation. A federal solution to the Irish problem, then, would presage the wholesale reconstruction of the British Empire into a more binding union. Secondly, since federalism stressed ideas of local autonomy and self-government within a larger union the view that it should be extended to include the whole of the United Kingdom possessed a certain logic. Why limit the federal solution to Ireland ? The reconstitution of the United Kingdom as a federal state would remedy many of Britain's outstanding problems: it would solve the Irish problem; it would make for more efficient government by relieving the central legislature of purely domestic concerns; it would, correspondingly, facilitate more time for the discussion of imperial affairs; and it would pave the way for imperial federation.

Federal ideas tended, therefore, to become enmeshed in the Irish question in a very complicated way. A century ago discussion about federalism and Ireland led assuredly to 'Home Rule all round' and imperial federation. The issue which sparked federal ideas into life during the 1880s was Gladstone's attempt to remedy Irish grievances by introducing home rule. His first Home Rule bill of 1886 fired the imaginative hostility of most MPs who soundly rejected the legislation, but it also provided fertile soil for the nourishment of federal ideas. A small minority of imperial federationist MPs used the epic parliamentary debate on Irish home rule as an opportunity to push their own grandiose cause. However, it was Joseph Chamberlain who was chiefly responsible for shifting the emphasis of the debate towards the federal principle.

Chamberlain was a consistent opponent of any home rule scheme which threatened the imperial connection. Since Gladstone's legislation implied the departure of Irish MPs from Westminster and since Chamberlain possessed a much stronger conception of imperial unity than did Gladstone, the basis for major disagreement was clear. Chamberlain's federal ideas, however, appear to have developed in a somewhat haphazard fashion. They were both confused and confusing. During 1885 he wrote to his Radical colleague and friend, Charles Dilke, acknowledging the fact that federation would involve 'the entire recasting of the British Constitution and the full and complete adoption of the American system'. Later, in May 1886, he reiterated his faith in the federal principle and made no secret of where he thought the central issue lay:

The retention of the Irish representatives is
clearly the touchstone. If they go, separation
must follow. If they remain, federation is
possible whenever local assemblies are
established in England and Scotland.[13]

On 9 April, 1886, Chamberlain kindled a fire which
spread throughout the House of Commons when he
claimed that the solution to the Irish conundrum
might be found in 'some form of federation'.[14] He
rejected the American and the German federations as
suitable models for Britain and Ireland, yet he
offered no detailed federal proposal to the House of
Commons. From that moment on the nature of the
parliamentary debate changed quite significantly.
Almost every participant commented upon the strengths
and weaknesses of the federal panacea. And several
MPs exploited the opportunity to urge 'Home Rule all
round' upon the Prime Minister. Gladstone,
predictably, refused to consider this; it was far too
complicated and there was no evidence that 'the wants
and the wishes' of England, Scotland, Wales and
Ireland were the same.[15]
But the debate about federalism was not allowed
to peter out. Chamberlain further enlivened it when,
on 1 June 1886, he made another unexpected
intervention for the federal cause:

You may find - I will not say the details - but
the lines of such a plan in the present
constitution of Canada; not, however, in the
relations between Canada and this country -
those are the wrong lines, and lines against
which I protest, and which mean separation - but
in the relations inter se of the provinces of
Canada and the Dominion Parliament. These are
the relations which I, for one, am perfectly
prepared to establish tomorrow between this
country and Ireland.[16]

The sense of confusion and misunderstanding generated
by Chamberlain's dramatic initiatives can easily be
appreciated. His ideas seemed disorganised and
hasty. Yet though they appeared to be expedient they
were beginning to take shape and to make sense. The
Canadian analogy could be misleading in several ways
but it had the merit, in Chamberlain's mind, of
providing some form of home rule while keeping the
United Kingdom and the empire intact.
The public debate about federalism and Ireland
continued to simmer throughout the 1880s and 1890s.

Even so redoubtable an intellectual as Edward Freeman felt compelled to admit that 'there seemed to be more of a tendency to federation in Britain that he had imagined.'[17] The imperial federationists, of course, could be relied upon to keep the issue before the public. But the Liberal party, too, began to gravitate in this direction. Lord Rosebery wrote to Gladstone in 1889 arguing that the longer the Liberals prevaricated in evaluating the details of the next Irish Home Rule Bill, the more it would 'approximate to the federal principle'.[18] Another leading Liberal, Hugh Childers, informed Gladstone that the 'Federal idea' had been gaining ground in Scotland where Scottish Home Rule was growing rapidly and he believed that federalism had either to be formally adopted or firmly repudiated by the Liberal party once and for all.[19] Neither home rule nor federation attracted sufficient parliamentary support during these years to bring about constitutional reform however, and the failure of Gladstone's second Home Rule Bill in 1893 was something of a watershed in the debate about Ireland.

Federal ideas, however, lived on. The Round Table movement played an important role in the reshaping and resurfacing of these ideas as 'Home Rule all round' during the years between 1910 and 1914.[20] Federalism aroused considerable interest in 1910 during the Constitutional Conference, assembled to resolve the conflict between the Commons and the Lords, and again between 1913 and 1914 when the United Kingdom hovered on the brink of civil war. Philip Kerr and Lionel Curtis were active behind the scenes attempting to exert pressure at home and abroad in their quest to make the links between constitutional reform in the United Kingdom and organic union of the Empire. Attempts to persuade key political figures about the need for a Royal Commission to examine the whole constitutional machinery, however, failed. The movement had to be satisfied with its own private study. Part of their discussions were subsequently published as articles in The Round Table in August and December 1911 and the whole study was issued anonymously as a book in 1912 entitled An Analysis of the System of Government Throughout The British Empire.[21]

According to John Kendle, the only positive gain from these early plans were those findings from the study which bore fruit in the criticisms levelled by Leo Amery and Lord Robert Cecil at the financial aspects of the Government of Ireland Bill in 1912-1914. The influence of the movement, however,

is indisputable. Federal ideas had come of age.
Besides Kerr and Curtis, the activities of Frederic
Scott Oliver are especially interesting. A Unionist
and much respected political thinker, Oliver had
immersed himself in the problem of constitutional
reform during 1910 and he became one of the most
enthusiastic and forceful advocates of federalism
during these years. Along with J. L. Garvin, editor
of The Observer, he carried his campaign into the
heart of Unionist circles. While Garvin used his
newspaper to support the federal cause and
continuously bombarded leading Unionists with lengthy
letters and memoranda on the Irish question and 'Home
Rule all round', Oliver infiltrated the Unionist camp
with his federal ideas by approaching Austen
Chamberlain and Arthur Balfour directly. His
influence in helping to shape the intellectual
climate was considerable; he had, in Kerr's words,
'ploughed the hard soil' so as to prepare it to
receive Round Table ideas later on.[22]

Curtis, meanwhile, had scored a great success on
his own terms. He persuaded the young Winston
Churchill to consider the federal ideas circulating
within the Round Table. As First Lord of the
Admiralty who had introduced the second reading of
the Government of Ireland Bill in the House of
Commons, Churchill was an obvious target for Round
Table activists. His receptivity to their ideas,
however, must have come as a surprise. In a major
public speech during September 1912 he urged his
Dundee constituents to consider the notion of a
federal United Kingdom. His conception of a
reconstructed Britain included national parliaments
for Ireland, Wales and Scotland, and regional
legislatures within England - all subordinate to an
imperial parliament. Churchill's primary interest in
this constitutional innovation was twofold : he
viewed it as a solution to the Irish problem and he
could accommodate the Dominions in a new central
government of the Empire. Ireland, federalism and
empire were thus still intimately associated in
Churchill's thinking. His political thoughts 'helped
in making federalism a major talking point once more
in party and intellectual circles; and it remained at
the forefront of the political stage until the early
summer of 1914'.[23]

Neither the Irish problem in particular nor the
question of British constitutional reform in general
had been solved when the First World War broke out.

Both issues were 'temporarily forgotten' in 1914.[24]
The promotion of federal ideas in these two areas,
however, was resurrected in 1917-1918. According to
Kendle, the chief driving-force behind this revival
was Oliver. His personal influence upon leading
Unionists in general and upon Lloyd George, Austen
Chamberlain and Edward Carson in particular seems to
have been crucial. His personal contacts were of
vital importance and his single-minded commitment to
the federal cause ensured that the 'the main topic of
conversation was federalism'.[25] Chamberlain was
especially amenable to the idea - he regarded it as
'the best compromise available'. Federal ideas
received wide coverage in the British press and
loomed large in Scottish and Welsh home rule circles.
Indeed, such was the ubiquity of federal ideas in
Britain that Oliver himself estimated that about
fifty Unionists, ninety Liberals and an uncertain
number of Labour MPs wanted 'federalism for its own
sake'.[26]

It is clear that by April 1918 both the British
Prime Minister, Lloyd George, and his War Cabinet
minister, Austen Chamberlain, were agreed upon a
scheme of Irish home rule which would 'fit in with a
Federal plan' - it would facilitate 'Home Rule all
round'.[27] Oliver's influence upon Chamberlain was
striking. He prompted him, along with his brother
Neville, to exhume their father's interest in the
federal solution for Ireland. Exposure to Joseph
Chamberlain's ideas 'reaffirmed Austen's conviction
that federalism was the only way out of the
difficulty.[28] The federal solution was undoubtedly
the zeitgeist of 1918 and Pinder and Ionescu are
correct to emphasise how close the British government
came to proposing a practical federal arrangement for
Ireland. Interest in federalism did run high in the
country. But, as Kendle has astutely observed,
'federalism had become topical and possible because
of the Irish problem but ultimately it was the Irish
problem which made it impossible to adopt or even to
examine it seriously'.[30]

Since the establishment of Ulster in 1921
political science terminology regarding the Irish
problem has undergone significant changes. We no
longer accept the blurring of alternatives implicit
in the fuzzy, embryonic thinking of the Round Table
activists: 'Home Rule all round', devolution and
federation are not acceptably synonymous labels for
major constitution reform. For over fifty years
since the Irish partition the relationship between
federalism and the Irish question has been weak

precisely because it has been more clearly defined.
The constitutional settlement and the loss of empire
have combined to isolate and radically alter the
conventional perception of federalism regarding
Ireland. Before its decline the Round Table movement
did come to the conclusion that the Irish question
and the wider United Kingdom issue were not
inextricably intertwined. They were obviously
related - as they, in turn, were then linked to
imperial union - but they were not necessarily
inseparable. The Kilbrandon Report of 1973 confirmed
this position. One Northern Ireland representative
sat on the Royal Commission, but Northern Ireland
already had a separate regional assembly, albeit with
limited powers and functions, from 1921. The Irish
question was conveniently ignored.

This did not mean that federal ideas were
completely absent in the Report. As Anthony Birch
has indicated, 'eight of the thirteen members of the
Commission favoured the creation of legislative
assemblies for Scotland and Wales' and the logical
concomitant of this proposal was 'the creation of an
assembly for England, or several assemblies for the
regions of England, thus giving the United Kingdom a
federal or quasi-federal form of government'. Birch
was surprised that it was 'rejected outright by the
Commission'; in his view 'the merits of federalism
ought to be carefully weighed against the
alternatives'.[31]

In conclusion it is clear that federal ideas
regarding the Irish problem have had considerable
significance during the last century. The nature of
the Irish problem has changed quite dramatically in
this period but the notion of a specifically federal
solution has never been far below the surface of
informed opinion. Today 'the Irish problem' tends to
be considered in isolation rather than as a part of
the 'multinational perspective' of the United
Kingdom. But its shadow did fall across the
Kilbrandon Report and the current proposals of the
New Ireland Forum, analysed by Neil Collins in
Chapter Six, suggest that federalism may yet prove to
be as ubiquitous in the 1980s as it was a century
ago.

Europe

> 'The nations of Europe must constitute
> themselves into some form of federation .... we
> shall never abolish war in Europe unless we ....
> take up a completely new citizenship. We must

> cease to be mere Englishmen, Frenchmen, Germans
> and must begin to take as much pride in
> calling ourselves Europeans .... all schemes
> will fail which propose to unite Europe merely
> by adding together the States that compose it.
> The individual, and not merely the State, must
> enter into a distinct relation to the Federation
> .... the federation wanted is .... a real
> union of peoples.'[32]

These words were neither spoken nor written by one of
the continental founding fathers of post-war West
European unity. They have been culled from the
speech of a prominent Englishman who addressed the
Peace Society on the 'United States of Europe' in
1871. Sir John Seeley, Regius Professor of Modern
History at Cambridge between 1869 and 1895 and a
leading imperial federationist, conveyed an idea and
urged a political strategy which has formed an
intermittent theme in British thinking about Europe
for over a century.[33]

This statement may seem initially surprising.
The British, after all, have an established
reputation for maintaining a healthy distance from
what were perceived as purely continental European
affairs. Only when British interests were at stake
was any kind of direct intervention seriously
considered. This view amounted to a conventional
wisdom regarding Europe for virtually the whole of
the nineteenth and much of the twentieth century. It
was underlined in Churchill's famous dictum about
Britain being of Europe without being in it. But
this long-standing tradition of qualified aloofness
from European affairs did not prevent British federal
ideas from surfacing in a variety of forms in a
number of influential quarters. They attracted only
intermittent interest in the years between 1880 and
1914 but thereafter grew in prominence as Britain's
European and global position changed. Indeed, the
inter-war period can be said to have been something
of an intellectual watershed in terms of its
increasing receptivity to federal ideas. At both
elite and mass levels of British society federalism
gained widespread support as the means whereby war
could be averted. During and after the Second World
War, however, this perception of federalism changed.
It became a strategy for political change both in
Europe and throughout the world. And it is here that
distinctly British federal ideas played a key role;
they were absorbed in a curious way into the
continental European federal tradition which is

currently at the forefront of the movement for major
constitutional reform in the European Community
during the 1980s. It is a quite remarkable turn of
events.

This strange twist in the history of British
federal ideas concerning Europe, however, must be set
in its context. Its origins stretch back at least to
the years before the First World War. Relatively
little attention has been paid to this period but
there were some interesting developments. William T.
Stead, for example, was representative of the early
federal tradition which linked Empire, Ireland and
Europe. As editor of The Pall Mall Gazette and an
imperial federationist during the 1880s, Stead had
used his position as a leading British journalist to
publicise the federal cause and attack Gladstone's
naval policies for the empire.[34] As editor of the
Review of Reviews in the 1890s, Stead toured Europe
and wrote that 'this far-off, unseen event (A United
States of Europe), toward which the whole continent
has been moving with a slow but relentless march, has
come within the pale of practical politics'.[35] Sir
Max Waechter, a British industrialist of German
origin, also typified this tradition. Convinced that
Europe's national rivalries were nurturing a
dangerous and costly armament struggle which would
seriously weaken Europe's economic and moral position
in the world, he urged the peoples and governments of
Europe to move towards a federal system built around
Britain and Germany. Waechter had many European
contacts and was actively involved in the first
Congress for European Federation held in Rome in May
1909. He also established the European Unity League
in London in 1914 to work for a 'Federation of the
States of Europe on an economic basis'.[36]

British federal ideas regarding Europe, then,
were still largely academic before 1914. There was
certainly nothing resembling an organised political
movement on their behalf. Even among continental
Europeans 'the movement to unite Europe politically
did not really get under way before the First World
War'.[37] It was the War itself which gave British
federal ideas a fresh impetus. As Walter Lipgens has
observed, these ideas were supported at first only by
'a small section of the intelligentsia' but,
operating through 'a number of groups and
committees', they were marked by 'great
determination'.[38] Carl H. Pegg has claimed that
'some of the most impressive and optimistic
assertions of the European idea' in 1914 'were in
England'.[39] The Union for Democratic Control,

founded in London by Ramsey Macdonald, Charles
Trevelyan and Norman Angell, declared in its first
manifesto that: 'Policy should no longer be aimed at
a balance of power
but should be directed to establishing a European
federation of states'.[40] The widely read Review of
Reviews and the working-man's Daily Citizen both told
their readers that future peace and stability in
Europe depended upon the federal solution. In its
first issue after the outbreak of war, Review of
Reviews carried an article entitled: 'The United
States of Europe: The Only Way Out' and 'every issue
of the journal for many months carried at least one
article arguing the political organisation of
Europe'.[41]
        During the years between 1919 and 1939
Pan-Europa Union, founded by Richard
Coudenhove-Kalergi in 1923 as an all-party mass
movement, was the best organised association
advocating federation to emerge in Europe.[42] Its
impact in Britain was negligible but federal ideas
were championed in three other organisations: the
'New Europe Group', 'New Commonwealth Society' and
'Federal Union'. Based in London, the New Europe
Group was what Lipgens has described as 'the first
real European-federal group', presumably because of
its 'integral' conception of federalism - depriving
the nation state of its major political functions -
which it advocated with 'remarkable consistency' in
the 1930s.[43] The New Commonwealth Society was
created in 1932 as an organisation which advocated,
not federation, but a reorganisation of the
international states system. But this did not
prevent federal ideas from circulating within it.
The Society's founding figure, Lord David Davies,
promoted a conception of world order based upon
federal influences. His book, A Federated Europe,
published in 1940, depicted the United States of
Europe as a regional bloc in the League of Nations;
this was a 'confederal' scheme preserving the
decision-making integrity of the member states but
it, none the less, challenged traditional notions of
state sovereignty. The New Commonwealth Society was
the precursor of the third political organisation
reviewed here - and easily the most important - the
Federal Union.
        There is, as yet, no definitive study of Federal
Union in Britain. The two best surveys are those of
Nigel Forman and Walter Lipgens.[44] It is still
unclear how the movement was formed in the autumn of
1938, but Forman claims that the first recorded

meeting was on 14 September under the leadership of
Charles Kimber and Derek Rawnsley, two Oxford
graduates. They were joined in October by another
Oxford contemporary, Patrick Ransome, and together
they gained the support of several distinguished
public figures: Lionel Curtis, Lord Lothian, Barbara
Wootten, Wickham Steed and Sir William Beveridge.
The movement, as Lipgen's survey demonstrates,
reached the height of its effectiveness during
1940-1941, 'having grown with astonishing speed and
produced an equally astonishing output of books and
pamphlets'.[45] Barbara Wootten addressed the first
public meeting of Federal Union on 18 May 1939 and
its active local organisations numbered just over 20
in February 1940. The movement claimed an average of
200 press mentions each week during the early months
of the Second World War and by June 1940 it had 225
branches with 12,000 members.

Federal Union, according to Lipgens, 'received
strong backing and real momentum, from Clarence
Streit's famous book, Union Now, first published in
New York in March 1939. The chronology of events
outlined above, however, proves that it did not
inspire the movement's creation. Forman claims that
'the seminal publication which served to crystallise
much of federalist thinking at the beginning of the
War was The Case For Federal Union, written by W B
Curry'[46] and published as a Penguin special in the
autumn of 1939. He acknowledged his debt to Streit's
book but stated that he had been inspired to make the
attempt by the writings of H. G. Wells and Bertrand
Russell: the War had merely underlined the necessity
for putting these ideas into practice.

The movement's original objectives can be
summarised simply: it advocated a federation of free
peoples based upon Western liberal democratic
principles as a first step towards ultimate world
government. But this broad description of Federal
Union's aims concealed many disagreements about both
the scope of the proposed union and the political
strategy required to achieve it. As Forman has
emphasised, 'there was no specific mention of Europe
as the ideal unit for such a federation' although 'it
was certainly assumed that Europe was the priority
area in any attempt to preserve international
peace'.[47] Similar divergences of opinion existed
about strategy: should the movement remain exclusive
to those who were genuine federalists or should it
widen its membership to include influential people
from other organisations who might, in turn,
strengthen its appeal to the public ? This was a

dilemma identical to that which had confronted both the Imperial Federation League and the Round Table Movement many decades earlier. The failure of the federal idea as a peace aim, however, forced Federal Union to choose the latter course. Under the growing influence of Ronald W G Mackay during 1940-41,[48] the movement adopted the realistic strategy of political effectiveness rather than doctrinal purity. It sought to persuade politicians and government officials to include the goal of federation in any peace settlement for a reconstructed Europe and recognised that only by influencing political parties and their leaders could it hope to galvanise British public opinion on any significant scale.

Federal Union activists gained real inspiration for their objectives when Winston Churchill made his famous, desperate offer of a federal union with France on 18 June 1940. Some federalists continue to regard this as evidence of Britain's readiness 'to open its constitutional structure to innovation, and specifically to innovation of a federal type' in particular circumstances. Whilst it is true that Britain has 'historically shown no little flexibility and imagination in defining the relations between England and Scotland, Wales and Ireland,[49] the example of 1940 is none the less, somewhat unconvincing as a significant federal precedent. As Forman has demonstrated, Federal union 'totally misread the real motivation' behind Churchill's dramatic offer: it was 'no more or less than a belated initiative to try to stiffen the resolve of the crumbling Reynaud Government'. It did not amount to a recognition that the British state had outlived its usefulness, 'nor did it betoken a commitment to full federation on the part of the British government.[50]

A much more significant British contribution to a federal Europe has, however, been made in a much less spectacular way. Indeed, this is precisely why it has gone unrecognised for so long. The influence of British federal ideas upon Europe and the way in which this thinking has recently been transformed into practical action has only just begun to receive academic attention.[51] Altiero Spinelli's latest initiative in the European Parliament to revive and rejuvenate the European idea by proposing a new Draft Treaty on European Union provides the connecting link between the intellectual influences of the 1930s and 1940s and those of the 1980s. The most recent attempt to reform and construct the European Community bears all the hallmarks of federal

thinking. How ironic it is that the leading
protagonist of the federal cause in the Community
today should confess that the intellectual origins of
his federal ideas are rooted in 'English political
culture'.

The paradox can be simply explained. During the
period of his imprisonment and subsequent confinement
by Mussolini on the island of Ventotene, off the
Naples coast, Spinelli began to receive a steady flow
of political literature from his anti-Fascist
fellow-traveller, Luigi Einaudi. Einaudi, a
confirmed federalist, helped to convince Spinelli of
the need for a federal solution to Europe's problems.
But it was Einaudi's role in circulating British
federalist literature from Federal Union which was of
crucial importance. In this way Spinelli read and
absorbed British federal ideas. In particular, the
views and arguments of Lord Lothian, Lionel Robbins
and Sir William Beveridge made a strong impression
upon him. And the impact of these ideas was both
decisive and durable. The following extract from an
essay which Spinelli wrote in 1957 bears testimony to
this:

> We are used to thinking of the British as
> completely averse to any idea of federation, and
> they, themselves, seem to strengthen this
> impression by often repeating that this is ....
> very foreign to their method of thinking ....
> This is actually not so, however .... The idea
> that it is possible to bring about a
> supranational government by means other than
> conquest, i.e. through free consent of states,
> and that it is possible to divide sovereignty,
> assigning portions of it to different organs of
> the government, is a typically Anglo-Saxon
> conception .... We must conclude that the
> federal experience is very close to the British
> political spirit, and also that the British can
> easily understand the federal concept and its
> logical political and economic implications.
> Another proof of this understanding is seen in
> the federalist literature of the Federal Union,
> which is of first quality and even today
> superior to the average Continental literature
> on the subject, because of the coherence with
> which the problems are presented, obstacles
> examined and solutions proposed. It is
> interesting to note here that the most coherent
> federalist movement today is the Italian, which
> has absorbed a great deal from the study of this
> English federalist literature.[52]

I have examined the links between British federal
ideas and Spinelli's recent initiative, buttressed by
the European Parliament, elsewhere.[53] Suffice it to
underline here, once again, the significance of what
are British federal ideas, this time in the European
domain. Their importance is little-known at home and
it is not an exaggeration to claim that the weight of
the British Establishment would prefer this.
Spinelli's observations, then, provide a convenient
juncture at which to consider some concluding
reflections.

Conclusion

This brief historical sketch of British federal ideas
is important if we are to appreciate more fully the
nature of the double paradox with which we introduced
this chapter. These ideas have manifested themselves
sometimes clearly and sometimes in a very confused
manner. They have occasionally been prominent and
have often been peremptorily dismissed. However,
this historical outline does demonstrate a
continuous, unbroken tradition of federal ideas which
has been overlooked. Empire, Ireland and Europe have
provided the stimulus for these ideas during the last
century. Great Britain is not a federal state but
this does not mean that it lacks a significant
tradition of federal ideas. It is important to
remember that this is a tradition which arises out
of, and is a practical response to,
the perceived need for major institutional and
constitutional reform of the British state itself.
These federal ideas were indigenous and were directed
at the reorganisation of the British state. They
were related to Empire, Ireland and Europe also in
the sense that they sought to strengthen and
consolidate the state during a turbulent century
which has witnessed the decline of British influence
in world affairs. To this extent British federalism
has always been prescriptive, both as political ideas
and strategy, and as a political movement promoting
federal union.
 In the 1980s the federal tradition lives on,
albeit in a stultified manner. The tiny group of
British federalists in the European Democrat group in
the European Parliament underlines this basic
continuity of federal ideas. The federal current -
dormant for many years - seems to have resurfaced in
Europe with an impressive vigour. It is important
that we do not underestimate the specifically British
contribution to this recent revival. A century of

British federal ideas, however, will not easily convert federalism to federation. And it is the shift from federalism to federation that divides Part One of this book from Part Two. We shall now concentrate upon a number of different aspects of federation as they appear in Austria, Switzerland and West Germany.

Notes

1. See M. D. Burgess, 'Imperial Federation: Continuity and Change in British imperial ideas, 1869-1871', The New Zealand Journal of History, Vol.17, No.1 (April 1983), pp.60-80.

2. For an explanation of the League's appearance, see M. D. Burgess, 'Forgotten Centenary': The Formation of the Imperial Federation League, 1884', The Round Table, Vol.289 (January 1984), pp.76-85.

3. On Rosebery's imperial federationist ideas, see M. D. Burgess, 'Lord Rosebery and the Imperial Federation League, 1884-1893', The New Zealand Journal of History, Vol.13, No.2 (October 1979), pp.165-181.

4. W. E. Forster, 'Imperial Federation', The Nineteenth Century, Vol.17 (February 1885), pp.201-218.

5. See T. R. Reese, The History of the Royal Commonwealth Society, 1868-1968, (London 1968) and S. C. Y. Cheng, Schemes for the Federation of the British Empire, (New York 1931).

6. See M. G. Miller, 'The Continued Agitation for Imperial Union, 1895-1910: The Individuals and Bodies Concerned, Their Ideas and Their Influence', unpublished doctoral thesis, (Corpus Christi, Oxford, 1980).

7. A. H. Loring, 'The Imperial Federation (Defence) Committee, 1894-1906' United Empire, Vol.6, pp.341-346.

8. See J. E. Kendle, The Round Table Movement and Imperial Union, (University of Toronto Press, 1975).

9. Kendle, Round Table Movement, p.64, On Lothian, see J. R. M. Butler, Lord Lothian (Philip Kerr), 1882-1940, (London 1960).

10. Kendle, Round Table Movement, p.68.

11. Kerr to Curtis, 31 August 1910, GD40/17/2, Lothian Papers, Kendle, Round Table Movement, p.93.

12. Kendle, Round Table Movement, p.305.

13. Chamberlain to Dilke, 26 December 1885, S. Gwynn and G. Tuckwell, The Life of the Rt. Hon. Sir Charles Dilke, Vol.2 (London 1917), pp.199-201, and Chamberlain to Dilke, 3 May 1886, Dilke, Vol.2, p.217.

14. Hansard, (third series), Vol.304, 1206.

15. Hansard, 17 May 1886, Vol.305, 1143.

16. Hansard, 1 June 1886, Vol.306, 697.

17. E. A. Freeman to James Bryce, 4 July 1886, Bryce Papers (Bodleian Library, Oxford), Mss.7, ff.236-239. On Freeman's great academic debate with the imperial federationists, see M. D. Burgess, 'Imperial Federation: Edward Freeman and the Intellectual Debate on the Consolidation of the British Empire in the late Nineteenth Century', Trivium, (University of Wales Press), Vol.13 (1978), pp.77-94.

18. Rosebery to Gladstone, 11 August 1889, Gladstone Papers, (British Museum, London), Add. Mss. 44289, f.97.

19. Childers to Gladstone, 10 October 1889, Gladstone Papers, Add. Mss. 44132, ff.295-296.

20. On this subject, see J. E. Kendle, 'The Round Table Movement' and 'Home Rule All Round', The Historical Journal, Vol.11, No.2 (1968), pp.332-353.

21. Kendle, 'Round Table Movement', p.337.

22. Kendle, 'Round Table Movement', p.338.

23. Kendle, 'Round Table Movement', p.349.

24. See J. E. Kendle, 'Federalism and the Irish Problem in 1918', History, Vol.56 (1971), pp.207-230.

25. Kendle, 'Federalism and the Irish Problem in 1918', p.213.

26. Kendle, 'Federalism and the Irish Problem in 1918', p.214.

27. Kendle, 'Federalism and the Irish Problem in 1918', p.216.

28. Kendle, 'Federalism and the Irish Problem in 1918', p.215.

29. See J. Pinder and G. Ionescu, 'A British Lead to a Federal Europe ?'Government and Opposition, Vol.19, No.3 (Summer 1984), p.284.

30. Kendle, 'Federalism and the Irish Problem in 1918', p.230.

31. A. H. Birch, Political Integration and Disintegration in the British Isles, (London 1977), pp.156 and 169.

32. J. R. Seeley, 'United States of Europe', Macmillan's Magazine, Vol.23, (1871), pp.441-444.

33. On Seeley's political ideas, see D. Wormell, Sir John Seeley and the Uses of History, (Cambridge University Press, 1980).

34. See F. Whyte, The Life of W. T. Stead, Vol.1, (London 1925), pp.145-155.

35. W. T. Stead, The United States of Europe, (London 1899), p.30.

36. See The Times, 31 January 1914. The whole of p.6 is devoted to the projected Unity League, which had its headquarters at 39 James Street, London.

37. W. Lipgens, A History of European Integration, 1945-1947, (Clarendon Press, Oxford 1982), Vol.1, p.35.

38. Lipgens, European Integration, Vol.1, p.36.

39. C. H. Pegg, Evolution of the European Idea, 1914-1932, (University of North Carolina Press 1983), p.9.

40. Lipgens, European Integration, Vol.1, p.36.

41. Pegg, The European Idea, p.9.

42. For a detailed analysis of Coudenhove-Kalergi's activities, see A. Zurcher, The Struggle to Unite Europe, 1940-1958, (New York 1958).

43. Lipgens, European Integration, Vol.1, p.162.

44. See N. Forman, 'The European Movement in Great
     Britain, 1945-1954', unpublished M. Phil.
     thesis, (University of Sussex, 1973), Ch.3,
     part 1, pp.62-90 and Lipgens, European
     Integration, Vol.1, pp.142-153.

45. Lipgens, European Integration, Vol.1, p.142.

46. See Lipgens, European Integration, Vol.1, p.64
     and Forman, 'European Movement', pp.64-65. This
     is also confirmed in the short article by
     R. A. Wilford, 'The Federal Union Campaign',
     European Studies Review, Vol.10, (1980),
     pp.101-114.

47. Forman, 'European Movement', p.63.

48. R.W.G. Mackay, a relatively unknown Australian
     solicitor who had settled in England in 1934,
     was co-opted on to the Executive Committee
     of Federal Union in February 1940. He was
     Labour party parliamentary candidate during
     1935-1942, worked in the Ministry of Aircraft
     Production during 1942-1945 and became Labour MP
     for Hull North-West between 1945 and 1950 and,
     again, for Reading North in 1950-51. His most
     influential book, Federal Europe, was published
     in 1940 and he rapidly acquired widespread
     parliamentary respect as a man of independent
     conviction who could mobilise support for the
     federal solution across party lines in the House
     of Commons.

49. See Pinder and Ionescu, 'A British Lead to a
     Federal Europe ?', pp.281-282.

50. Forman, 'The European Movement', p.76.

51. See, in particular, J. Pinder, 'Prophet not
     without Honour: Lothian and the Federal Idea',
     The Round Table, Vol.286, (April 1983),
     pp.207-220 and M. D. Burgess, 'Federal Ideas in
     the European Community: Altiero Spinelli and
     European Union, 1981-1984', Government and
     Opposition, Vol.19, No.3, (Summer 1984),
     pp.339-347.

52. A. Spinelli, 'The Growth of the European
     Movement since World War II', in C. Grove
     Haines, (ed), European Integration, (Baltimore
     1957), pp.38-40.

53. M. D. Burgess, 'Altiero Spinelli, Federalism and
     the EUT: On the Trail of a Long Progeniture' in
     J. Lodge (ed), Whither Europe ? -
     European Union: The European Community in
     Search of a Future, forthcoming, (London,
     MacMillan Press, 1985).

PART TWO

8.   THE REVITALISATION OF FEDERALISM AND FEDERATION
     IN AUSTRIA[1]

     Richard Luther

Introduction

For many students of the Austrian political system -
be they native Austrians or external observers such
as this author - the subjects of federalism and
federation have never loomed very large. This is
understandable, given the fact that the Federal
Republic of Austria is widely held to be either not a
federal state at all or, at best, to be located at
that point on the federal spectrum where states
virtually cease to be federal.[2] The political
division within Austria which has attracted most
attention is that between the socialist and
clerical-conservative Lager. Yet even in this
respect recent writings have portrayed Austria's
political system as one in which the emergence of an
Austrian national identity has contributed to a
thoroughgoing reconciliation between the two
previously mutually hostile political subcultures.[3]
It may therefore appear somewhat paradoxical to
devote a chapter to federalism and federation in a
country widely characterised as highly centralised
and endowed with a homogenous political culture.
However, the assumption that federalism and
federation are irrelevant in Austria is mistaken.
First, the territorial dimension in Austria should
not be seen as of negligible salience when compared
to the party-political cleavage. It is inextricably
linked with the latter and in fact reinforces it.
Secondly, it would be difficult to conceive of any
federation in which federalism was totally absent and
in which it would not constitute a guide for, or
measure of, the performance of the federation.
Thirdly, not only has Austrian federalism continued
to exist, but it has of late in fact enjoyed a
considerable revival. Indeed, the impact of this
revival has led to tangible, albeit as yet limited,
changes in the Austrian federation.
     For reasons that will become clear in due
course, it is Vorarlberg, Austria's westernmost land,
that has been at the forefront of the revival of
Austrian federalism. Though survey data on popular
attitudes within Vorarlberg to the Federation are few
and often not very accessible, it is possible to
capture Vorarlberg's perception of the federal
political party which has for over a century enjoyed

a hegemonic position within the land. A second source of information is the text of a popular referendum held in Vorarlberg in June 1980 on proposals for federal reform. The proposals were endorsed by nearly 70% of the 90% of the electorate which voted. However, the main focus of this chapter will be the 'Pro-Vorarlberg Movement', a popular citizens' initiative launched in 1979, whose aim was twofold. First, it sought to enhance Vorarlberg's autonomy within the Austrian federal political system by means of the introduction of a special statute to regulate Vorarlberg's relationship to the Centre on terms considerably more favourable to the former. This first aim, however, was linked to a second goal. It was part of a general strategy whose ultimate goal was no less than the fundamental reconstruction of the Austrian federation in the direction of increasing the powers of the lander at the expense of the Centre. In pursuit of these twin aims Pro-Vorarlberg availed itself of a form of federalism that has a long history in Vorarlberg, namely, federalism based upon Catholic social theory and its principle of subsidiarity. This chapter therefore constitutes a study of how federalism has been used within an extant federation for the purpose of the latter's reform.

The structure of this chapter will be as follows. The next section will consider a number of factors which have enabled Vorarlberg to maintain its sense of distinctiveness within the Austrian federation. These include geography, history and the party system, as well as a distinctive form of federalism. The second section evaluates the nature of Vorarlberg's relationship to the federation in general and the Centre in particular during the years from the establishment of the Second Republic in 1945 until the launch of Pro-Vorarlberg in 1979. An important theme of much of this period was the lack of progress in the continuing attempts at federal reform. The frustration of these efforts helps to explain Vorarlberg's recourse to more populist measures. It is to the latter that the penultimate block of the chapter is devoted. It examines the birth of Pro-Vorarlberg and the varied responses to it. An equally important element is the investigation of the federalism contained in the Movement's petition. Finally, we shall consider what conclusions might be drawn from the developments we have outlined.

Vorarlberg and Austria

There are a number of factors which have helped
sustain since 1918 Vorarlberg's sense of
distinctiveness within the (German-) Austrian state.
Not least of these is the Land's geographical
location. A glance at any map shows its remoteness
from the federal capital. Vienna is further from
Bregenz in mileage terms than Bonn and only
fractionally nearer than Brussels or Paris. The
situation regarding travelling times is not much
different. Until the opening as recently as 1978 of
the Arlberg road tunnel, Vorarlberg's road link to
the rest of Austria through Tyrol - rather than via
West Germany - was frequently impassable during the
winter months. By contrast, some 80% or so of
Vorarlberg's frontier borders are on the foreign
states of Liechtenstein, Switzerland and West
Germany, with whom its road and rail links are
considerably better and with whose economies it has
long been closely related.[4]

Vorarlberg's history prior to and during the
establishment of the First Republic offers a further
explanation for the former's attitude within and
towards the Austrian federation. Before the fall of
the Habsburgs in 1918, Vorarlberg had been a Crown
land of the Dual Monarchy. The degree of political
independence which this entailed was minimal,
especially in the case of Vorarlberg, which lacked
even its own administrative system, being
subordinated instead to the Tyrolean 'Statthalter'
(Imperial Governor) located in Innsbruck. Though
this relative impotence during the Dual Monarchy
might make appeals to Vorarlberg's heroic and
independent past appear somewhat misplaced, there is
no doubt that a long history as a territorially
distinct entity has fostered a strong sense of
communal identity, even if this identity has more
often than not been expressed in terms of opposition
to the Land's perceived lack of political
independence. The struggle for greater political
autonomy within the Empire was a continuous, albeit
unsuccessful, theme throughout the last fifty or
sixty years of Habsburg rule.

Subsequent to the abdication of the Emperor in
1918, Landeshauptmann[5] Otto Ender observed that
'through the collapse of the Austro-Hungarian
Monarchy the Pragmatic Sanction has become null and
void. The 1867 constitution has also ceased to apply
and the Lander have attained independence'.[6] Nor was
this mere rhetoric, for Vorarlberg was then actively

considering a future outside the new German-Austrian
state, whose viability it was not alone in doubting.
Basing its case upon Wilsonian self-determination,
Vorarlberg was working on an Anschluss to
Switzerland. Indeed, a referendum held in the Land
in May 1919 showed over 80% favouring this option.[7]
That Vorarlberg did not secede was very much a
consequence of Allied pressure and apprehensions on
the part of Switzerland. Many of the arguments
raised in favour of the 'Anschlussbewegung' were the
same as those currently voiced in support of
Pro-Vorarlberg: geography, history, language and
culture.[8] However, one should not overlook the
significance of party political considerations.
Within Vorarlberg, the clerical conservative
Christian Social Party enjoyed a hegemonic position.[9]
At the national level the situation was very
different in 1918, with Socialist domination of what
was then still a unitary and not a federal republic.
Only after it adopted a federal constitution in 1920
and the Socialist federal government was replaced by
Christian Social governments, did Vorarlberg slowly
come not only grudgingly to accept the new state, but
also to identify with it.

We shall return to the asymmetry of the
Vorarlberg and national party systems shortly. At
this point it might be worth noting two other factors
that help to account for Vorarlberg's perception of
itself as different from the rest of Austria. The
first concerns the fact that Vorarlberg's experience
during and after the Second World War was markedly
different from that of eastern Austria. Not only did
it suffer considerably less war damage, but it was
also spared the economically debilitating effects of
being in the Soviet Zone of Occupation. Thus it is
not surprising that Vorarlberg prospered and that its
economic growth compares favourably with the overall
Austrian figures. The increased prosperity, combined
with higher birth rates, has contributed to
Vorarlberg's dramatic population increase since the
war.[10] Secondly, Vorarlberg has a widely read local
press, a matter of some significance, given the
growth in Austria since the 1960s of a territorially
undifferentiated national boulevard press.[11] The
Vorarlberger Nachrichten has a readership of roughly
132,000 while that of the rival Neue Vorarlberger
Zeitung is about 73,000.[12] Pro-Vorarlberg's success
was in no small part due to the fact that the editor
of the former paper was a signatory of the petition
and threw the full weight of his newspaper behind the
Movement. On the same theme of press and media

influence, it is worth recalling the impact during
the early years of the Second Republic of radio
broadcasting. The old black-red division between the
conservative west and socialist Vienna was
re-emphasised during this period because of the use
by the occupying Soviet authorities of the
Vienna-based radio station for propaganda purposes.
Such broadcasting merely served to confirm for the
Vorarlbergers their view of Vienna as being
ultra-red.[13]

It is the contention of this chapter that the
factor which best explains - or at least most
graphically illustrates - the political
distinctiveness of Vorarlberg vis-a-vis the rest of
Austria in general and Vienna in particular, is the
party system. To focus attention upon the party
system when seeking to understand the persistence
through time of the distinctive identity of the
constituent units of a federation is not new.[14] Most
students of Austrian politics have, however, pointed
to the integrative function of the party system.
This is to say, they have suggested that the Austrian
party system played a crucial role in the centripetal
tendencies of the federation.[15] Some authors in fact
contend that the parties have been so successful in
their integrative function that their adversarial
postures no longer reflect any significant social
division, but serve instead merely to rationalise
their own continued existence.[16] By contrast the
argument which this author wishes to advance is that
while the party system is an important factor
affecting the Austrian federation, the nature of the
role played by the party system depends upon the
degree of congruence or symmetry between national and
local political elites. In short, the party system
is most likely to have a centripetal effect in times
of harmony between local and national political
elites, while during periods when there is an
asymmetry in the party system, centrifugal pressures
are likely to prevail. Concomitantly, if one accepts
Sawer's claim that federal political systems are more
likely to move within the spectrum of federal states
rather than out of it,[17] demands for federal reform
are more likely to come from constituent units with
political leaders of the 'out'group nationally.
Vorarlberg offers a very good example of this
principle, as can be demonstrated by a consideration
of the electoral and party-political disparty between
the Centre and CVP-dominated Vorarlberg.

That the Austrian People's Party (OVP) enjoys a
hegemonic position within Vorarlberg is beyond doubt.

Since 1945 it has regularly polled between 50% and
70% of the votes at Landtag and National Council
elections[18] and has held at least five (and since
1974 six) of the seven seats in the Land
government.[19] Figure one is an index of
non-socialist voting at National Council elections
since 1919 and demonstrates graphically the disparity
between voting behaviour in Vorarlberg and in Austria
as a whole (the figures for Tyrol are included, since
Tyrol has recently also spawned a citizens'
initiative calling for reform of the Austrian federal
system in the direction of greater autonomy for its
constituent units).[20] Examination of the diagram
shows that the extremely high values in Tyrol and
Vorarlberg during the first Republic have, with the
exception of Vorarlberg's 1949 value, not been
repeated. Up until the mid 1970s there had in fact
been a general decline in non-socialist voting that
has, roughly speaking, paralleled the national trend.
However, the returns since 1979 tell a different
story. The rise at the 1979 National Council
election of Vorarlberg's degree of non-socialist
voting transpired at a time when the national trend
was the reverse. And although the national value for
non-socialist voting moved in an upward direction in
1983, it did so only by a mere three points, while
the Vorarlberg increase at the same General Election
was eight points.[21] Since the object of the
comparison is to highlight the disparity in voter
alignments and not merely absolute levels of
non-socialist voting, reference to figure two should
prove interesting. This graph depicts the change in
the disparity between the returns in Vorarlberg and
Tyrol and those nationwide. At least two points
stand out. First, Vorarlberg has, with the exception
of 1920 and 1945, consistently demonstrated a higher
degree of deviation from the all-Austrian levels than
Tyrol. Indeed, at times the differences have been
huge (e.g. 53 points in 1923). Secondly, the Second
Republic peaks of 1949-53, 1966 and 1979-83 coincide
respectively with the times of greatest propaganda
output by the Soviet occupation forces in Vienna,
with the election immediately following the Fussach
incident (see below) and with the elections either
side of the launching of the Pro-Vorarlberg Movement.
This appears to substantiate the hypothesis that the
political events with which we shall concern
ourselves in the subsequent section, have accentuated
the distinctive voting patterns and made politically
salient the whole question of Bund-Land
relationships.[22]

Before proceeding to examine how and why reform of
the Austrian federation became politically salient,
it would help to point out the implication of the
factors mentioned this far for Austrian federalism.
The first point to be made is that the greatest
support for a federal state form has traditionally
come not from Vienna, but from the rural hinterland.
Thus at the very outset of Austria's republican
history it was the success of the activities of rural
Lander such as Vorarlberg and Tyrol which forced the
urban metropolis of Vienna to concede a federal
political system. Secondly, it is important to note
the party-political nature of this division. It is
from strongly conservative, OVP-dominated Lander such
as Tyrol and Vorarlberg that most of the arguments in
defence of the powers of the constituent units of the
federation vis-a-vis the metropolitan Centre have
come. This party-political dimension has in fact
become increasingly significant since 1970, when the
Socialist Party of Austria (SPO) started a period in
office at the national level which is (at the time of
writing in February 1985) as yet unbroken. As a
corollary of this factor, one is forced to conclude
that the most fruitful source of information for a
student of Austrian federalism are the pronouncements
of the OVP and related bodies and individuals. For
it is primarily from within the OVP camp that
latterday calls have come for the reconstruction of
the Austrian federation along more decentralised
lines.
     To understand Vorarlberg's self-perception and
its view of the federal state it is therefore
necessary to consider the political ideology of the
christian democratic OVP and its First Republic
predecessor: the Christian Social Party. Crucial to
both parties is Catholic social theory, whose key
concepts are personalism, mutualism, but above all
subsidiarity. Based upon theories of natural rights,
this latter principle found its most famous
expression in Leo XIII's 1891 'Rerum Novarum' and was
re-stated by Pius XI and John XXIII in 1931 and 1961
respectively.[23]   It reads as follows:

> It is a fundamental principle of social
> philosophy, fixed and unchanged, that one should
> not withdraw from individuals and commit
> to the community what they can accomplish by
> their own enterprise and industry. So too, it
> is an injustice and at the same time a
> great evil and disturbance of right order, to

transfer to the larger and higher collectivity
functions which can be performed and provided
for by lesser and subordinate bodies. In as
much as every social activity should, by its
very nature, prove a help to the body social,
it should never destroy or absorb them.[24]

A study of the manifestos and policy statements of
the Christian Socials and OVP shows the persistence
of the ideas of an organic society. While the
Christian Socials stressed Christianity as a general
principle,[25] the protection of the Catholic Church[26]
and identified the three 'founding pillars' of
society as family, professional group and
settlement,[27] the manifestos of the post-war era have
considered in much greater detail the practical
application of notions such as subsidiarity and
solidarity to Austrian political life.

The 1952 'Everything for Austria' manifesto, for
example, advocated solidarity and a 'healthy
federalism' (sic. federation) as alternatives to
class-based politics and centralism. Indeed, it was
stated that 'The (Party's) individual aspirations in
all areas are determined by the fundamental idea of
solidarity'.[28] In 'What We Want' in 1958 it was said
of democracy that it:

> rests upon the idea the the people possesses the
> maturity to govern itself. The inescapable
> corollary of this is that lesser communities
> must also be enabled to decide by themselves
> upon matters directly affecting them. As a
> general principle, higher collectivities should
> only take from the lesser that responsibility
> which the latter cannot itself carry. In
> accordance with this principle, extensive
> self-administration is to be secured for the
> Bundeslander, the communes and professional
> bodies. However, the necessity still
> remains for a living bond between the lesser and
> higher communities.[29]

Clearly, this represents an organic view of society
and constitutes, in all but name, a definition of
subsidiarity. In 1965 the word subsidiarity was used
for the first time in an OVP manifesto; moreover, its
use was explicitly with reference to the nature of
the Austrian federation.

The relevant section of the 'Klagenfurter
Manifesto' stated:

The Federation is only to exercise functions
which cannot be fulfilled by the
self-administration of the Lander and communes
or by society's interest groups and other small
communities. Conversely, the Federation is to
apply itself energetically to those functions
that exceed the capabilities of those
collectivities (the principle of subsidiarity).
The Austrian People's Party sees in the federal
structure of the Republic, as envisaged by the
constitution, a valuable vitalization of public
life, a proven school for political activity, a
precondition for the strengthening of the
consciousness of one's homeland and the
opportunity for greater attention to the
diverse conditions prevailing in the individual
Lander and communes. This form of state also
promotes a rational and cost-effective
administration.[30]

Finally, the 1972 'Salzburger Programm' listed second
in its enumeration of the Party's fundamental
principles: 'subsidiarity, as protection against an
omnipotent state'.[31] This latter concern has in the
last ten years been mentioned with greater frequency
especially in sections of the press predisposed
towards the OVP. Those of the OVP who had for many
years advocated that the Austrian federation be
reformed in line with the idea of subsidiarity have
themselves commented upon the way in which the
commitment to this reform of some of their fellow
party members has increased in direct proportion to
the length of time that the OVP has been excluded
from central government.[32] The omnipotent Centre
must therefore be interpreted as an omnipotent SPO
Centre.

       To have dwelt at some length upon the expression
of Catholic social theory in the pronouncements of
the OVP is justifiable on a number of counts. First,
the OVP has long enjoyed a hegemonic position within
Vorarlberg, as Figure One below illustrates.
Secondly, given the extent of the influence of the
Catholic Church in Vorarlberg, the aforementioned
principles can be taken as widespread amongst the
population. Finally, both the Pro-Vorarlberg
petition and the amended format which was endorsed by
70% of the voters in a Vorarlberg referendum were, as
will be shown below, predicated upon the principle of
subsidiarity.

Federal Reform in Austria 1945-1979

Having considered a number of the most important
factors which help explain the maintenance of
Vorarlberg's sense of distinctiveness within Austria,
it is now time to examine the attempts at federal
reform which have been made during the Second
Republic. As will become apparent, it was the
persistent failure of these endeavours, combined with
Vorarlberg's growing disenchantment with the
socialist government of Kreisky, which acted as
catalysts for the launch in 1979 of Pro-Vorarlberg.
      For the first ten years of the Second Republic,
demands for increased Lander autonomy were
politically a non-starter. The reason for this was
the call for national unity in face of the presence
on Austrian soil of armies of occupation. The
signing in 1955 of the State Treaty changed all this,
allowing feelings of resentment to be voiced about
the continuous centripetal tendencies exhibited in
Austrian constitutional and administrative reforms
from as early as 1925 and 1929.[33]
      On 16 November 1956 the
Landesamtsdirektorenkonferenz set up the so-called
'Committee of Four' in which the following Lander
were represented: Carinthia, Upper Austria, Tyrol
and Vorarlberg.[34] The remit of this committee was to
prepare a draft of demands designed to reverse the
centralising trend and its proceedings were very
lengthy, something due in no small measure to the
adoption of the principle of amicable agreement as
the basis of all decisions.[35] This consociational
technique, combined with the desire to remain
ideologically neutral in order to avoid allegations
of party-political bias, led to the drafting of a
'Forderungsprogramm' (programme of demands) that was
both minimalist and legalistic. It was not until
1964 that the draft was finalised and presented to
the Federal Government as the Lander's counter to the
former's call for 'Notopfer' (emergency sacrifices)
on the part of the Lander in order to balance the
federal budget deficit. This Forderungsprogramm der
Bundeslander 1964 was followed by a 1970 and 1976
version. While the original rationalisation of the
demands for greater Lander autonomy was based upon
the claims that a more cost-effective administration
would ensue, later justification stressed the
benefits of what was hailed as a revitalisation of
the federal political system and of democracy
itself.[36] The 1974 constitutional amendment[37] was
the first substantive result of the movement for
greater Lander autonomy that had started eighteen

years previously. This slow progress had frustrated
both the individual participants such as Dr. Grabherr
and public opinion generally.

In 1964 two events demonstrated the strength of
feeling in western Austria against what was perceived
as unwarranted central interference. The first was a
national popular initiative calling for greater
independence in broadcasting, the signatures for
which were collected in late summer and autumn.
Since the SPO was generally held to be the group
exerting the greatest influence on broadcasting, the
fact that most signatures came from Vorarlberg and
Tyrol[38] is not without significance. A more
spontaneous protest came on 21 November at the
proposed christening of a new ship at Fussach, on
Vorarlberg's Bodensee coast, by an SPO Federal
Minister. Thousands of Vorarlbergers turned out and
forcibly prevented the ship being named Dr. Karl
Renner in memory of the SPO's famous Chancellor.
Instead, an impromptu ceremony gave it the name
'Vorarlberg'. Two more popular initiatives, one in
1969 on the introduction of the forty-hour-week and
one in 1975 against the Socialists'abortion law,
reaffirmed the extent of anti-socialist sentiment in
Vorarlberg. The former petition was signed
by nearly 900,000 persons, but only 2.5% of these
were from Vorarlberg. Conversely, the proposal that
the SPO's abortion law be severely curtailed received
32.7% of its signatories from Vorarlberg.[39]

From 1945 until April 1966 the Austrian Federal
Government was, as everyone knows, composed of
members of both of Austria's Lager, namely the SPO
and OVP. Although this consociationalism[40] had given
the Second Republic a stability unknown to Austria in
the inter-war years, the side-effects of such
'amicable agreement'[41] led in the 1960s to mounting
scepticism about the continued value of this mode of
decision-making. First, elections appeared to have
lost their traditional significance, serving merely
to prompt, via the 'Proporz' (ratio), minor
adjustments to the number of posts allocated to the
OVP and SPO in the political and administrative
branches of the executive, as well as in a host of
public corporation and nationalised industries.
Secondly, not only had the National Council been
reduced to a ratifier of Cabinet decisions, but the
Cabinet itself had become a mere rubber-stamp for
decisions made in the Coalition Committee and other
extra-constitutional bodies. Thirdly, the extension
of Proporz to so wide a range of institutions was
felt to have increased, at the expense of the

principle of merit, the influence of the party
book.[42] Finally, it was becoming apparent that the
deadweight of this consociational structure was
simply no longer output effective; symptomatic of
this immobilism was the frequent recourse to
'Junktim'.[43]

The creation in April 1966 of an OVP
single-party government did, of course, not mean the
end of consociationalism in Austria, but it did
signify the start of a new phase in which majority
rule became more acceptable. The 1970 and 1971
National Council elections were of great significance
for OVP Lander, since they resulted in the setting up
in Vienna of single-party SPO governments. Moreover,
while the first Kreisky government was a minority
government, the second had an absolute majority.
Thus for a period of about nine years prior to the
launch of Pro-Vorarlberg, there had been an absence
of participation in the Federal Government by the
party dominant in Vorarlberg and Tyrol (i.e. the
OVP). This was felt especially strongly in
Vorarlberg, for whom it furnished proof - if that
were needed - of the lack of congruence between
themselves and the Centre. Whereas this lack of
symmetry as between local and federal political
elites might otherwise have been dampened by the
consociational practices of a functional mid-range
elite such as the Landeshauptleutekonferenz and the
Landesamtsdirektorenkonferenz, inter-alia, these
latter channels were no longer able to satisfy
demands but were seen instead as excessively
bureaucratic and slow moving. (Witness the eighteen
years that has elapsed from the Lander's first call
for the reversal of the centripetal trend of Austrian
politics until the Federal Government's limited
response in 1974). Furthermore, the electoral
success of the SPO at the federal level had led to a
large increase in the number of SPO men in posts that
had previously been filled according to Proporz. As
for the Bundesrat, not only was Vorarlberg
represented by a mere three delegates, but, because
of its negligible powers, the Bundesrat has never
been an effective guarantor of Lander interests. Nor
was it useful as a party-political counter to the
National Council, since the balance between OVP and
SPO was so even, that procedural regulations more
often than not resulted in SPO majorities.[44] While
Tyrol, for example, had been fortunate in being able
to compensate to some extent for these
disadvantages by virtue of having in Landeshauptmann
Wallnofer a charismatic and forceful politician who

enjoyed very good personal relations with both
Chancellor Kreisky and former Finance Minister
Androsch, Vorarlberg's Landeshauptmann Kessler lacked
these advantages.

Since the early 1970s there had therefore been a
lack of effective overarching elite accommodation
between the OVP decision-makers at the Land level and
their federal SPO counterparts. These changes meant
that the territorial issue took on a new
significance. In 1975 Tyrol and Vorarlberg founded
the Institute for Federal Research in Innsbruck,
through whose endeavours they aim to increase public
knowledge of and sympathy for federalism and
federation. The output of the Institute has been
prolific[45] and it has gained considerable esteem.[46]
On 5 November 1978 Austria held its first national
referendum. The issue was whether or not to bring
the nuclear plant at Zwentdorf on stream. The fact
that the issue was 'forced' via referendum is a sign
of the change from amicable agreement to majority
rule and the use of this decision-mode undoubtedly
served as a hint for those in Vorarlberg who were
disillusioned by the seemingly endless process of
bargaining. Despite its attempts to portray itself
as neutral, the SPO was held to be for putting
Zwentdorf on stream and the OVP against. Vorarlberg
had always been against nuclear plants, but the
results of the referendum none the less involved a
censure of the SPO government and demonstrated
graphically the east-west divide in Austria (see
figure 3).

The National Council elections of 1975 resulted
in no change in the composition of the parliament,
nor of the Government, but on 6 May 1979 the SPO
increased its vote and its absolute majority improved
by two seats, something which had[47] appeared very
unlikely six months previously. Confronted with no
prospect of the OVP resuming power at the Federal
level for at least four years and exasperated by the
snail-like progress of the Forderungsprogramm, a
group of Vorarlbergers got together in the spring of
1979 to discuss the feasibility of launching in the
Land a popular initiative on the territorial issue.
The forthcoming Landtag elections (October 1979) were
considered a propitious moment, since politicians
are, in Dr. Grabherr's words, 'more susceptible at
such times'.[48]

The Pro Vorarlberg Movement

During the summer of 1979 the Pro-Vorarlberg movement
was formed and its petition drawn up. While the 46
signatories are representative of the Land
geographically, an analysis of their occupations
shows an underrepresentation of manual and routine
white-collar groupings.[49] The driving force and
technical expert of Pro-Vorarlberg is retired Landesamtsdirektor,[50] Dr. Elmar Grabherr; he was
responsible for the professional drafting of the
legal petition. The movement avoided any publicity
whatsoever during its formative phase; the reasons
for this were twofold. First, since the prime
concern of the signatories was to cut through the
politics of compromise and accommodation which had,
they felt, frustrated all previous reform efforts
they wanted to avoid involving the parties and
bureaucracy for fear of the Movement's demands also
becoming the victim of procrastination and
appeasement. Secondly, their aim was to remain
party-politically neutral and it was felt that an
unheralded launch would be most consistent with a
truly 'popular' initiative. Accordingly, it was not
until immediately before the launch on 10 September
1979, that an attempt was made to find the one
Landtag deputy required formally to submit the
proposal to the legislature. Nor was support of the
press sought until the final hour, though the
contribution of the Vorarlberger Nachrichten was to
prove crucial, allowing 'a minimum of organisation to
reap a maximum of success.[51]
    The petition[52] took the form of a request of the
Vorarlberg Landtag that, in view of Vorarlberg's
distinctive geographic position, history and
consciousness, a referendum be held on the question:
'Should Vorarlberg receive, via consultation with the
Federation within the framework of the Austrian
Federal State, its own statute .... ?' The text went
on to detail what the content of such a statute
should be. Among the functions to be devolved upon
Vorarlberg, the most important were: 1) the power to
decide independently upon the legislative and
administrative process of the Land and 2) powers to
raise revenue commensurate with the Land's
responsibilities. Moreover, the Vorarlberg Landtag
was to receive 3) a constitutionally entrenched
right of consultation and veto regarding all
constitutional amendments affecting the Land and 4)
similar rights <u>vis-a-vis</u> ordinary legislation deemed
by the Landtag to endanger Vorarlberg's interests.

There was also to be 5) the establishment outside
the existing Federal Constitution of a Commission of
Arbitration to adjudicate on contentious issues
relating to the interpretation or application of the
statute and, finally, 6) the prohibition of its
unilateral amendment or nullification.

Despite the Movement's hopes to the contrary,
Pro-Vorarlberg was held by many to be but a
thinly-veiled OVP proxy intended to promote the
party's prospects at the forthcoming Landtag election
in particular and its campaign for federal reform in
general[53]. It was not so much the detailed executive
and administrative re-arrangements sought by
Pro-Vorarlberg that caused this suspicion, but the
justification offered for this proposed restructuring
of the Land's relationship to the Federation. Point
one of the proposed statute read: 'The Land
Vorarlberg has the unrestricted right of legislation
and execution in all matters which it is equally able
to carry out for Vorarlberg'. In the appendix to the
petition the following justification was offered:

> Fundamental to all social policy is the
> principle that individuals and small communities
> have the right and also the duty to fulfil by
> themselves all the functions that they are able
> to. A balanced distribution of functions also
> militates against the abuse of power ....
> Accordingly, Vorarlberg is to have a natural
> relationship between her and the federal state.
> In future, the Federation is only to regulate
> matters which Vorarlberg cannot herself do
> better.

The parallels between the demands of
Pro-Vorarlberg and the pronouncements of the OVP (see
above) are self evident. The basic principle that
both seek to have adopted as the guideline governing
the rearrangement of the federal state is that of
subsidiarity. Indeed, Dr. Grabherr has confirmed
that this is his intention, conceding that
subsidiarity is the crux of the petition and the rest
merely detail relating to its application[54]. Given
this concurrence, it at first appears surprising that
it was the Freedom Party of Austria (FPO) and not the
OVP that was Pro-Vorarlberg's most wholehearted
supporter. The OVP, while generally positively
inclined towards the Movement, did have its doubters.
In particular, some sections of the party were
opposed to Vorarlberg receiving a special statute,
preferring instead equal treatment for all Lander

(the principle of solidarity). To call for special treatment was, they felt, to invite accusations of particularism and selfishness. Moreover, there was unease about the popular origins of the demands. The sudden appearance of a seemingly well-planned and well-orchestrated campaign threatened the previous monopoly of the parties in this area. However, to have allowed a popular call for the reform of the Austrian federal system to fail, or to have been seen not to support it, was practically unthinkable. Thus the federal party used the opportunity to press home at the federal level its demands for reform, initiating in the National Council a Parliamentary Enquiry on Federation.[55]

The Vorarlberg SPO's response to Pro-Vorarlberg was not uniform; one group, led by the Chairman of the Parliamentary Party in the Landtag (Winder), was strongly opposed to it, while the leader of the Vorarlberg party (Meyer) was in favour of a less overtly negative stance and preferred a neutral posture. Outside the SPO itself, a counter to Pro-Vorarlberg crystallised under the name of 'Pro Austria'. It attacked the citizens' initiative for being particularist, racist, inimical to the unity and general welfare of the Austrian nation and for its elitist origins.[56] The response of the Federal (SPO) Government to Pro-Vorarlberg was to try to play down the latter's importance. Although Kreisky suggested a willingness to discuss some of the issues he stressed that the Lander must for their part be prepared to discuss his government's counter demands. These included increasing the Federation's powers in the field of environmental protection, setting up district parliaments and enhancing the powers of the communes.

The passage through the Vorarlberg Landtag of the Pro-Vorarlberg petition commenced on 20 November, when it was submitted by Landtag Members Battlogg and Ess (respectively, the Chairmen of the Parliamentary OVP and FPO) and then referred to the Legal Committee. During the months of January, February and March the Committee debated the petition and drew up its own 10 Point Programme, which was approved by the OVP and FPO. A minority proposal by the SPO was defeated. It had called for a double referendum, with the electorate being asked whether it wanted the Vorarlberg Land Government to pursue more vigorously the demands contained in the 1976 Forderungsprogram der Bundeslander and, in a separate question, whether it wished Vorarlberg to secure more rights for the communes and the individual citizen.[57] Three days

later, on 28 March, the Landtag resolved in a plenary
session to hold a referendum on 15 June on its 10
Point Programme. The parties supporting the
resolution were those of the Land Government (i.e.
OVP and FPO). The SPO was opposed to the resolution.
    The 10 Point Programme differs in some respects
from the petition of Pro-Vorarlberg, with the
deletion of the demand for a special statute for
Vorarlberg, the addition of demands for the
strengthening of the position of the communes. The
question put to the electorate was as follows:

> Should representatives of the Land enter into
> negotiations with the National Council and the
> Federal Government which would be open to the
> Lander and whose aim would be to secure, within
> the framework of the Austrian Federal State,
> more independence for the Land (Lander) and
> strengthening of the communes as defined by the
> 10 points mentioned hereinafter ?[57]

There were also differences in the powers to be
devolved; for example, the Land Government's proposal
did not call for the transfer of social insurance to
the Land. However, although the original demands had
been toned down, the signatories or Pro-Vorarlberg
were by and large content, because the 10 Point
Programme had retained the crucial principle of
subsidiarity. In the explanatory literature sent to
all voters stood the following:

> Spearheading the demands is the principle upon
> which the division of powers between the
> Federation and Lander is to be based: What the
> Lander can resolve as smaller communities should
> not be arrogated to itself by the Federation.
> If this guiding principle is adhered to, then
> the preconditions for citizen immediacy,
> cultural diversity and economy are favourable.

The result of the referendum of 15 June on the
Land Government's 10 Point Programme was hailed by
Pro-Vorarlberg as a vindication of the latter's claim
to constitute the representative voice of the
Vorarlbergers; 69.3% of a 90% turnout voted in favour
of the proposal[59], giving the Vorarlberg Government a
strong mandate to negotiate for federal reform.
However, there was some uncertainty as to how best to
proceed. Landeshauptmann Kessler held talks with
Chancellor Kreisky and other Landeshauptleute and it
was decided that the Vorarlberg package would be

articulated through the Landeshauptleutekonferenz
(LHK), though not necessarily integrated into this
body's Forderungsprogramm. Concern was expressed by
people who feared that this would lead to a stifling
of the demands[60], but talks continued. At a meeting
of the LHK on 27 October in Graz, it was agreed that
Kessler and Wagner (the SPO Landesshauptmann from
Carinthia) would join their opposite numbers from
Tyrol and Vienna in negotiating with the Federal
Government on behalf of the LHK[61]. Meanwhile, the
Landesamtsdirektoren were to prepare, for an
extraordinary General Meeting of the LHK scheduled
for February 1981, a report on the compatibility of
the Vorarlberg packages and the LHK's
Forderunssprogramm. Subsequent meetings were to
allow Vorarlberg's demands to be presented to the
Federal Government. These arrangements were welcomed
because they allowed the Vorarlberg Landeshauptmann
to negotiate directly with Chancellor Kreisky.

Though progress was - from Vorarlberg's
perspective - extremely slow in coming, there were a
number of changes in the following four years.
First, the Federal Government agreed, in the
interests of expediting a partial realisation of
Lander demands, to withdraw its counter-demands. A
second, though less promising change, was the
inclusion into the process of bargaining over the
Forderungsprogramm der Bundeslander of the demands of
two other associations: namely, the 'Osterreichischer
Gemeindebund' and the 'Osterreichischer Stadtebund'
(Austrian Association of Communes and Austrian
Association of Municipal Authorities respectively).
This extension of the number of parties to the
negotiations was not as detrimental to the progress
of the consultations as had been feared by some. A
third and much more constructive signal came in the
new Sinowarz government's declaration of its
commitment to the 'co-operative federal state' and
its intention to continue negotiations on the
Forderungsprogramm. Finally, and most significant of
all, was the introduction of a Bill proposing a
number of specific changes. These include granting
the Landeshauptleute the rights to participate in the
discussions of the Bundesrat, as well as the
important proposal that any legislation seeking to
reduce the powers of the Lander be subject to the
approval of the Bundesrat. Moreover, the Bill
includes a reduction in the power of the Federal
President to dissolve a Landtag.[62]

That these and other measures will reach the statute book is likely. The extent to which the credit for such achievements should be given to the efforts of Pro-Vorarlberg is difficult, if not impossible, to judge. However, what can confidently be claimed for the Pro-Vorarlberg Movement and the ensuing referendum is that it has contributed to placing the question of the reform of the Austrian federal system very firmly on the political agenda. All three of Austria's major political parties have held conferences on the issue[63] and there have been numerous parliamentary debates and Committees of Enquiry.[64] International symposia have taken place[65] and various organisations with differing degrees of party-political commitment have hosted their own meetings at which federal reform has figured prominently, if not exclusively.[66] Opinion polls were commissioned on the population's perception of the federation[67] and the output of academic literature on federation has increased apace.[68] Finally, other petitions calling for the reform of the Austrian federation have sprung up. In addition to Pro-Tirol, the Salzburg FPO submitted to the Bundesrat a petition requesting detailed reforms of the latter.[69]

Conclusion

This chapter has made a number of points in respect of both Austrian federalism and Austrian federation. It has been argued that the revitalisation of federalism in Vorarlberg has been in large measure a response to the Land's perception of its increasing impotence vis-a-vis the Centre. We have pointed to the perceived ineffectiveness of consociational techniques for the processing of Lander demands for greater autonomy. Emphasis has been placed upon the disparity between the party systems of Vorarlberg and the Centre. The significance of this lay partly in the fact that single-party SPO government at the Centre from 1970 meant that for the first time since the establishment of the Second Republic, the OVP - Vorarlberg's hegemonic party - was not represented in the Federal government. The party-political disparity between Vorarlberg and the Centre was also significant as a sympton of ideological differences in general and differences of federalism in particular.

In addition to discussing federation, we have devoted considerable attention to federalism in Austria. Since the focus has been upon federalism in Vorarlberg, and given the paucity of data on popular attitudes to the federation, we have concentrated upon the main institutionalised expressions of Vorarlberg federalism. These were the ideology of the OVP, the proposals of the Vorarlberg government as subsequently endorsed by 69.3% of the voters and, above all, the federalism of Pro-Vorarlberg.

There are numerous conclusions which might be drawn from this study. There is no doubting that Austria has recently experienced a considerable revitalisation of federalism. The extent to which this will result in changes in the structure and techniques of the Austrian political system is, however, as yet unclear. Some changes have occurred, but it remains to be seen how far these innovations are consolidated. One might speculate that the return of an OVP Federal Government could well reduce Bund-Land tensions and thus call a halt to demands for federal reform. Alternatively, Socialist opposition could be articulated in terms of federalism, though that would be unlikely, given the absence of a strong tradition of federalism in the SPO.

A central argument of this book is that it is useful to distinguish analytically between federalism and federation.[70] It might be helpful to conclude by summarising what we believe to be the practical value of this conceptual distinction. First, we believe that analysing federal political systems by reference to both federalism and federation leads to greater attention being accorded not only to the distinction between federations, but also to that between federalisms. Thus this chapter has demonstrated that Austrian federalism contains a strong element of Catholic social theory, something unfamiliar to those versed only in Anglo-American federalism. Beyond highlighting differences in the content of federalisms, the second merit of the analysis adopted in this book lies in its promotion of the study of the relationship between federalism and federation. It has not been our intention to suggest that federalism determines federation. The relationship is clearly symbiotic. None the less our study has illustrated how, in an asymmetrical party system, a federal ideology may be very attractive for the 'out' group nationally. Moreover, the examination of Pro Vorarlberg showed that within the Austrian federation, federalism has been utilised both for purposes of political mobilisation and for the legitimation of group demands. A final and related point is that our analysis directs attention to the dynamics of federal political systems. We believe that more work needs to be done on this area. This would necessitate a repudiation of the type of vitriolic attack made by Riker[71] and others against the 'ideologists' of federalism. Instead we should recognise federalism qua ideology and therefore examine it not in terms of epistemology, but by reference to content, political sociology and function <u>vis-a-vis</u> the federation.

FIGURE 1

Index of non-socialist voting.

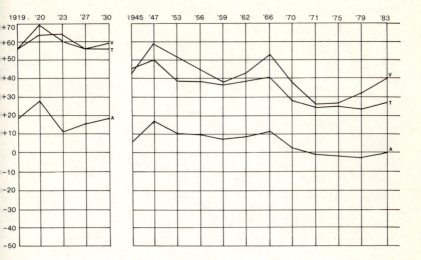

V = Vorarlberg   T = Tyrol   A = *Austrian national average*
(including V and T)

FIGURE 2

Distance on the index of non-socialist voting as between Tyrol and
Vorarlberg and Austria

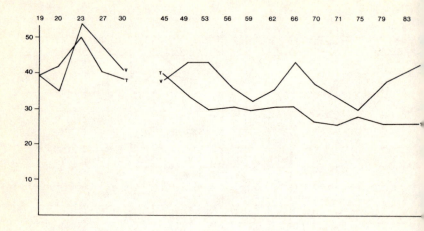

FIGURE 3

Percentages of voters voting "no" at the Zwentdorf (nuclear)
referendum of 5th November 1978

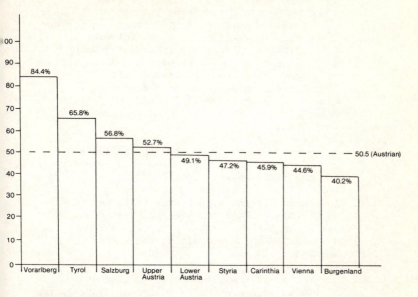

Source: R. Bretschneider, Wahlen & Wähler in Österreich 1978/79 in A. Kohl – A. Stirnemann (Eds)
Österreichisches Jahrbuch für Politik 1979. Vienna 1980, p6.

Notes

1. This is a revised version of a paper given at the E.C.P.R. Joint Sessions at Aarhus, Denmark in 1982 and entitled: 'Federalism from the Standpoint of the State Federated: The Case of Vorarlberg Austria'. The aim of the present chapter is to examine the links between federalism and federation in recent developments in the Austrian political system. A wider range of factors have been examined in Luther, K. R. 'The Increasing Salience of the Centre-Periphery Dimension in the Federal Republic of Austria'. Paper given at the E.C.P.R. Joint Sessions at Barcelona, 1985.

   The author wishes to express his appreciation to the Austrian Ministry of Science and Research for their financial support.

2. An example of the former view is to be found in K. C. Wheare, Federal Government, (London, 1963) while the latter view is articulated by G. Sawer, Modern Federalism, (Victoria, Australia, 1969).

3. See for example R. Stiefbold, 'Elites and Elections in a Fragmented Political System', in Sozialwissenschaftliches Jahrbuch fur Politik, Vol IV, (1975) pp.119-228 or W. T. Bluhm, Building an Austrian Nation, (New Haven, 1973).

4. For details of distances, road links, etc. see E. Grabherr, Vorarlberger Land, (Bregenz 1981). A recent account of Vorarlberg's history is to be found in K. H. Burmeister, Geschichte Vorarlbergs, (Vienna 1980).

5. The Landeshauptmann is the head of the Land Government and is thus analogous to a 'Ministerprasident' in the Federal Republic of Germany. The Landeshauptleutekonferenz is in turn analogous to the Ministerprasidentenkonferenz.

6. Cited in P. Pernthaler, Die Staatsgrundungsakte der osterreichischen Bundeslander. Eine staatsrechtliche Untersuchung uber die Entstehung des Bundesstaates, (Vienna 1979) p.23.

7. See D. Witzig, Die Vorarlberg Frage, (Basel 1974) or O. Ender, Vorarlbergs Schweizer - Anschluss - Bewegung von 1918 bis 1924, (Dornbirn 1952) or I. Zuderell, Die Anschlussbewegung Vorarlbergs an die Schweiz 1918-1921, (PhD, Innsbruck 1946), or H. K. Cohen, The Vorarlberg Question 1918-1922: Failure of the Movement for Union with Switzerland, (PhD Cambridge 1975).

8. The two latter points are connected, relating to the different ethnic or 'Stamm' origins of the indigenous Land population and the eastern Austrians, who are mostly of Bavarian extraction. The Vorarlbergers are of Allemanisch stock, which helps account for their distinctive dialect and is seen by many Vorarlbergers as the explanation of why they are, in contrast with the rest of Austria, industrious and clean-living.

9. The 1919 Landtag election returned 22 Christian Socials to the 30 seat chamber with 64% of the popular vote, see Burmeister, 183f.

10. 1939 Vorarlberg's population constituted 2.37% of that of the whole of Austria. By 1979 it had reached 4.02% Source: Demographisches Jahrbuch Osterreichs 1979, Ed.: Osterreichisches Statistisches Zentralamt, (Vienna), p.207.

11. The 'Kurier' and 'Kronenzeitung' have a joint readership in excess of 2.5 million in a country with a total population of 7.5 million. See F. Czoklich, 'Massenmedien', in Weinzerl and Skalnik (Eds.) Das neue Osterreich, (Graz 1975), p.259ff.

12. Figures taken from S. Morscher, 'Pro-Vorarlberg' in A. Kohl, and A. Stirnemann, (Eds.), Osterreichisches Jahrbuch fur Politik 1980, (Vienna 1981), p.36.

13. See H. Feichtlbauer, 'The Media' in K. Steiner, (Ed), Modern Austria, (Palo Alto, California, 1981). See also F. Mayer, 'Wo stehen wir heute ?' in Die Presse, 4.12.1980.

14. See for example, G. Lehmbruch, Parteienwettbewerb im Bundesstaat, (Stuttgart 1976), as well as W. H. Riker Federalism, Origin, Operation, Significance, (Boston 1964), D. Truman, in A. W. MacMahon Federalism Mature and Emergent, (New York 1955) and even Wheare, Federal Government.

15. Eg. G. Sawer, Modern Federalism.

16. See esp. R. Stiefbold, 'Elites and Elections'.

17. Sawer, Modern Federalism, Ch.11.

18. See Verbindungsstelle der Bundeslander (Ed.) Die Wahlen in den Bundeslandern seit 1945, (Vienna 1981), p.70f.

19. Ibid p.35. See also Vorarlberger Nachrichten (V.N.) of 21.11.79 for the declaration of intent of the new Vorarlberg government.

20. On 16 November 1979, 'Pro Tirol - Fur ein Osterreich der Bundeslander' was launched in Innsbruck. Though it was conceived independently of Pro-Vorarlberg and pursued a different strategy, the manner in which its demands are framed show an underlying ideological affinity with Pro-Vorarlberg. For a copy of the text of the petition, see Die unabhangige Zeitung fur die Universitat Innsbruck and Westosterreich, Vol II, Nr 6-7, 30.1.1980, 15ff. For a comparison of the background of Pro-Vararlberg and Pro-Tirol, see R. Luther, 'Increasing Salience', (1985).

21. The figures for 1983 exclude the returns for the two 'green' parties, which polled a total of 3.29% overall, 4.65 in Vorarlberg and 2.69 in Tyrol. This was done because of difficulties in their location in terms of the socialist/ non-socialist dichotomy. Even if their voters had been included on the socialist side of the equation, the overall picture would be little different. The indices of non-socialist voting for Austria as a whole, Tyrol and Vorarlberg would be 3.18, 23.76 and 35.06 respectively, instead of 0.11, 26.45 and 39.71. This would indicate an insignificant decrease in comparison with 1979 of non-socialist voting overall, with an equally miniscule increase in

Tyrol's figure, while Vorarlberg's non-socialist voting in 1983 constitutes an increase of 2.76 points.

The sources of the data for figures 1 and 2 as follows: re: 1919-30 correspondence from Austrian Central Statistical Office. Re: 1945-79 cf Osterreichisches Statistisches Zentralamt, (Ed) <u>Die Nationalratswahl vom 6 Mai 1979</u>, (Vienna 1979) p. 54, Re: 1983, cf F. Plasser and P. Ulram, 'Die Nationalratswahl 1983: Dokumentation, Analyse und politische Konsequenzen', in <u>Osterreichische Monatshefte</u>' 1983/4, p.130.

22. It is of course not contended that the voting of Vorarlberg and Tyrol is merely a dependent variable. It obviously both enhances and reflects cleavages.

23. A. Freemantle, <u>The Papal Encyclicals in their Historical Context</u>, (New York, Mentor-Omega, 1963), pp.166ff, 228ff and 342ff respectively.

24. <u>Ibid</u>, p. 342.

25. K. Berchtold, <u>Osterreichische Parteiprogramme 1868-1966</u>, (Vienna 1967), p.355 ('Proclamation of the Christian-Socials to Party Members' of 26 November 1918).

26. <u>Ibid</u>, p.365 on 'Party Manifesto of the Viennese Christian-Socials', 16.11.1919.

27. <u>Ibid</u>, p.372 in 'Linz Manifesto of the Austrian Christian Workers', 13.8.1923.

28. <u>Ibid</u>, p.380.

29. <u>Ibid</u>, p.388.

30. <u>Ibid</u>, p.399 Brackets in original. N.B.: Cost effectiveness is clearly not a primary, but a secondary consideration.

31. A. Pelinka and A. Kadan, <u>Die Grundsatzprogramme der osterreichischen Parteien. Dokumentation und Analyse,</u> (St. Polten 1979) p.190.

32. Interview in July 1981 with Dr. B Stamfer in Innsbruck.

33. These were the first two major revisions of the 1920 constitution, whose provisions were already decried in many circles as giving too much power to the Centre.

34. P. Pernthaler, Das Forderungsprogramm der Bundeslander, (Vienna 1980) p.16 See also C.Altenstetter, Der Foderalismus, (Heidelberg 1969), p33ff. It is worth mentioning that the venue for the meeting establishing the Committee of Four was Bregenz and nearly 13 years later, to exercise a leading role in the Pro-Vorarlberg Movement. N.B.: The Landesamtsdirektorenferenz is a meeting of all the Heads of the civil services of the various constituent units of the Austrian federation.

35. P. Pernthaler, Forderungsprogramm, p.15, footnote 19.

36. Ibid p.17.

37. BGBI Nr 444. For an evaluation of the amendment see F. Ermacora, 'Bundesverfassungsgesetznovelle 1974. Erfullung des Landerforderungsprogramms' in Juristische Blatter, Vol.97 (25.1.1975).

38. M.A. Sully, Political Parties and Elections in Austria, (London 1981), p.165. See also F. Czoklich as in footnote 11 above, esp. pp.264-467.

39. M.A. Sully, p.165.

40. See for example G. Lebmbruch, A Non-Competitive Pattern of Conflict Management in liberal Democracies: The Case of Switzerland, Austria and the Lebanon, and P. Pulzer, The Legitimatizing Role of Political Parties, both in K. McRae (ed.) Consociational Democracy Political Accommodation in Segmented Societies, (Toronto 1974). See also A. Lijphart, Consociational Democracy, World Politics, Vol.21 (1969) pp.207-225; R. Stiefbold, 'Elites and Elections'.

41. See Jurg Steiner, Amicable Agreement versus Majority Rule: Conflict Resolution in Switzerland, (Univ. North Carolina Press, Chapel Hill, 1974).

42   The popular initiative on broadcasting (see
     above) was one example of an expression of
     concern about this tendency and was supported by
     the so-called 'independent' newspapers.

43. This is the term for the 'package deal' whereby
     one side votes for a policy to which it
     fundamentally objects in return for reciprocal
     action by the other side on a different issue.

44. Article 36 para.1 of the Federal Constitution
     states 'The Lander succeed each other in
     alphabetical order every six months to the
     chairmanship of the Bundesrat'. Since the
     chairman has no voting rights and more Lander
     are OVP than are SPO, this acts to the
     disadvantage of the former.

45. Over 30 volumes in eight years, as well as
     numerous reports.

46. For a list of the extensive activities see the
     'Berricht uber die Lage des Foderalismus in
     Osterreich', Ed.: Institut fur
     Foderalismusforschung, Vienna. Vol.II (1977),
     pp.85-92; Vol.III (1978), pp.175-190; Vol.IV
     (1979), pp.173-180; Vol.V (1980), pp.225-232;
     Vol.VI, (1981) pp.57-62; Vol.VII (1982),
     pp.65-68.

47. R. Bretschneider, 'Wahlen und Wahler in
     Osterreich 1978/79' in A. Kohl and A. Stirnemann
     (eds.) Osterreichtisches Jahrbuch fur Politik
     1979, (Vienna 1980) pp.7-15.

48. Interview with Dr. Elmar Grabherr in Bregenz,
     17 July 1981.

49. A socio-economic classification based upon the
     Registrar General's Classification of
     Occupations 1970, (OPCS, London HMSO) shows 30%
     in Class I, 28% in Class II and 42% in Class
     III. The author is, of course, aware of the
     limitations of these statistics.

     An interesting extension of the sociological
     approach to Pro Vorarlberg is to be found in
     Markus Barnay, Pro Vorarlberg Eine
     regionalistische Bewegung, (Bregenz 1983).
     Barnay adopts a critical stance vis-a-vis the

Movement, rejecting its claims to 'popular'
origins. Instead, he argues that Pro Vorarlberg
is best perceived as an attempt by a local elite
to enhance its own power. Barnay's book was
kindly brought to our attention by Dr. Wolfgang
C. Muller of Vienna University after completion
of this chapter. We are also grateful to Dr.
Muller for his comments on an earlier draft of
the latter.

50. The Landesamtsdirektor is the Head of the Land
Civil Service. See footnote 34 above.

51. Interview with Dr. Elmar Grabherr in Bregenz on
17 July 1981.

52. For a copy of the text of the petition see V.N.
of 11.9.1979, or 7. Beilage im Jahre 1979 zu den
Sitzungen des XXVIII. Vorarlberger Landtages.

53. See Austrian press after 10 September 1979,
especially the Wiener Zeitung, (W.Z.) Arbeiter
Zeitung (A.Z.) and Furche.

54. Interview as in footnote 51.

55. Both the Federal FPO and OVP supported the
holding of this Enquiry. For the text of the
Enquiry see: Stenographisches Protokoll.
Parliamentarische Enquette 22. Janner 1980 (XV.
Gesetzgebungsperiode des Nationalrates) Thema
'Foderalistische Viefalt in der
bundesstaatlichen Einheit'. Ed: Osterreichische
Staatsdruckerei (Vienna 1980). Re: the doubts
held by some OVP members see, Furche, 5.12.1979.

56. See 9. Beilage im Jahre 1980 zu den Sitzungfen
des XXVIII. Vorarlberger Landtages.

57. Unterlagen zur Volksabstimmung am 15.Juni 1980,
Ed: Amt der Vorarlberger Landesregierung,
(Bregenz 1980), p.3.

58. Ibid, p.8.

59. See V.N. 16.6.1980 for a detailed breakdown of
the returns in the districts and individual
communes. N.B.: Voting was compulsory.

60. E.g. V.N. 31.7.1980.

61. For reports of the Graz meeting see the V.N. and
    Tiroler Tageszeitung (T.T.) of 28 and 29 October
    1980.

62. See Bundesgesetzblatt No.74, of 22.3.1983.

63. The OVP on the 22-23 of September 1980 (cf. V.N.
    19.9.80); their Landeshauptleute on the 3rd of
    January 1980 (cf W.Z. of 4.1.80 and V.N. and
    Neue Tiroler Zeitung (NTZ) of the same date).
    The FPO's Deputies Conference debated federation
    on the 21st of November 1979
    (Saltzburger Nachrichten (S.N.) of 22nd.11.79)
    and the SPO at Mallmitz on 18.1.80 (cf T.T.,
    A.Z., N.T.Z., Presse and W.Z. of 19.1.80).

64. E.g. the Federalism Enquiry of the National
    Council as in footnote 55 above; a discussion in
    the Bundesrat on the 14.12.79 (cf V.N.
    15.12.79); so-called 'Experten Hearings' in the
    Vorarlberg Landtag on the 26.2.80 (cf V.N.
    28.2.80).

65. E.g. International Christian Democratic
    Conference on 8-9 November 1980 in Bruneck (T.T.
    10.11.80) and a symposium on the 20-21 November
    1980 in Graz entitled 'Federalism as an
    organisational principle in the modern state',
    (cf V.N. 18.11.80 and 28.11.80).

66. Examples are legion, we shall cite but a few:
    the 25th Annual Conference of the SPO on
    15.11.79 (cf W.Z. 16.11.79 and A.Z.
    16.11.79); the 28th Annual Conference of the
    Vorarlberg OVP in Blundenz on the 21st of June
    1980, (cf V.N. 23.6.80); the 60-year
    celebrations of the Austrian constitution (cf
    V.N. 2.10.80); the 800th Anniversary of Styria
    (cf A.Z. 24.6.80); the Conference of OVP
    Mayors on the 21st of June 1980 in Innsbruck (cf
    V.N. 23.6.80 and W.Z. 22.6.80); the Symposium on
    the origins of the Austrian State and the
    "Contribution of the Federal Lander to the
    creation of the Federal Constitution" in
    Salzburg (cf S.N. and T.T. of 23 and 24.4.80);
    the "Foderalismus Enquette" of the Austrian
    Management Club in Salzburg, (cf S.N. 12.1.80,
    A.Z. 19.1.80 and Die Wirtschaft of 15th-21st of
    January, 1980); and the conference hosted
    jointly at the Salzburg Chamber of Trade on the

23.11.79 by the Salzburg Land Government and the Austrian Academy for Leadership Personnel, (cf W.Z. 24.11.79).

67. See S.N. 6.2.80 and 9.4.80.

68. See the relevant reports of the Institut fur Foderalismforschung as in footnote 43.

69. For the text see Informationsblatt des Institutes fur Foderalismusforschung 19.1.81 (Nr 1/1981), Innsbruck.

70. That is also the distinction elaborated in this author's as yet unfinished doctoral thesis entitled 'Federalism and Federation in Austria, Switzerland and the Federal Republic of Germany: A Comparative Study'.

71. W. H. Riker, 'Federalism', in F. Greenstein, & N. Polsby, Handbook of Political Science, Reading M.A. (Vol.5) p.156.

     See also W. H. Riker, Federalism, Origin, Operation, Significance, (Boston 1964) esp. pp.137-155; W. H. Riker, 'Six Books in Search of a Subject, or Does Federalism Exist and Does it Matter', in Comparative Politics, 11 (1969) pp.135-146; G. Sawer Modern Federalism (esp. Ch.9) and F. Neumann in A. W. MacMahon (Ed.) Federalism Mature and Emergent (New York 1955).

9. CONSTITUTIONAL REFORM IN SWITZERLAND:
    TASK-DISTRIBUTION, POLITICAL IDEALS AND
    FINANCIAL INTERESTS

    Ulrich Kloti and Kurt Nussli

Introduction

Switzerland has been a Federal state since 1848. The
basic ideas of federalism and subsidiarity are most
clearly expressed in Article 3 of the Federal
Constitution which defines the responsibilities:
'The cantons are sovereign as far as their
sovereignty is not restricted by the Federal
Constitution, and as sovereign cantons they exercise
all those rights which are not transferred to the
federal power'. The result of this constitutional
clause is a very complicated distribution of tasks at
the federal and cantonal levels, and at the level of
those communes which are - depending upon the canton
to which they belong - more or less autonomous. The
relations between the authorities of these three
levels have become very close and intertwined. And
as the State has had to accept new tasks and
responsibilities so the problems of task-distribution
have increased. The relative simplicity of the
earlier federal order has been transformed.
     Despite its undoubted merits, the Swiss
Confederation is widely acknowledged to be in need of
reform. Committees of experts which studied the
state structure and the decision-making process
agreed that a complete revision of the Federal
Constitution was necessary. In their view federalism
was in danger of eclipse. Even the most essential
parts of the basic idea of Swiss federalism had
already disappeared. During the 1970s this tide of
informed opinion led to specific reform proposals and
a parliamentary petition which provided the impetus
for a 'New Distribution of Tasks Between the Federal
Level and the Cantons'. The first package of
measures is due to be implemented in the mid-1980s.
Our purpose in this chapter is to evaluate these
recent efforts at major constitutional reform.
Consequently the first part of the analysis describes
the permanent changes which have occurred in the
conventional conception of Swiss federalism as a
result of the reform process, while the second part
examines the difficulties in the way of implementing
the reforms in the federation.

The Changing Concepts of Federalism and the Long Road
to Reform

In 1975 a study group appointed by the Federal
Department of Justice and Police published a report
entitled 'The Distribution of Tasks between the
Federal Level and the Cantons'. The group found the
reason for the problems of the federal welfare state
to be mainly a 'general crisis of performance and
coordination'. The increasing complexity of
responsibilities caused not only an awkward
overlapping of responsibilities but it also resulted
in gaps at the level of legislation and execution.
According to the report, the arbitrary distribution
of tasks between the federal level and the cantons no
longer guaranteed their effective implementation.
The smaller cantons, for example, were overburdened.
The federal level, however, was often unable to
participate in the implementation of tasks simply
because it lacked the responsibility. The report
alluded to an 'impenetrable entanglement of
coordinating committees and systems' which results
when there is a lack of congruence between the
interdependencies of tasks and the interdependencies
existing between the administrative units.
Task-realisation is endangered because the
task-distributing power and the financial power are
only partly congruent. Revenues are spent less
economically and the connection between the public
services and taxes is not made sufficiently clear to
the citizen.
    With this diagnosis the report suggested two
main remedies in order to achieve a redistribution of
tasks between the federal level and the cantons:
improved public services and support for cantonal
sovereignty. These goals, however, were not without
certain contradictions. For example, support for the
cantons involves disentangling the responsibilities
for the tasks and concentrating the tasks of the
federal level upon smaller areas. Yet an increase in
efficiency can probably be best achieved by further
centralisation and an appropriate coordination of
activities at the federal level. And these would be
activities which have so far been separated. The
report did not seek to favour one level at the
expense of the other, but it is clear that cantonal
sovereignty was the main priority. To this extent it
demonstrated little understanding of the demand for
disentanglement between the federal and cantonal
levels.

None the less the Federal Department of Justice and Police attempted to bring the difficult and controversial topic of a reform of the federal system into public debate. Their own document, 'Elements of a New Distribution of Tasks between the Federal level and the Cantons', sought to secure the future of the Cantons as important centres of democratically legitimised political decision-making by giving them adequate authority for sovereign legislation. Above all the document revealed a massive overload at all levels and in all policy areas. The remedy, it argued, lay in an increased coordination between the political units as well as more economical use of money and staff.

In 1978 the Conference of the Cantonal Finance Executives published a contribution to the debate entitled, 'A Model of a New Distribution of Tasks between the Federal level and the Cantons', in which the cantonal perspective was expressed. Their starting-point, not surprisingly, was the diminution of cantonal sovereignty. The document emphasised that since the maintenance of the federal order was an undisputed goal the imperative lay in comprehensive legislative authority for the cantons. It also stressed the need for a clear order of cooperation if an unambiguous federal structure of authority was to be re-established. This had particular implications for finance, especially as regards the restructuring of financial distribution from 'earmarked' to 'non-earmarked' contributions. These cantonal ideas concerning concrete regulations in particular policy areas thus demonstrated, for the first time, a desire for the disentanglement of task implementation.

This was confirmed by the cantons when in 1978 - aware of the model outlined by the cantonal Financial Executives - they responded to the propositions from the federal level. In their Vernehmlassungen (Consultation of interests) they emphasised the priority of policy goals over purely financial aims. They also reiterated the overriding need for consolidating the position of the cantons as autonomous centres of democratic decision-making in order to maintain and support the federal order. Almost unanimously the cantons rejected a new task-distribution which would transfer all legislation to the federal level and consign them to mere administration. They feared that in the long term such a system would threaten their sovereignty by converting them into virtual administrative districts of the federal level. Moreover, they

considered existing federal regulative activities to
be both too complex and too tangled, and they viewed
increased cantonal autonomy to be a partial remedy
for this. By the late 1970s, then, the cantons had
crystallised their preferences regarding the new
reform proposals: they preferred the traditional
distribution of tasks according to policy areas; they
welcomed a redistribution of responsibilities which
restricted the federal level to basic and general
legislation; they considered an increase in
inter-cantonal cooperation to be necessary; and some
of them expressed a desire for more participation in
federal policy-making.

In 1979 the Federal Department of Justice and
Police appointed a new committee to identify and
solve the growing problems of task complexity between
the federal and cantonal levels. In its initial
report based upon 'First Propositions' the committee
pointed out that task-distribution had always been
linked directly to the changing implementive
capacities of the participating units. When in the
1960s only the federal level had successfully
achieved its targets, entanglement was extended.
However, this position changed dramatically during
the early 1970s, thus excluding increased
centralisation as a feasible option in the goal of
task-redistribution between the federal and cantonal
levels. By the late 1970s the committee believed
that quite the reverse was necessary: cantonal
autonomy was to be supported and the efficiency of
federal implementation was to be improved by a
deliberate disentanglement of the policy areas.

Early in 1980 these recommendations were
presented to the cantonal governments, the political
parties and the various interested lobbies and
associations for another Consultation of interests.
The conclusions drawn from this were almost identical
to those agreed in 1978. Clearly, the time for
action had arrived. On 28 September 1981 the Federal
Council submitted a message to the Federal Parliament
on the first measures of task-redistribution. The
content of its message was obviously founded upon the
various preparatory and consultative negotiations of
the previous years. It recognised the preservation
of the development of the federal order as the
overriding objective, and underlined the need to
improve national services. But its emphasis upon the
sovereignty of the cantons and upon the need to
increase their autonomy was unmistakable. The
Cantons were to receive special assistance with their

existing tasks and their former responsibilities were
to be restored. Federal interference with cantonal
task-implementation was to be consciously reduced and
deliberate efforts were to be made to avoid the
uneconomic overlapping and administrative
inefficiencies of federal-cantonal interdependence.
Political cooperation rather than administrative
entanglement was one of the guiding principles.
Concerning finance, the Federal Council was
especially categorical. The existing procedures of
the subvention system were too bureaucratic. They
led to an unacceptable overlapping of
responsibilities which were as uneconomic as they
were hidebound. Worse than this they stifled
cantonal initiatives. In summary, the central
recommendation of the Federal Council was the
disentanglement and the simplification of the
federal-cantonal relations.

The Federal Parliament's reaction to these broad
aims was overwhelmingly favourable. Both
parliamentary chambers are currently active in
efforts to translate these goals into action.
Indeed, the committee-president of the Lower House,
Standerat Binder, who had formerly been instrumental
in pushing for reform, was especially enthusiastic
about these proposals. He pinpointed five primary
goals as crucial. First, the principal of
subsidiarity is cardinal to the general support for
Swiss federalism. Secondly, the various tasks are to
be disentangled efficiently without reducing the
level of public services. Thirdly, it is important
to recognise that the cantons will have to solve the
same problems in different ways. Fourthly, the
present Swiss State structure has to be simplified
from the standpoints of economy, democracy, and
intelligibility, and must be brought closer to the
citizen. Finally, the financial arrangements between
the federal and cantonal jurisdictions must be
modified by more generous considerations for the
cantons.

These primary objectives amounted to a strategy
of wholesale decentralisation. However, the Federal
Council supported it, knowing that it was
representative of a wide-ranging body of opinion.
Only the left-wing political parties opposed the
general trend of opinion, fearing that it might mean
a return to the old Confederate Union and that the
cantons would be incapable of implementing what had
become federal responsibilities. Their position,
however, remained isolated, But we must not assume
that certain striking differences of opinion did not

exist among those who advocated new models of task-distribution in Switzerland during the 1980s. Indeed, there were many significant differences which exposed divergent views of Swiss Federalism and had serious implications for the nature of the federal state.

A Change of Preferences: From Coordination To Disentanglement

If we examine the nature of the reform proposals since 1975 there have been a number of significant changes in emphasis between several broad objectives. Both the general ideas which underpin the reforms and the particular strategies implied to achieve them have been transformed. Indeed, many of the original goals and strategies have been completely overturned. The 1975 report, for example, considered the main problems of Swiss federation to be due to the lack of cantonal and national efficiency. There was a general crisis of performance and coordination, and it was assumed that only a very few large policy areas could be handled by the cantons alone. By 1981, however, the Federal Council was suggesting the contrary position. It argued that existing levels of efficiency in the national, cantonal and communal structures were far higher than the previous twenty years, and that the cantons, in particular, had achieved more manoeuvrability for realising their goals than the Federal level. Indeed, the cantons had revealed a remarkable ability to fulfil new and extended tasks. The Federal Council clearly felt uncomfortable both about increasing entanglement and declining cantonal independence.

This shift of emphasis changed the goals of reform. The original three goals - support of the Federal order, improved national public services and economical federal task-implementation - had previously been accorded similar importance but this had altered significantly by 1981. The cantons had narrowed their objectives to one: support of the Federal order. This was the result of their growing identification of a stable Federal order with enhanced cantonal sovereignty. It was accompanied, too, by a reassessment of the various forms of entanglement. The 1975 report had been quite critical of strategies of disentanglement whereas the first propositions of 1979 had acknowledged their validity, and both the Federal Council and the Parliament concurred with this in 1981.

Even the goal of disentanglement itself was not immune to changing perceptions. During the reform discussions the models of task-distribution were also subject to re-evaluation. The 1975 report attempted to link new forms of task-distribution to general task-implementation at federal and cantonal levels. Its desire to underline the connections between certain policy areas, however, was blunted when the Federal Council returned to support for the cantons. By concentrating upon the distribution of tasks according to policy areas, the Federal Council sought to allocate large policy areas to them (as states) for autonomous regulation and financing. Against this kind of support, all rival models of task-distribution lost their competitive edge.

In similar vein the various forms of cooperation between federal and cantonal levels were also subjected to re-evaluation. Whereas the 1975 report had contemplated the possibility of new forms of cooperation in order to attain parity between the entanglement of tasks and juridical responsibilities, and even toyed with the idea of establishing collective decision-making bodies for joint tasks akin to the West German model, the drift of official opinion by 1981 was in the opposite direction. The Federal Council demanded the liberation of the cantons from what it considered to be the unnecessary influence of the federal level. Furthermore, it linked some cases of uneconomical overlapping and administrative inefficiency directly to those tasks which involved federal-cantonal cooperation. The signs were clear: reform had come to mean not more but less federal-cantonal cooperation. Even in the realm of financial relations the picture had changed. The financial implications of such a shift towards the cantons were obvious - it entailed greater fiscal obligations. However, no such recognition was publicly endorsed either by the Parliament or the Federal Council. The cantons, it appeared, had achieved their overriding goal - increased autonomy with the minimum of financial burdens.

In summary, then, there has been a major change in the paradigm of reform and in its strategic implications. An improvement of the general federal performance together with new forms of cooperation, a redistribution of responsibilities and a new financial order has given way to support for the older traditional notion of cantonal autonomy in its conventional forms and patterns. Entanglement with central federal coordination has succumbed to disentanglement with decentralised cantonal autonomy. The wheel appears to have turned full circle.

The Dominance Of The Status Quo ?

The redistribution of tasks between the federal and
cantonal levels has from the outset given rise not
only to the development of conceptual ideas, but also
to concrete propositions. In the federal documents
of 1975 and 1977 many new suggestions have been made
which have wide-ranging policy implications. They
deal with the new distribution of tasks as well as
with the regulations concerning finance. These
propositions were the subject of critical evaluation
by the cantons which, in turn, added their own
suggestions. Let us now examine some of these
proposals and comment upon their implications.

Redistributions of Responsibilities: Only Weak Decentralisation

The original and paramount goal of the propositions
made by the federal level was an improved
coordination of federal and cantonal activities.
Most of the 22 suggestions made in the two documents
of 1975 and 1977 concerning the redistribution of
responsibilities start with an urgent emphasis upon
increased coordination. Subsequently in 17 cases
either a transfer of authority to the federal level
is demanded or at least a coordinating and
harmonising intervention by the federal level
(especially via basic or general legislation) is
considered necessary. In contrast only a handful of
federal propositions contemplate more authority for
the cantons.

Not surprisingly, the cantons viewed things
differently. Only 13 of their 35 propositions
intended to increase federal influence while the
other 22 amounted to clear restrictions on federal
activities. These competing perspectives are sharply
focused in the propositions concerning
decentralisation. Here seven further suggestions
were added to the single proposal of the federal
level. And they are especially underlined in
regulations concerning entanglement between the
federal and cantonal levels. Typically cantonal
suggestions have a predominant orientation towards
decentralisation whereas federal perspectives favour
centralisation.

Notwithstanding these important differences, the
federal level and the cantons have concurring
opinions about several tasks. For example, five
suggestions made by the federal level and tending
towards decentralisation have been accepted by the

cantons while another six of the 17 proposals advocating centralisation have also been agreed. In three cases the suggestions made by the federal level are virtually identical to those propounded by the cantons and in five other examples a discernible support among some cantons exists for federal priorities. Upon reflection, then, it is remarkable that so little has been achieved to date in the area of task redistribution. Our discussion so far has been somewhat general and it is useful to look at some concrete examples concerning federal-cantonal task relationships.

With regard to the actual redistribution of tasks, only one proposition, strictly speaking, has been put into practice, namely, the renunciation of a federally regulated domestic education. It is also true that a redistribution of responsibilities has been achieved with regard to the scholarship system, but this occurred only in the course of the reform process. It was not a discrete proposition. Originally it was agreed that the federal level was to stipulate minimum standards for scholarship in a general law, but this idea was ultimately omitted from the first package of task redistribution. Instead it was decided that the federal level would regulate only the question of juridical residence in this matter - all materially essential responsibilities were attributed to the cantons.

Four further propositions can be added to this example, albeit that they have been only partly effected. These are as follows:

1. Extension of the federal responsibility concerning the law of research.

2. Federal regulation of the beginning of the school year within the context of general legislation related to primary schools.

3. Restriction of federal responsibilities to only general instructions concerning the laws of city and physical planning and of environment preservation.

4. Restriction of federal responsibilities to only general instructions concerning the law of wild fauna preservation and hunting.

Of the other propositions only six have been accepted within the second package referred to earlier. With only one exception they intend to place restrictions on the federal level regarding both basic and general legislation. About 40 suggestions, however, were eliminated during the preparatory negotiating process. It is significant that 27 of these suggestions sought either a redistribution of competences in favour of the federal level or at least support for increased federal intervention to the effect of coordinating general regulations. Only three of these survived: the cantons effectively nullified 24 of these 27 propositions. But it should also be noted that among the eliminated suggestions were several that provided for restrictions and renunciations of federal responsibilities. The concessions were not all one-way traffic.

Most of those propositions which suggested centralisation or centralised entanglement had already run into difficulties during the consultation of interests in 1978. For example, proposals designed to attribute a leading position within the welfare service to the federal level and the idea of regulating the basic principles of penal law within the federal law met strong opposition, as did the notion of a federally centralised coordination of hospital planning. In contrast many propositions concerning decentralisation or decentralised disentanglement passed the consultation of interests, but foundered during the course of the reform process. This occurred, for example, with the renunciation of federally regulated teaching of sport in primary schools and with the shaping of regional economic support as a collective task at federal and cantonal levels. Surprisingly enough, among the many propositions which failed to survive were some that had actually been presented in identical fashion by both the federal level and the cantons, and had received positive evaluation by the cantons during the 1978 consultation of interests, such as the cantonalisation of house-building support.

The general implications of this activity can be reduced to a single clear judgement: a concrete redistribution of authority has not occurred. Only a weak decentralisation has emerged. Nevertheless, it is striking that the propositions aimed at a decentralisation of responsibilities, or at least at a restriction of federal intervention, seem to have had the best chance of success compared with those suggestions tending in the reverse direction. In most successful cases this has not occurred in the context of the first package; rather it has been either a development arising outside the actual task redistribution or, as it were, a rennaissance of former propositions within a second package of task redistribution. This judgement becomes even more valid when we learn of the clear predominance of propositions concerning decentralisation among all those propositions accepted for the second package.

New Financial Regulations : The Federal Level Will Continue To Pay

In contrast to the propositions concerning the redistribution of responsibilities, the federal and cantonal suggestions regarding financial regulations are distributed somewhat differently among the three categories 'centralisation', 'entanglement' and 'decentralisation'. From the federal level standpoint the overriding concern has been to reduce financial responsibilities. Twelve out of eighteen suggestions were intent on transferring these responsibilities to the cantons or at least to reduce the contributions either partly or wholly. Shared financing was scarcely mentioned and propositions designed to shift the entire financial responsibilities to the federal level were restricted to two noteworthy exceptions: the assumption of state contributions to annuity insurance and to disability insurance; and the complete assumption of both costs and maintenance of the national road network.

In comparison, half of the cantonal propositions concerning finance implied a decentralisation of responsibilities, but they were only partly congruent with federal preferences. Indeed, the federal level and the cantons agreed upon only two issues: the renunciation of federal subventions for primary schools and the renunciation of federal contributions to house-building. As regards shared financing the cantons were also at variance with the federal level; they either adhered to existing arrangements or sought to extend them. Clearly, the focus of our attention in this area is upon the overall tendency of the negotiations to be about the decentralisation of financial responsibilities.

Nine out of 24 propositions directed towards reducing federal financial responsibilities were discussed and agreed; two more are to be debated in the second package. The consequences of these discussions are the renunciation of federal contributions to: educational establishments;

domestic education studies; food and disease control; practical training of hospital staff; building and management of homes for the aged; and sports facilities. Furthermore, some federal contributions have been renounced for civil defence and cantonal scholarships, while assistance for refugees becomes one of the rare shared responsibilities. All of these are propositions concerning decentralisation which have only been developed during the course of the reform process and successfully implemented in the first package of task redistribution. But we must not overlook the fact that many proposals concerning decentralisation have failed. Among the 13 propositions that were neither realised within the first package nor despatched to the second one are, notably, those which had already been rejected by virtually every canton during the consultation of interests in 1978. Overall, however, those suggestions for a transfer of financial responsibilities to the cantons - indicating decentralist impulses - have been relatively successful.

Correspondingly, suggestions in the reverse direction have been less successful. Only one of the seven propositions of the federal level and the cantons has become a resolution (annuity insurance), but a later proposal to transfer the costs of standardised civil defence material to the federal level did ultimately succeed. In contrast, the renunciation of cantonal contributions to disability insurance, mentioned earlier, has been despatched to the second package, while the question of transferring the financial responsibilities of costs and maintenance of the national road network to the federal level also ultimately failed.

Propositions concerning entanglement are different. These have, in practice, been much more straightforward. Whereas only one out of ten suggestions have been realised in the first package of task redistribution - the continued investment contributions for penal institutions - two further proposals were successfully agreed outside the actual task redistribution process: federal contributions to city and physical planning; and federal subventions to cantonal expenditures for road construction. Indeed, six propositions were accepted for the second package, among them such key activities as federal participation in the financing of cantonal universities and federal contributions to agriculture. In the course of the reform process further suggestions concerning shared financing were

added and successfully implemented. Such new
categories are, for example, federal contributions to
model experiments in penal policy, public civil
defence buildings, sports associations and improved
housing conditions in mountain areas. By contrast,
only a handful of proposals concerning entanglement
could be viewed as having failed. The outstanding
tendency in the new financial regulations, then, is
to effect a transfer of responsibilities to the
cantons, a trend also reflected in the propositions
presented in the preparatory process of the second
package for a task redistribution. But there has
also been a marked shift towards shared or mixed
financing. From being scarcely mentioned by the
federal level, it has been increasingly incorporated
into the new financial regulations by cantonal
insistence. In total, 15 propositions fall into the
two categories 'decentralisation' and 'entanglement',
but only four into the category 'centralisation'.
This clearly underlines the restricted financial
opportunities of the federal level. However, the
anticipated reduction in shared financing which we
would expect from a genuine disentanglement programme
of reform is also conspicuously absent.

Conclusion: Almost Everything Remains As It Was

What are we to make of these complex reform
proposals ? Clearly, the difficult and protracted
redistribution of tasks between the federal level and
the cantons is expressive of the need to reform the
Swiss federal state. In the course of the reform
process innumerable propositions were presented,
sometimes including quite far-reaching intrusions
into the established patterns of task distribution
and financial regulation. During the reform process,
now lasting over ten years, previously adversarial
views have largely disappeared. The questions of
federal state efficiency and economical task
implementation are no longer the priority goals of a
new task distribution. Increased cooperation between
the federal level and the cantons, and the
appropriate entanglement of state activities which
have formerly been separated and uncoordinated are no
longer discussed. Instead the focal point now is
simply the maintenance of the federal order, meaning
unilateral disentanglement in the sense of a
redistribution of responsibilities in favour of the
cantons.

This change in the original position is also reflected in the concrete propositions for task redistribution. In the beginning the federal level decisively emphasised improved coordination which, in many instances, would have required extended federal responsibilities. Today, in contrast, most of the newly accepted propositions for the second package of a task redistribution tend towards increased cantonal responsibilities. This is especially significant if we pause to reflect upon the major trend of centralisation within other federations. Perhaps only Canada can be earmarked as an example similar to Switzerland in this respect.

Returning briefly to financial relationships between the federal level and the cantons, the overall impression of a shift from centralising entanglement to decentralising disentanglement is only partially accurate. While the majority of suggestions accepted in the first package demand a reduction of federal services, the number of suggestions accepted for the second package in favour of continued shared financing equals the number of propositions for demanding a redistribution of the financial burden on to the cantons. This is probably because disentanglement ideas relating to the federation as a whole, despite the rhetorical efforts, nearly always lag behind financial priorities. From the perspective of purely financial priorities, disentanglement appears less attractive even if ideas related to the federation as a whole suggest the contrary. This is because in most cases such disentanglement leads to the renunciation of federal contributions which, correspondingly, increases cantonal budgets. In general, then, the notion of a massive shift of the financial burden to the disadvantage of the cantons has had a significant braking effect upon the impulses for major reform. Hence disentanglement of responsibilities in the sense of genuine decentralisation is quite clearly restricted in the Swiss federation.

Regarding both the policy content and the performance capacity of the federation, it is undoubtedly unsatisfactory that, on the one hand, a decentralisation of authority is demanded but realised only in a minor degree, while, on the other hand, shared financing is maintained to a large degree and, consequently, federal money is continually used for the financing of what are

cantonal tasks. This does not, however, come as a
real surprise. It is clearly the direct result of
strong cantonal influences. Without their agreement
the federal level can neither succeed in the
effective redistribution of responsibilities
concerning the rights and obligations of the
constituent units of the federation nor can it
seriously reduce federal contributions to the
cantons. We thus come to the conclusion that in the
quest for legislative authority in the reform process
the cantons clearly won the competition. They
tenaciously defended their member-state sovereignty
and were successful against centralising trends.
Hence, even if the current decentralising
disentanglement does not adequately fulfill the prior
expectations concerning the disentanglement
programme, the threat of centralised entanglement has
been effectively nullified.

In conclusion, then, the redistribution of tasks
between the federal level and the cantons
demonstrates that federalism as a principle of
political organisation remains the dominant idea
governing the reform and survival of the Swiss
federation. But the Swiss example cannot be used as
evidence to support a theory of centralising
convergence in federations. The fact that
federations are not immune to centralising trends
does not imply that every federation tends inevitably
and irreversibly towards centralisation. In
Switzerland, at least, everything remains almost as
it was.

REFERENCES

Official Documents

BERICHT "Aufgabenteilung Bund - Kantone" vom 20.
August 1975.

Aufgabenteilung zwischen Bund und Kantonen:
GRUNDZUEGE des Ist-Zustandes 15.1.1977.

ELEMENTE einer Neuverteilung der Aufgaben zwischen
Bund und Kantonen 21. August 1977.

FINANZIELLE BEZIEHUNGEN zwischen Bund und Kantonen,
9. September 1977.

BERICHT der Expertenkommission fur die Vorbereitung
einer Totalrevision der Bundesverfassung, 1977.

ZUSAMMENSTELLUNG der Ergebnisse des
Vernehmlassungsverfahrens zur Neuverteilung der
Aufgaben zwischen Bund und Kantonen 1977/1978,
September 1978.

MODELL fur eine Neuverteilung der Aufgaben zwischen
Bund und Kantonen, Bern 1978.

ERSTE VORSCHLAEGE zur Neuverteilung der Aufgaben
zwischen Bund und Kantonen, 31. Juli 1979.

ERGAENZUNGSBERICHT "Verkehr" und Finanzausgleich",
November 1979.

ZUSAMMENSTELLUNG der Ergebnisse des
Vernehmlassungsverfahrens zur Neuverteilung der
Aufgaben zwischen Bund und Kantonen, (1980), 1981.

BOTSCHAFT uber erste Massnahmen zur Neuverteilung der
Aufgaben zwischen Bund und Kantonen, 28. September
1981.

ZWEITES PAKET von Vorschlagen zur Neuverteilung der
Aufgaben zwischen Bund und Kantonen, Januar 1984.

Secondary Sources

A. Benz, 'Zur Dynamik der foderativen
Staatsorganisation', in: Politische
Vierteljahresscchrift, 25 Jg., Jeft 1, (April 1984).

S. Bieri, Fiscal Federalism in Switzerland, (Canberra
1979).

W. Bussmann, Attempts to Reform Swiss Federalism,
(forthcoming).

T. Fleiner, The Concept of the Constitution of
Switzerland, Kleine Institutsreihe, Nr.7, (Riehen
1983).

U. Kloeti, and K. Nuessli, Erste Vorschlage zur
Neuverteilung der Aufgaben zwischen Bund und Kanton,
Kleine Studien zur Politischen Wissenschaft, (Zurich
1981).

Kloti and Nussli, Foderalismus zwischen Rationalitat
und Selbstblockierung. Ein Beitrag zur Theorie und
Empirie der Politikverflechung in der Schweiz,
(forthcoming).

W. Reinmann, Judicial Modes of Decentralisation:
Distribution, Delegation and Use of Competences,
Prepared for the Second National Congress of the
French Political Science Association, (Grenoble
1984).

F. Lehner, The Political Economy of Interlocked
Federalism: A Comparative View of Germany and
Switzerland, (Bochum 1982).

K. Nuessli, Foderalismus in der Schweiz: Konzepte ,
Indikatoren, Daten, (forthcoming).

U. Schmid, and U. Kloeti, Interlocked Federalism in
Switzerland: How does it Affect Bureaucracy ?
Prepared for the Workshop on 'Comparative Federalism
and Federation in Western Europe', ECPR Salzburg
1984.

H. Stalder, 'Unternehmen Aufgabenteilung', in O. K.
Kaufmann, A. Koller, A. Riklin, Die Zukunft von Staat
und Wirtschaft in der Schweiz, Festschrift zum 60.
Geburtstag von Bundesrat Kurt Furgler, 332 S. (Zurich
1984).

10. THE AMBIVALENT ROLE OF THE BUNDESRAT IN THE WEST GERMAN FEDERATION

Tony Burkett

Introduction

The nexus between federalism and parliamentarianism within the West German model is one in which the all-pervading formalism that invests the constitutional model has been forced into an uncomfortable accommodation with the realities of the party conflict as well as the encroachment of the federal government over the constituent provinces. We shall focus on the evolved relationships between the Federal Government and the lander at that point where checks on federal competence are exercised by the constituent provinces. This is not to say that the crucial, interpretative and controlling role played by the Federal Constitutional Court (FCC) in regulating the balance of power between the federal centre and the lander will be ignored or that its importance is not acknowledged. An examination of the legislative checks and balances within the West German federation is rather intended to show how developing political practice has been forced to conform to the demands of constitutional formalism, affecting at the same time the role of the Court as well as the parliamentary system. The reader's attention is drawn to the detailed and authoritative examination of the FCC by Philip Blair, now the standard work in English and one which achieves the relative miracle of leading the Anglo-Saxon mind through the maze of legal complexities which are the very heart of German constitutionalism.[1]

The Origins of West German Federalism

West German federalism had its origins in the unification in 1871 of the separate principalities and states, most of which had participated in the customs union, 'Zollverein', of the 1840s. The 1871 Constitution scarcely followed the federalist principles put into practice a century earlier in the United States either in form or spirit. The system was a reflection of both Prussian domination and the disparate administrative, legal and political structures of the constituent states. The principal departure in form from that of the USA was that the German model introduced a parliamentary system, albeit a rudimentary one. The executive was scarcely responsible to parliament, ministers nominated by the Chancellor in the awesome figure of Bismarck were crown appointees, reflecting the domination of Prussia and its monarch. Checks and balances were rudimentary both in terms of the powers of the federal parliament and of the relationship between the constituent states, (lander), and the federation.

Rather was the adoption of federation an administrative and political convenience. It allowed for disparate administrative structures and practices already established in the constituent states to be maintained and with them the maintenance of the existing and pre-unification political structures. The period 1871-1914 left federal traditions that had failed to reduce Prussia's hegemony and to achieve national integration. Local separatisms remained as marked as they had been before 1871. The parliamentary model was weak and ineffective as a check on the executive.

Following their defeat in the First World War, both Germany and Austria adopted revised forms of federation in which the influence of the jurist, Hans Kelsen, was particularly marked. As a reflex against the absolutism of the Prussian monarchy and the Bismarckian traditions of weak parliamentarianism, the balance between the executive and the legislature was tipped heavily in the latter's favour. The framers of the Weimar Constitution of 1919 retained the parliamentary model within a federal political system, strengthening both the powers of the legislature over the executive but also those of the federation vis-a-vis the provinces which were also reduced in number. Both reforms were to prove counter-productive. Parliamentary control over the weakened Chancellor was to lead eventually to the exercise of presidential emergency powers, a republican reversion to the spirit if not the forms of 1871. Strengthening the powers of the federation was no less critical in undermining the Weimar Republic. Reducing the powers of land initiative served to deepen the resentments of local politicians especially in conservative provinces against the new republicans who had now replaced the aristocratic nominees of the Kaiser in Berlin. It was these local resentments which helped to maintain local separatisms yet again and which through the 'pure' PR voting system used in Weimar were reflected in the splintered party system that was a root cause of parliamentary and executive instability in the Republic. It was both local separatisms and resentments of the federal government as much as hatred of the 'November Criminals' upon which the Nazis were able to build the voting strength post-1928.[2] The Nazis were also able to exploit the federal system after 1930 when they used their strength in some land governments as a launching pad for their assault on the Republic as a whole.[3]

Ironically enough it was as a reaction to Hitler's centralised state that the Parliamentary Council, under pressure from the occupying Americans and French, reintroduced a federal system in the Basic Law of 1949. There appears to have been little consideration of the fact that it was through the exploitation of the federal system that the Nazis were able to weaken and destroy the Weimar Republic.

In the three-quarters of a century since unification therefore the German federal model had succeeded in one broad aim shared by all federal systems, namely, that of local autonomy. But it was at the expense of the other aim of federalism: the achievement of national political integration. And there had been another casualty - German parliamentarianism.

Although the West German federation follows some of the configurations associated with Commonwealth federations, like other West European federations (Austria especially) it weds parliamentarianism to the federal model. Where it and Austrian federation part company from almost all other forms of federation is in their division of powers.

Federalism ? Or Cooperative Federalism ? Or Executive-Legislative Federalism ? Or Administrative Devolution ?

In his first chapter Blair sets out the German federal model with a clarity and economy that are deceptive in the light of the complexities of the legal-formalism which follow.[4] He takes the opportunity to sketch out the principal features of the German system and deals with a central problem which confronts the student of federation. Is it a federation ? His central conclusion is that it is a matter of opinion. Unlike another English specialist, Nevil Johnson,[5] who entertains no doubts, or K. C. Wheare[6] who has nothing else, Blair suggests that the German model is best considered for its uniqueness and thereafter depicts it as 'cooperative federalism' - an epithet commonly used by German authors often defensively. 'Defensively' because the system has been dismissed as not being a federal one by American scholars as well as Wheare.

The phrase 'executive-legislative' federalism was
first coined by Peter Merkl in 1959[7] and is a more
pertinent phrase than 'administrative devolution'
though not totally satisfactory. Merkl's article
dealt with the crucial and unique departure of German
federation from most other models by concentrating on
the division of powers between the Federation (Bund)
and Lander, what Johnson refers to as the 'horizontal
division' of powers,[8] in contrast to the USA system
which is 'vertical'. In fact the Basic Law divides
powers vertically as well as horizontally.

Article 73 of the Basic Law assigns certain
powers exclusively to the Bund (e.g. defence, foreign
affairs, citizenship, currency and communications).
The federation has exclusive powers to legislate in
these matters and executive power to administer such
laws (Article 87). Residual powers are by inference
a matter for the legislative and executive
competences of the Lander. In this respect therefore
there is a 'vertical' division of power.

However, the number of residual powers left for
the Lander to exercise are minimalised by the
category of 'concurrent powers' (Article 74). It is
this catalogue of powers and how they are exercised
which contains the horizontal division in practice.
Article 74 lists a wide, detailed and large number of
legislative powers called 'concurrent' and Article 72
devolves the power to legislate on these matters 'as
long as, and to the extent that, the Federation does
not exercise its right to legislate'. In almost
every case the Federation has exercised that right.
However, it is the Lander which execute these federal
laws 'as a matter of their own concern' (Article 83).

Thus this 'horizontal division' of powers
between legislative and executive competences applied
as it is to the wide catalogue detailed in Article 74
is what gives the German federation its unique form.
And since the federation has made full use of its
right to legislate in the area of these concurrent
powers it is at this point that the German federation
departs from other models and where the relationship
between the federal centre and the constituent units
is critical. For although the principle established
here is that the federation legislates and the Lander
administer, the spirit of 'cooperative federalism' or
'executive- legislative federalism' is reinforced
later where the Basic Law (Article 91) allows 'Joint
Tasks' between the two spheres of government.
Assigning legislation to the Federation and
administration of federal laws to the Lander,
intended to divide and balance power between the two

spheres of government, is in fact a means of coupling
rather than separation albeit one in which the
tensions between the federal centre and the
constituent units are focused and expressed.

Before turning to examine this particular focus,
however, Wheare's dismissive appraisal of the West
German federation as mere 'administrative devolution'
can be considered and itself dismissed on the grounds
that it misses the point. It is true that the power
of administration is devolved on the Lander, but by
the constitution and not by the Federation. It is
not devolved duties which the Lander exercise, but
devolved power. On this subject Blair makes an
interesting point in respect of Northern Ireland
pre-1972 where the provincial government had powers
'considerably in excess of those of the members
states of some federations'. That Stormont was
stripped of those powers by Westminster indicates the
constitutional primacy of the Mother of Parliaments
which had only 'leased' some legislative and
administrative powers to the province. The Federal
Government in Bonn, and hence the Bundestag, enjoys
no such constitutional primacy and thus the phrase
'parliamentary sovereignty' is meaningless in a
German context. Wheare seems to have overlooked the
crucial point: that there is a world of difference
between 'administrative devolution' and
'constitutionally-conferred administrative
devolution'. Nor should it be forgotten that the
Lander possess some exclusive legislative competence
over their residual powers (police, education,
cultural matters and the right to insert local
provisions into federal 'framework' laws).[16] The
Lander also have exclusive control of certain tax
revenues and the right to share certain taxes with
the Federation (Article 106).

What seems finally to dispose of Wheare's
cursory and grudging dismissal of West German
federation (a case based largely on the grounds that
it does not conform to his model) are the rights
which the Lander enjoy with respect to federal
legislation, to the federal budget and to the
appointment of half the members of the Federal
Constitutional Court. The instrument by which those
powers are exercised is the Federal Council
(Bundesrat). It is here that the ambivalence of the
relationship between the two spheres of government is
located. That ambivalence, suggested above, shrouds
and obscures the division of the balance of powers
between these spheres. Indeed, this
institutionalisation of Land participation in the

federal competence of legislation is a device whose
existence may give Wheare a leg to stand on after
all. Can one really talk of a system being federal
when it permits one sphere of government to
participate in and (as we shall see) exercise a veto
over the competence of another ? For the Bundesrat
is not an elected body like the American Senate which
is constitutionally detached from the states its
members represent. The Bundesrat is a confederal
chamber consisting of representatives of Land
governments, not Land electorates or even the Land
parliaments. Thus while it exists to articulate
Lander rights over federal law, using where it will
its veto and powers to amend, the Bundesrat exists
not only as a check on federal government but also as
its partner in the processing of federal law.

   At the same time it should be noted that the
federal government for its part has the right to
supervise the administration of federal law by the
Lander, a system of control not exercised through the
machinery of the Bundestag but by the bureaucracies
of federal ministries.[11] Thus this division of
powers, almost unique to the West German
federation,[12] is hedged about with checks and
balances focussed largely within the Federal Council,
where Land interests can be deployed to veto and
amend federal government legislation and where the
federal budget is subjected to the same processes.
Furthermore, this constitutionally prescribed
relationship between Bund and Lander has undergone
some changes not envisaged by the framers of the
Basic Law and which reflect and are a manifestation
of the centripetal tendencies that are evident within
the West German federal system.

The Bundesrat

Within the deliberations of the Parliamentary Council
there was a minority which advanced the 'Senate'
principle for the Federal Council. This would have
gone against German traditions and towards the
American one by having the Council directly elected
on a Land basis on the lines of the American Senate
although with the more heavily populated states
having more members than the smaller ones. However,
the traditionalist view triumphed and the Bundesrat's
composition today reflects the earlier practice of a
membership drawn from the ministers of the Lander.[13]
Thus the principle is one of Land government
participation not Land participation as the Basic Law
lays down. The 41 representatives from the ten

provinces (which are given 5, 4 or 3 places according to population size) represent Lander government interests. Which ministers actually appear at any one plenary session of the Bundesrat will usually depend on the matter under consideration. Each Land delegation casts its votes as a block and it is practice that the decision of how that bloc vote is cast is determined by the cabinet of the Land and not its local diet (Landtag).

The reasoning behind the existence of the Bundesrat is based on the federal division of power; its membership also reflects the role which the Lander play in administering federal law. That being so, the opinion of the Lander and the expertise of their bureaucracies are reflected in the legislative role of the House. To begin with, the Bundesrat is allowed to initiate legislation but has used this power comparatively rarely – an average of 5% of all bills since 1949 were Bundesrat bills.[14] It has the right to examine and comment on all bills proposed by the Federal Government before they are submitted to the Bundestag, as well as that of 'filling in' federal framework law. Finally the Federal Council is responsible for examining what in Britain is called 'delegated legislation' (a function which the Bundestag does not have).

The Bundesrat's processing of legislation follows the pattern of the Bundestag's practice: three readings and a Committee stage. The power exercised by the Bundesrat is determined by the type of bill proposed, i.e. whether it is a so-called Enfaches Gesetz (simple law) or a Zustimmungsgesetz (a law that needs consent). (See Figure 1)

The diagram shows that the interplay of Bundestag and Bundesrat in legislation is very complicated and has many stages, not least being the part played by the Vermittlungsausschuss (Mediation Committee). To explain the essence of the procedure: the Bundestag has either a suspensive or an absolute veto in federal legislation according to the type of law. In both cases it is necessary to use the Mediation Committee to carry through the respective legislation. For this purpose the constitution provides for a body of twenty-two members, who make up the Vermittlungsausschuss. The Bundestag delegates eleven members according to party strengths in the House, and the Bundesrat sends the other eleven members, one member for each Land including West Berlin. This committee comes into operation when there is dissent over a law. In cases where the Bundesrat is objecting to a simple law it has sole

appeal to the committee; in case of an absolute veto
both the federal government and the Bundestag have
the right to invoke the committee. There are four
possible recommendations:

- a change of the disputed parts of the bill,
- a scrapping of the bill altogether,
- a proposal to leave it unchanged,
- no proposal because an agreement could not be
  reached.

Various deliberations in the Bundesrat and the
Bundestag will follow.[15] If the Bundesrat is not
willing to follow the proposals of the Mediation
Committee it will apply its veto. In cases of simple
laws the Bundestag can overrule this veto with the
same majority with which the Bundesrat applied it.
Where a simple majority of the Bundesrat was in
favour of the veto, a simple majority of the
Bundestag is enough to reject the veto and finally
pass the law; but if it was a two-thirds majority
veto then the Bundestag will need a two-thirds
majority in order to overrule the veto and carry
through the legislation. If it is a
Zustimmungsgesetz and the Bundesrat cannot accept the
mediation proposal it has the power (after several
additional stages of mediation) finally to reject the
bill. In that case not even a unanimous vote of the
Bundestag could pass the law.
     From this short explanation of the federal
influence in legislation there follow two important
observations: clearly, the question whether a law is
a 'simple' one or one needing the Bundesrat's consent
is of extreme importance. Unfortunately the Basic
Law does not contain a comprehensive grouping of all
possible legislative issues. The respective
regulations are scattered all over the Grundgesetz.
Most significant is Article 79 (2), whereby all
amendments of the constitution require the
Bundesrat's consent, and Article 84: if laws have to
be executed by the Lander on their own responsibility
the Bundesrat has the power of absolute veto as
described above. This has wide implications for the
number of laws which can only be enacted with
Bundesrat approval since the vast majority of federal
laws is administered by the Lander.
     The Federal Constitutional Court (which has to
decide on the nature of a law in cases of doubt) has
tended to increase the power of the Bundesrat by
ruling that the existence of just one
'consent-needing' clause in a bill necessitates the

Bundesrat's consent to the whole bill. Mainly because of the breadth of this interpretation the actual proportions of Zustimmungsgesetze in relation to simple laws amounts to 60:40. Originally it was intended to restrict their number to about 10% of total legislation. This low figure can no longer be regarded as valid after the decision of the Federal Constitutional Court that amendments to an existing consent-needing law are automatically subject to the Bundesrat's approval no matter what their actual content is.

The second, and politically crucial, problem is raised by the existence of opposing majorities in the two houses. Until 1969 - the beginning of the Social-Liberal coalition - the CDU/CSU held power in the Bundestag and also had a majority in the Bundesrat. Thus, dissent over bills was rare, although one must always bear in mind that 'equal party majorities' in both institutions do not necessarily guarantee perfect harmony. After all, the Bundesrat is a medium in which the interests of the Lander rather than parties ought to be brought into the federal decision-making process. The interests of a CDU-delegation from Schleswig-Holstein and an SPD-delegation from Bremen in securing the livelihood of the North Sea fishermen are much more likely to be congruent than those of the same North German CDU-delegates and their Bavarian colleagues who want to subsidise their small mountain farmers from the same funds. Nevertheless, a CDU/CSU-majority in the Bundesrat is very unlikely to make life difficult for its party comrades in the Bundestag by obstructing major political plans for legislation and thus possibly bringing about an election defeat or damaging the party's public image of unity.

After 1969 an SDP/FDP-coalition in the Bundestag was confronted with a conservative party majority in the Bundesrat. More than ever before the Bundesrat became an instrument of party conflict and occasionally formed an effective opposition to the majority in the Bundestag. The number of vetoes from the Bundesrat increased considerably and many of the reform policies of the Brandt-era were defeated in the Bundesrat. The counter-argument that only twenty-one laws have been defeated since 1969 - a small number considering the total of 1205 laws passed during the same period - is not convincing. It is not the quantity which is significant but the nature and scope of the laws rejected. Many of these bills were defeated because of their political objectives rather than because they infringed Lander rights. They were not generally concerned with highly specialised matters, but reflected basic differences in party outlooks and beliefs. In fact the Bundesrat with its CDU/CSU-majority formed a high threshold against the far-reaching changes in society, at least until 1974 when Chancellor Schmidt replaced Brandt and a period of caution arose out of the economic recession.

Furthermore, one must not only count the bills that were actually lost due to the Bundesrat's opposition. Many of those laws that were passed after successful mediation emerged in a considerably altered version in which the demands of the opposition were accepted in order to ensure Bundesrat consent and thus avoid the loss of the whole bill. It is also very likely that many proposals of the cabinet or the majority in the House are drafted with an eye to the opposition's anticipated demands and that they already integrate these demands to such an extent that the final bill is acceptable to the opposition majority in the Bundesrat.

Federal Encroachment

The 'party politicisation' of the Bundesrat was scarcely foreseen by the Parliamentary Council and academic and legal opinion is divided on whether the Council was intended to reflect party as well as Lander interests. Certainly the encroachment of federal politics into the arena of Lander ones is to be seen in more than the development of partisan conflict especially in the period 1969-83. Yet it cannot be denied that it was the powers of the Bundesrat's over-legislation which brought the Council into the arena of party conflict. The 'creative tension' between Bund and Lander focused in the Bundesrat and the ambivalence of the federal principle upon which it is based, especially in a period of intensive partisan activity, absorbed Land politics into the federal arena. And the extension of that tension, minus its creativity, seriously disrupted the relationship between the two Houses.[16]

Between federal elections party struggles in Bonn flowed into the provincial capitals both between and during Land elections. In an effort either to keep or increase their Bundesrat seats, the parties began to deploy senior party figures from Bonn as candidates for Land premierships. The leading party luminaries in federal politics campaigned in the provinces with the result that Land elections, like

British by-elections, became plebiscites on the parties' records in federal rather than local politics. It seems unlikely that the creation of the CDU/FDP coalition with majorities in both Houses will restrain this development.

In any case, the process of federal encroachment is not restricted to the manifestations of party conflict. Since 1949 there have been other developments which have continued to increase the centripetal tendencies within the West German federation. Particularly noteworthy are the establishment of a federal police authority - the Bundeskriminalamt (BKA) - based on the Verfassungschutz, and the development of the federal border police into a branch of the BKA. The origins of this encroachment in an area where the Lander had virtually exclusive rights and an intrusion not resisted by them, stem from the terrorist phenomenon in general and the Munich massacre at the 1976 Olympics. Education, too, has been an area where Land exclusivity has been subject to federal encroachment, albeit on a limited scale. The burgeoning of higher education in the 1960s was made possible largely by the provision of federal funds while the imperative of technological education led to the establishment of a federal ministry to deal with its development. In any case, the Lander themselves have adopted machinery to coordinate their education services and to align standards in teaching and public examinations.

Membership of the European Community has also played its part in the process of reducing Land competences in the area of economic development. In protecting their interests the Lander have to rely on the ability of federal ministers and, however disappointing the result of Community bargaining, the Lander have never yet rejected the deals made on their behalf. Moreover, their right to do so has not so far been tested in law.[17] In addition, there are extra-institutional pressures which have affected the federal system. Blair notes that there are increased demands from the citizen for equality of treatment, demands which push the Lander to maintain identical standards of public service, a right enshrined in the Basic Law and upheld by decisions of the Federal Constitutional Court (FCC).

Conclusion

There is a final epithet which has been applied to
West German federation but one which has been
deliberately withheld until this final discussion.
Karl Hesse claims that the Federal Republic has
become a 'unitary Federation'.[18] His arguments are
concerned more with legal matters than with political
issues and it is the Federal Constitutional Court
that is the object of his concern. The argument is
deeply entrenched within the complexities of German
legalism but, put simply, Hesse is concerned at what
he sees as attempts by the FCC to impose political
value judgements which have failed to protect the
'federal principle' from centralising tendencies.
Since the author of this chapter has little
competence in German legal issues, the subject is
clearly not a matter for pertinent comment here. Yet
even a passing acquaintance with the subject of
federation requires an acknowledgement that courts
and the interpretation of constitutions lie at the
heart of all conflict resolution within federal
systems. Is the requisite requirement of a book of
rules and reference a built-in universal component of
federation per se ? Or is it that the legal
formalism which is both a tradition and a basis of
German political practice has strengthened the legal
impetus towards centralisation ? The dominance of
legal norms, which is a central feature of the West
German political 'style', is considered to be a major
'conflict avoidance syndrome' by such diverse authors
as Dahrendorf, Sontheimer and, more recently, Blair.
But such legal norms may be more than a reflection of
the dominance of legal arbitration to be found at the
centre of German federation. Could it be that the
acceptance of legal norms as the major resolution
mode in 'non-federal' political and social conflict
has tended to inflate the FCC and the expectations
made of it beyond the role it was intended to play as
arbitrator in disputes on federal/constitutional
matters ?

We must return, however, to the main issue at
the heart of this chapter: the role of the Bundesrat
and its function as the instrument of Land
participation in the federal legislation process.
Some acknowledgement must be given to the factors
which have led to the party politicisation of the
Federal Council. Clearly, the intensification of
partisan conflict, especially over the Ostpolitik
issue, has been of crucial significance. Yet is it
not the structure of the Bundesrat itself and the

ambivalence of both structure and function in
relation to the federal principle which can be viewed
as a constitutionally-based centralising feature ?

Finally there is one issue which has not been
discussed in this chapter: the relationship between
Land governments and Land parliaments. The West
German tradition and practice seem to be that the
Landtage, by convention, neither mandate nor even try
to influence Land ministers' actions within the
Bundesrat. This observation is crucial to our
evaluation of the West German federation. If the
Bundesrat enshrines the federal principle by enabling
the Lander to participate in federal legislation,
what are we to make of the fact that it is now the
Land Governments which have pre-empted this role ?
Perhaps we should view this as a major departure from
the German federal principle.

FIGURE 1 – USE OF MEDIATION COMMITTEE*

A For laws to which Bundesrat approval is mandatory

B For laws to which Bundesrat approval is not mandatory

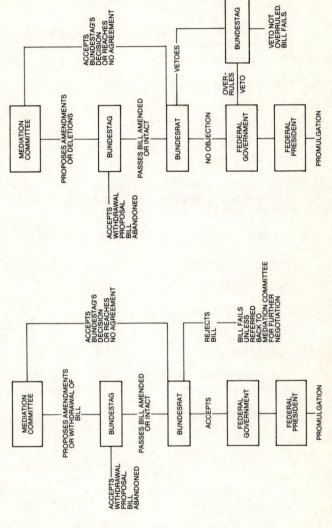

Source: Trossman 'Der Deutsche Bundestag'.

* Following 3rd Reading in the Bundestag and formal consideration by the Bundesrat

Notes

1. P. Blair, Federalism and Judicial Review in West Germany, (Oxford 1981).

2. J. Noakes, The Nazi Party in Lower Saxony, (Oxford 1976), pp.123-37.

3. K. D. Bracher, Die Auflosung der Weimarer Republik, 5th edn. (Ring Verlag, Villingen, 1971), Ch.VI.

4. Blair, Federalism, Ch.1.

5. N. Johnson, Government in the Federal Republic of Germany, (Oxford 1981).

6. K. C. Wheare, Federal Government, 4th edn. (London, 1963), p.26.

7. P. Merkl, 'Executive-Legislative Federalism in West Germany', The American Political Science Review, Vol.53, (1959), pp.732-41.

8. Johnson, Government in the Federal Republic.

9. Blair, Federalism.

10. Ibid.

11. Scharpf, Reissart and Schnabel, Poliltikverflechtung: Theorie und Empirie des Kooperativen foderalismus in der Bundesrepublik, (Kronberg, 1976), pp.13-66.

12. I am aware that the Austrian federation shares features in common with those of the BRD.

13. J. Golay, The Founding of the Federal Republic of Germany, 2nd Impression, (Chicago, 1963), pp.53-67.

14. P. Schindler, 'Parlaments - und Wahlstatistik fur die 1. bis 8. Wahlperiode des Deutschen Bundestages', in Zeitschrift fur Parlamentsfragen, Vol.1, (April 1981), pp.5-20.

15. Ingo von Munch, Grundbegriffe des Staatsrechts II, (Stuttgart 1976), p.145.

16. Members of the Bundesrat have the right to address plenary sessions of the Bundestag, an opportunity often exercised.

17. I am grateful to Suzanne Schuttemeyer of the journal _Zeitschrift fur Parlamentsfragen_ for bringing this point to my attention and allowing me access to some unpublished research.

18. K. Hesse, _Der Unitarische Bundestaat,_ (Karlsruhe, 1962).

11. CONCLUSION

Michael Burgess

This study has looked at the twin concepts of federalism and federation from a number of different angles in eight states of Western Europe. It has also examined the nature of the relationship between these two concepts as it exists in these West European states. The most difficult problem which emerges from this study is how precisely to define the relationship between federalism and federation in our eight states. What do these individual discussions and analyses reveal about this problem ?

Clearly the relationship is not simply causal. Spain and Belgium, for example, may never become conventional federations in the sense that we have here defined federation. They may seek solutions to their particular differentiations which do not arrive at federation. And the notion of 'federalising' may not, therefore, be particularly helpful when attempting to understand and explain precisely what their respective goals have been. This notion might lead to serious misconceptions. How, for example, do we accurately classify a state which is said to be 'federalising' but which does not achieve federation ? There is a strong temptation to regard it as, in some sense, either incomplete or even a failure. This in turn arises from a dangerous assumption which may be inadvertently smuggled into the general debate about federation, namely that federation is the ultimate good. Only when a state achieves federation, according to this view, can it be considered as a complete and successful entity.

Our purpose in this book has been neither to reify nor deify federation. It is only one among many rival alternative remedies for combining diversity and integration. Each diversity is both compound and unique, and must work itself out according to its own perceived end. Preconceived notions of federation may be arrogant, coercive and highly authoritarian - the very opposite of what is intended. Our initial conceptual distinction between federalism and federation, then, must guard against what may gravitate towards an invidious teleology. We do not suggest an ultimate moral purpose.

Similarly no sweeping claims are made here regarding our conceptual distinction as an analytical approach to the subject of federal union. It may be taken to be a useful approach which avoids the rather sterile debate of the last thirty years and it may be

revealing for what it informs us about the nature of
modern federalisms. The chapter on Austria by
K. R. Luther, for example, is indicative of this.
But our main difficulty - having made the conceptual
distinction - is how to put federalism and federation
in a defined relationship which will facilitate
empirical research. Careful attention to case
studies is an obvious pre-requisite, but the
relationship between federalism and federation
remains at present unclear. One simple answer is
that different forms of diversities produce different
solutions. But, as we have already argued, they do
not always produce federations.

This study raises additional problems for the
empirically oriented student. The way that the
federal principle has been employed here must not be
allowed to limit its applicability to different
political traditions. Our intention in this book is
not to reduce its meaning to what in global terms
would be a parochial understanding. We merely wish
to identify and underline the significance of a
distinct European tradition. Furthermore, we accept
that the reader will find in this text sufficient
material to support a variety of approaches to
federalism and federation which can then be
operationalised at different levels in different
political systems. Indeed, it is to be hoped that
future writers pursue these routes of federal
enquiry.

The question of which particular approach to
adopt when examining federalisms and federations will
perforce remain controversial. Each approach must be
assessed on its own merits and drawbacks. However,
it might be especially useful to encourage political
science research on those matters which can be
generally categorised as 'problem-solving'. Here our
conceptual distinction may be peculiarly relevant.
If we can identify and understand the changing
demands and requirements of contemporary federalisms
we might begin to appreciate how federations change
in response to such impulses. Chapter Nine on
Switzerland provides a good insight into the push and
pull of intrastate negotiations on centralist and
decentralist themes in a federal state in the 1980s.
It is impossible to overlook the stark contrast
between Centralist and cantonal perceptions and
perspectives of decision-making. Cantonal resilience
- the hard outer shell of the constituent unit of the
federal state - is staunch. Similarly the case study
of West Germany in Chapter Ten directs our attention
towards problems of institutional relationships and

constitutional/legal interpretation which directly
affect the process of federal government. It may be
the case that the federal state structure remains
intact but that the daily practice of government as
regards the lander, as constituent units of the
federation, has altered quite significantly. Here
federation clearly impinges upon federalism.

The gist of our conclusion, then, is that the
conceptual distinction between federalism and
federation would seem to offer valuable lines of
enquiry in the pursuit of practical relevance. It
enables us to see federation as problem-solving
rather than as a finite goal. It also encourages us
to look at movements for change in a different light.
The activation of federalisms leads to a particular
type of political mobilisation which may not be
satisfied either with measured decentralisation or
administrative deconcentration. The federal idea is
qualitatively distinct from conventional
decentralisation and devolution; it is a separate
concept. However we regard the idea, it must be
rescued from the tendency in current political
science literature to impoverish the concept by
merging its identity with notions of decentralisation
and devolution. If the federal principle is allowed
to sink to a mere footnote in the contemporary debate
about centralisation and decentralisation we shall be
unwitting collaborators in a hazardous enterprise.
And the victim would be political science itself.

CONTRIBUTORS

Michael Burgess is Senior Lecturer in Politics at
Plymouth Polytechnic, England.

Tony Burkett is Professor of European Studies at the
University of Loughborough, England.

Neil Collins is a Lecturer in Politics at the
University of Liverpool, England.

Frank Delmartino is Professor of Politics at the
University of Leuven, Belgium.

Ulrich Kloti is Professor of Politics at the
University of Zurich, Switzerland.

John Loughlin is a Research Associate at the European
University Institute, Florence, Italy.

Richard Luther is a Lecturer in Politics at Preston
Polytechnic, England.

Antoni Monreal is a Lecturer in Politics in the
Faculty of Law at the University of Barcelona, Spain.

Kurt Nussli is a Research Associate in the Institute
for Political Research, University of Zurich,
Switzerland.

INDEX

Index